Days of Shame

Coward-McCann, Inc.
New York

Contents

CONTENTS

Illustrations will be found following pages 96 and 208

Prologue

THE McCarthy episode was, short of war, one of the most dramatic and provocative events in this century if not in all American history. It is unlikely that fate will ever again assemble a similar cast or write a comparable script.

The story reached its climax in the spring of 1954 when a cloud of terror blanketed the United States. Like a gigantic, tumultuous hurricane it dominated the thoughts and actions of the American people, disrupting their emotions, distorting their judgment. Sanity seemed to go into hiding, opinions whirled to the outer edges of human thought. There was no compromise, no courage to laugh at the basic absurdity. Even now, pockets of this strange phenomenon are evident.

At the center of the disturbance, stimulating the confusion and pumping power into the dissension was one man—Joseph Raymond McCarthy, junior Senator from Wisconsin—a brutal demagogue to some, a godlike savior to others. To no one was he unimportant.

As a United States Senator from Michigan and a member of the Senate Government Operations Committee, it was my privilege to live through those days in the center of the action. I was, along with McCarthy and Senators Dirksen and Mundt, one of the majority GOP members of the committee. The Democrats were Senators McClellan, Symington, and Jackson.

7

The pattern for the final act in McCarthy's uproarious career began with the attempts of a legal counsel of the committee (Roy Cohn) to save his friend (G. David Schine) from serving his country as an Army private

From this simple and selfish whim of two young men who seemed to be demonstrating a rare kind of irresponsibility, the entire country was swept into a tornado of emotional nonsense. It turned husband against wife, brother against brother, changed close friends into snarling enemies, disrupted the political pattern of the Nation and sent messages over all the oceans that the United States had gone stark, raving mad.

Each citizen found he must declare himself, stand up and be counted. He must be either "for" McCarthy or "against" him. Somehow it had been arranged—almost, it seemed, by cosmic direction—that if you were for him you were a "red-blooded patriot"; if not, you were a "Commie lover."

In the late spring of 1954, a committee hearing, featuring Senator McCarthy vs the United States Army, became the focal point of the Nation. The controversy had raced far beyond the question of whether or not David Schine should be required to serve his country like any other young man. This was McCarthyism on trial.

The hearings spurted a strange, psychotic force into millions of American homes. The reputations of dozens of people, both prominent and unimportant, were scarred. The rule book went out the window and no referee could control Joe McCarthy.

Eventually, the hearings ended and Senator McCarthy faced in the U. S. Senate a resolution for censure. Here was the reckoning, the mirror of public opinion, and the resolution was passed. The tragic ending of Joe McCarthy's life was near.

Conversations in this book between myself and other veterans of this war on Capitol Hill are not offered as word-for-word, but are reasonable constructions and expansions re-created from memory.

My gratitude goes to many of those mentioned in this story

for the time they gave and the effort they made to help me put it together, and to Roger Treat for research and editorial advice.

There are lessons to be learned from the McCarthy era and conclusions to be drawn. Each citizen must draw his own and, in this book, I have tried only to tell it as I knew it from the committee table.

This is the way it was.

—CHARLES E. POTTER

DAYS OF SHAME

CHAPTER 1

Ike Was Furious

DURING the noon recess of the first day of the Army-McCarthy hearings in May 1954, I went to my office and found a message that President Eisenhower would like to have me come to the White House early that evening. He suggested that I keep the visit confidential and come in the north gate entrance on East Executive Avenue.

The hearings had been called to order that morning after the Army had charged that Senator Joseph R. McCarthy, chairman of the Permanent Subcommittee on Investigations of the Senate Committee on Government Operations of the United States Senate, and its chief counsel, Roy Cohn, and other members of the staff, had sought by improper means to obtain preferential treatment for one Pvt. G. David Schine, formerly a consultant for the committee.

McCarthy and Cohn had filed countercharges, claiming that the Secretary of the Army, Robert Stevens, Counselor for the Army, John Adams, and Assistant Secretary of Defense, H. Struve Hensel, had been responsible for the Army charges in an effort to induce Senator McCarthy to stop investigating Communist infiltration into the Army and misconduct on the part of Hensel.

There had been a lot of loud and irresponsible statements in the press and now we were on camera with television displaying the hearings to an audience estimated at 20 million.

I was one of the seven-man committee, a member of the Republican majority, along with Senators Acting Chairman Karl Mundt of South Dakota, Everett Dirksen of Illinois and Henry Dworshak of Idaho, who was filling in for Joe McCarthy. The Democrats were John McClellan of Arkansas, Stuart Symington of Missouri, Henry Jackson of Washington.

My administrative assistant drove me to the White House shortly after six o'clock, and I found that the guard on the gate was expecting me. Another guard escorted me to the elevator and up to the living quarters on the third floor. The President was standing by the window looking out over the balcony at the back lawn of the White House. He suggested drinks, mixed them himself and we chatted for a few minutes.

Finally he said, "What happened up there today, Charlie?"

"It was terrible," I said. "The whole thing is a disgrace to the Senate. He did all the impossible things you might expect him to do and twenty million people were watching."

"You mean McCarthy?" Eisenhower asked.

"Yes. Within a minute after the hearing officially opened, he made his first move. He said the charges against him were not being brought by the Army but by what he called Pentagon politicians."

The President snorted.

"That was only the beginning," I said. "The next thing he did was make believe he didn't know who Struve Hensel was and demanded that Hensel get up and identify himself. This was nothing but heckling and clowning for his audience of twenty million. I though Hensel was going to get up and strangle him right there."

"There are certain rules and regulations for hearings," the President said.

"There aren't any rules and regulations for Joe McCarthy,

14

Mr. President," I answered, and we both laughed, but there was nothing funny about it.

"A lawless man," the President said. He got up and walked to the window again and stood there looking down at the fountain on the White House lawn. I could see that he was deeply disturbed.

"You might as well know it all, sir," I said. "General Miles Reber was the first witness. He testified about the original McCarthy appeal for a commission for Schine. Reber was the liaison officer for the Senate but he has been transferred to Germany since then. There was nothing important about his testimony. He merely reported the extraordinary efforts that his office made to find a spot for Schine because, naturally, he knew it was a hot case. But the boy was completely unqualified for any kind of commission. Reber told all this and about the excessive amount of phone calls, putting pressure on him, and then Joe sailed into him."

"Sailed into him? For what?"

"Not exactly into him but into his brother."

"His brother?" the President asked. "What in the name of God has his brother got to do with it?"

"Nothing at all. His brother, Samuel Reber, retired from the State Department service a few months ago. He was Acting High Commissioner in Germany at the time Schine and Cohn made that trip through Europe. You probably know all you want to know about that episode. So today—and I still don't want to believe it happened—McCarthy asked Reber, that's General Reber, if he failed to get a commission for David Schine because Reber's brother, Sam, had been forced to quit the State Department since he was being investigated as a security risk."

Eisenhower whirled around from the window.

"Surely you can't be serious?" he said.

I nodded.

He slammed his fist down on the desk.

15

"Go ahead," he said, "what happened then?"

"Reber was ready to explode. I don't know how he restrained himself. There must be something about that West Point training that makes it possible for a man to control his emotions. But then we wrangled for two hours about it, for two hours, and the whole country watched us. The question was would General Reber, as a witness, be permitted to make a statement in answer to this slander of his brother? I won't go into all the details because it was insane. Mundt, the presiding officer at this hearing as acting chairman, had great difficulty maintaining any semblance of order."

Eisenhower was on his feet again, angrily pacing back and forth behind his desk. He was listening intently.

"Finally," I said, "it was agreed that Reber could make a statement, and he said that he had no knowledge of any security investigation against his brother. What more could he say?"

"Is there no way the committee can control this man?" Eisenhower asked.

"He has what he calls points of order, Mr. President," I said. "He brings up a point of order and then he makes a speech."

"The Army can take care of itself," Eisenhower answered. "Bob Stevens should be able to take care of the whole thing when he takes the stand. When is that scheduled?"

"He's already on the stand. It started late this afternoon, and he's in trouble already. He hardly got his mouth open before McCarthy started taking shots at him."

Eisenhower snapped around in surprise. He came back to his chair and sat down. "What happened?" he asked.

"McCarthy is determined to trip him up, smudge the evidence, and keep up a steady fire of harassment. This seems to work for him. It always has. And, of course, he will get big headlines in the papers tomorrow."

The President took my glass and mixed me another drink

and I was happy to get it. All of a sudden the tension of the day was draining my strength. I went on with the report.

"Stevens had an opening statement, of course," I said. "He referred to my letter to him which I wrote when Charlie Wilson first called me about this Army report. In it I told Stevens that I had received many inquiries concerning external pressure for preferential treatment in behalf of Schine. The letter asked if Schine had received any preferential treatment and if any member of the subcommittee twisted any arms in the Pentagon for him. Stevens testified that, in answer to my letter, he had furnished copies of the Army report to me. And just about then Joe plowed in. He made a big thing about how Stevens should not be speaking for the Army but only for himself. He is trying to prove his point, no matter how ridiculous it is, that Stevens is responsible for this hearing because he wants to block Joe's search for Communists in the Army. This would be funny if it were not so degrading."

"I was told that McCarthy was trying to blame Hensel," Eisenhower said.

"Oh yes, Hensel got it, too, the other day," I answered. "Sometimes it's Hensel, sometimes it's Stevens. Sometimes it's Adams. It all depends on what Joe happens to be thinking at the time. Or maybe it depends on the phase of the moon."

"Psychopathic, yes."

"Anyway, McCarthy made a big show out of whether or not Stevens was speaking for Stevens or for the Army. There was some scuffling back and forth between Mundt and Jenkins, and Joe seemed to win his point with them, that Stevens was speaking for himself. Then Bob went on with his opening statement explaining the case and explaining the Army's complaint. He got through that without any more interruptions and then he was excused from the chair temporarily while General Walter Smith testified. He'll be back on the stand tomorrow, and I'm afraid he's going to take a beating. He's not capable of coping with Joe."

17

"Surely he can take care of himself," the President said. "He represents the Army of the United States. Isn't that enough? He has my full support. Surely the Secretary of the Army can take care of himself."

"I'm afraid it's too late," I said. "The cards are stacked against him now and, to be fair, he stacked them himself. If he had slapped Cohn down when the whole thing started, this hearing would never have happened. But there are a lot of if's connected with this. Anyway, we are in it now and the only good thing that can happen from now on will be the final day of it."

"Did Smith have any trouble?"

"General Smith? No, none at all. Most of his testimony was a copy of a letter he had written to Bob Stevens. The letter told of a phone call from Roy Cohn asking Smith's advice about the Schine case. Cohn had told him that General Reber and the other Army authorities had not been cooperative, that they had promised to arrange a commission for Schine and had not done so.

"He did not tell General Smith that the promise of a commission was not a promise at all but only Reber's statement that, from what Cohn had told him, Schine was qualified for a commission. Unfortunately, what Cohn had told him was not altogether accurate. Schine had never been an officer in the Transport Command, although Cohn said that he had. Smith called a General Hull, I think it was, and found that there was no commission available for Schine.

"Cohn appeared at Smith's office the next day and, during their conversation, asked if the CIA could not arrange to have Schine commissioned because of his experience as an investigator. Smith offered to telephone Allen Dulles and ask about the possibilities but Cohn backed off. He told Smith that the CIA was a juicy subject for future investigation and it would not be right to ask them at that time to do a favor for Schine. Incredible, isn't it, Mr. President?"

18

"It must be stopped, Charlie. It must be stopped now. I do not intend to get into a public brawl with this man, but nothing in the past year and a half has brought me more anguish. Sherman Adams, some of the others, think I should denounce him publicly, go to the mat with him and settle it once and for all. I won't deny that my normal tendencies would be to do just that. But this office, my position as President of this country, demands more dignity. I cannot brawl with every irresponsible person who becomes a problem. The newspapers are attacking me because I do not do this. I wish I could ask them why they have helped to create this man, this situation." He leaned back in his chair, looking thoughtfully at the ceiling.

"A large section of the public supports him, Mr. President," I said. "You know this, of course. I know it too, although I hate to believe that it's true. But my mailbag tells me it is. Ever since it was published in the papers that I asked for this Army report I have been getting hundreds of letters denouncing me as a Commie coddler, a Pinko, a traitor. They were on my telephone at home at all hours of the day and night. Women, men, drunk, sober, they all believe in Joe. I had to have my phone cut off. There is a certain amount of rabble, of course. Thousands and thousands of them all over this country. But there are plenty of others who are not rabble. In the Senate, in the House, in the Pentagon, top businessmen, clergymen, they all believe that he is sincerely dedicating his life to saving the country from Communism."

"Charlie, what can be done right now?"

"Not a thing that I know of, Mr. President," I answered. "The time for action, for courage, was long ago, four years ago when this whole thing started. But some people learned to be afraid of Joe McCarthy soon after that. They saw what happened to Senator Tydings and Senator Benton and to General Marshall. Around the Hill they knew about his almost psychopathic determination to hurt Margaret Chase Smith. No one may know of all the hoodlum tactics he used against Margaret, but I happened to have been closer to that than almost anyone up there. But each one knew some of it, and I'm afraid a great many of us decided to live by the law of self-preservation."

"It was different in the Army," the President said. "If a soldier was guilty of rebellion, he would be put in a stockade."

We sat there in silence for a few minutes, and my heart went out to Dwight Eisenhower. He had led the armies of the Allies to a great victory in the most horrible war in history. Now he was in a new kind of war, a deadly back-alley struggle with one man who was willing to destroy his own political party for the sake of his own political glory. Eisenhower was a man of principle and self-discipline; McCarthy was neither.

"I am sure Bob Stevens will be able to take care of the whole dispute," Eisenhower said again, "and I hope it will be cleaned up in the next couple of days."

He just didn't understand. He hadn't been there. He hadn't watched the flogging of dozens of witnesses who had been summoned to the dozens of hearings. He had not seen them stripped of all dignity, smeared with unsupported accusations, suffocated by the realization that their own government, which guaranteed them so much of freedom, would deny them even the basic rights of a criminal in a court of law.

After McCarthy's incredible attack on General George Marshall, Eisenhower had been infuriated. After all, Marshall had reached far down in the ranks to pick Eisenhower for Commander-in-Chief of the Allied forces. Despite this, he had refused to, as he said, "engage in a gutter-type brawl with McCarthy." He limited his retort to a mild statement of his support of Marshall.

Then, when McCarthy had snarled to the world that General Ralph Zwicker was unfit to wear the uniform of the U. S. Army, the President was privately seething but again did not speak out publicly in Zwicker's support.

McCarthy seemed to take a special delight in shooting, verbally, at outstanding military men. There had been episodes when he had thrown his bombs at Douglas MacArthur, and his swipes at General Eisenhower himself were becoming more frequent and more impertinent.

When Joe had seen fit to rip and tear through the State Department, the U. S. Information Agency, when he had threatened the security of the CIA, there had been no public objection from the White House.

I knew this policy was not the result of Eisenhower's own determination after he had learned all the facts. Cynically, many top Republicans believed that McCarthy's antics resulted in votes for the party and there was no question that this was true. The question was—how many of a man's principles can be thrown away for the sake of votes?

"Charlie, can the man possibly believe these slanderous things he's saying? Does he think anyone in his right mind would believe that Bob Stevens and the other top men in the Pentagon are part of a Communist conspiracy?"

"Mr. President, he may have convinced himself by now that he believes it. But if you backed him in a corner and injected some truth serum, you might learn that the whole thing is a game with him. One outrageous statement results in one large headline, two statements make two headlines. If he calls some defenseless government office clerk a Fifth Amendment Communist, he gets a small headline. If he implies General Marshall is part of an infamous Communist conspiracy, he gets the big headline. He obviously has the press completely bamboozled. They rise to the bait on every one of his statements and later either praise it or denounce it. They never seem to have the good judgment to throw it in the wastebasket where the unsensational stories go.

"It has become a nasty little game, and, if you go back through the memory, you find that Joe gets bored with it very quickly if one particular act of vandalism is not scoring with the headlines."

"I cannot believe that any man would have the indecency,

21

the bad manners, to deliberately befoul some of the people McCarthy has attacked for no better reason than to get publicity," the President said.

"That's right," I answered, "he is being used too. He uses the press and other people use him. He has become the voice of a strange collection of people and groups, many of whom despise each other but are locked together in support of Joe McCarthy. They make strange teammates. Many Catholics are behind him and so is the Ku-Klux Klan. The intellectuals who happen to know what Communism is all about, and are dedicated to opposing it, stand side by side with thousands of morons who don't know what anything is about but will follow any rabble-rouser. I don't think he himself has any particular political philosophy or ambition. I think he enjoys the position he has, the freedom for mischief and the immunity from counterattack that the Senate gives him. He is an overage delinquent who has found out that he can throw mudballs at anyone without taking the spanking that he needs."

The President got up again and began prowling up and down the room, hands in pockets, head bowed. I felt sure that he was involved in thoughts which were new to him—that Joe McCarthy was a man about whom it was impossible for anybody to maintain neutrality, that he was a man of extremes and that his effect on others was always extreme. Some who had fought him openly had lived to mourn over their own political corpses. Those who had attempted the policy of neutrality, the shut-your-eyes-and-it-will-go-away strategy, as Eisenhower had, had learned that this was no barricade.

As I sat waiting for the President to speak again, it came to me that I should have added to the list of McCarthy's supporters a lineup of all the disgraceful racial bigots and American Fascists. And, although I hated to admit it because I was a member of the American Legion and the Veterans of Foreign Wars, many of their local branches were noisy supporters of every irrational blast at Communism that McCarthy fired. One post of the Veterans had recently made itself ridiculous by accusing the Girl Scouts of America of being a Communist front because it supported the United Nations.

Antics like this should have been the object of gut-splitting laughter from coast to coast, but in those days, the few people who had sense enough to laugh had learned to be wary. Big Brother was beginning to take shape and, in the early 1950's, he was Big Brother Joe.

The President stopped prowling. I knew he had reached some conclusion and it was something he was not going to put into words.

"Charlie, do everything you can. Keep in touch with me. I want you to come back soon."

It was not quite dark as I walked out through the north gate of the White House grounds.

CHAPTER 2

It's Blackmail

I HAD tried to block the Army-McCarthy hearings when the story had started to pop. I was the first one on the committee to know that the fuse was getting short and I had gone to McCarthy's office right away. I gave him the story and told him we might be able to dampen it if we got rid of Roy Cohn, who seemed to be the culprit in the Army charges.

"I have a few friends left in the press," Joe said. "Not many, but a few. They can make it rough for you, Potter. They can make you look bad."

He was shaking his finger under my nose in that gesture that was such a prominent ritual of his investigations and would become even better known in the weeks ahead.

It was the first time I had ever been under the gun with him and I wondered why he was attacking me. It was the Army, not me, that was shooting at him.

"This is important, Joe," I said. "You can't win by denying it, or counterattacking or making some silly charge against the Army. Roy Cohn is trying to set up a soft touch for Dave Schine and we've got to get rid of him."

"I will not fire Cohn," McCarthy said. "The Army is trying

to blackmail me into stopping our investigations. That's all it amounts to. Roy hasn't done anything wrong."

"Threatening to wreck the Army if Schine doesn't get a soft berth isn't wrong?"

"Roy didn't do that."

"Of course he did it, Joe," I said. "If you'd read this report you'd find thirty-four pages of what Roy did. You made some pleas yourself. These are monitored phone calls that the Pentagon recorded. When the public gets this, the stuff will hit the fan."

Again I tried to hand him the bulky report as we stood in his office in the Old Senate Building. He was restless, moving around the room, shuffling the thick piles of papers that always covered his desk.

"They don't have the whole story there," he said. "It's blackmail. They're using Dave Schine for a hostage."

He seemed to consider that theory for a moment, weighing it, looking out the window at the clean-washed sky of a windy spring morning. Then, for a moment, his grin came through. "Hell, Charlie," he said, "I don't care if they ship Schine to Siberia. But Roy worries about him."

He had that ability to change roles, sometimes several switches within a few minutes. He could be Prince Charming or Mr. District Attorney or good old Joe, the drinking man's buddy, or the outdoorsman tramping through the Wisconsin woods or the rabble-rouser deftly juggling the emotions of his audience.

He could be any of them and better than most men could be even one of them. But he couldn't be any of them long. I often wondered which was the real Joseph Raymond McCarthy.

When he had started his war on Communism in government with his speech at Wheeling, West Virginia, in early 1950, he had been hunting blindly for an issue. He had never shown any particular distaste for Communism until Wheeling. In fact, he had welcomed the support of the strong Communist elements in Wisconsin, particularly within the CIO unions, which had thrown their support to him in 1948. The Wisconsin Reds were pleased with McCarthy's statement that "Communists have the same right to vote as anyone else, don't they?" and his praise of Stalin's proposal for world disarmament . . . "a great thing, and he must be given credit for being sincere about it" . . . and they rallied behind him to defeat young Bob La Follette whom they considered a much more effective enemy.

But the speech at Wheeling had exploded in the newspapers throughout the country and McCarthy, a hungry rebel, suddenly had a cause. Now, seven years later, he would have bitten the head off anyone who said Communists had a right to vote, or even to breathe, and he was ready to start punching at me that morning.

"No, Potter," he said as he turned from the window. "If you try to force me to fire Roy it will be anti-Semitism, and Winchell and Sokolsky would have plenty to say about that."

So this would be his attack—Charles Potter, racial bigot. There wasn't any use protesting, although he knew that I knew that he knew it was absurd. And up to now I was one of the few human beings he had not attacked.

"Joe," I said, "Dirksen and Mundt agree with me. The whole committee is going to be clobbered and it will be justified if we let Cohn get away with this. We've held still for a lot of nonsense from that boy. This rumor has been going around the Hill for weeks. Why shouldn't Schine serve his draft time just like any other young fellow? You're a veteran. You were in the Pacific when the guns were going off. This youngster wants a joy ride in peacetime. Nobody can condone this."

Maybe I was a little harsh about Schine but I think any combat veteran would have felt the same. I had been wounded three times between the Normandy beach and the Ardennes Forest in Germany nine years before. I had tangled with a German land mine in France one bitter cold morning shortly after the Battle of the Bulge had been resolved and I had lost my left leg at the hip, my right one below the knee. I had learned to live without them and without resentments. However, I could not find enough tolerance to be pleased with a young man who was determined to spend his Army career on the playboy circuit while hundreds of thousands of other young men served their time.

Joe McCarthy surprised me with his willingness to arrange a goldbricking tour of duty for Schine. At least he was prepared to back up Roy Cohn. And now he was ready to lay his political future on the line to support Cohn.

"It's blackmail," he said. "The Army wants me to stop digging out Communists. The report" (he pointed to it) "is not true. It's a fraud dreamed up by the Army to get me off their back."

"Joe, you had better read it before you deny it," I said. "These are monitored conversations. They're not something some Army press agent dreamed up. They quote you word for word. They say you told John Adams that Schine was no help to the committee, that he was a pest who wanted to get his picture in the paper. It says you called Schine a nuisance but that you didn't want Cohn to know you thought so."

"It says that?"

"It says that. Why are you afraid to fire Cohn, Joe?"

He turned his back on me again and stood looking out the window, hands in his trouser pockets, the big shoulders hunched forward like a boxer waiting for the attack; the champion heavy-weight boxer of Marquette University that he had been long before life became one massive tornado against him as it was this week of March in 1954.

The big guns were blasting him now. President Eisenhower, Adlai Stevenson, Secretary of Defense Charlie Wilson, Senator Flanders, Ed Murrow on television, Drew Pearson in his column, the murderous cartoons by Herblock in the Washington *Post*, were all zeroed in on this strange, haunted man. I knew him well, and yet I didn't know him at all.

Great chunks of our biographies could have been inter-

27

changed. I was born and raised in the small town of Lapeer, Michigan; he only a few hundred miles westward across the lake at Grand Chute, Wisconsin. He had gone to Marquette; I to Eastern Michigan. Both of us had enlisted early in the war: he, in the Marines, had served in the Pacific; I, in the Army, had been sent to Europe.

We had returned and found our way to Washington. For the past year we had been two of the four Republican majority members of the same committee—its official title: the Special Subcommittee on Investigations for the Committee on Government Operations of the United States Senate.

That unwieldy title had long since been forgotten. We were the "McCarthy committee" and had been even before Joe became chairman under the Eisenhower majority in 1953.

It had not been a dull year.

Now as he turned around and faced me I knew that there was no hope for a rational approach to this problem. I braced myself for some more thumb in the eye and knee to the groin.

"It's that Bob Stevens," Joe said. "I'll have him fired."

"Maybe he should be," I answered, "but not for the reason you think, and don't forget he's the Secretary of the Army. Maybe he should be fired for not stopping this nonsense about Schine the first day it started. No one on this committee had any right to pressure the Army, especially when you were investigating at Fort Monmouth and other places. That dispute was between Schine and his draft board. You made a plea for a commission for him and that was turned down because he wasn't qualified and that should have been the end of it."

"Roy didn't do it," he said, and there was a snarl in his voice now. "It's blackmail."

"Joe, you can't make that stick."

"It's an answer, isn't it?"

"It's absurd. The Army of the United States, ten million men, resorting to blackmail because one young punk doesn't

28

want to serve his country like every other young man must?"

"If I got rid of Roy it would be the greatest victory the Communists have scored up to now. He's indispensable."

I smiled to myself. I wondered if Joe had ever heard of Stalingrad. I had the feeling he was working up his case, using me as the dummy in a practice scrimmage that would become the strategy when he faced the press. And he had seized on the one tiny, raw nerve end in the Army's charges. He'd found it without even glancing at the 34 pages of embarrassing revelations in the report that I was trying to give him.

Why had Bob Stevens, Secretary of the Army, and John Adams, Army Counsel, wasted hours and hours of their time, plus the efforts of their staff, on G. David Schine, an unpaid spearbearer on Cohn's staff? Schine was a young heir to millions but he wasn't the first young man of that mold to be drafted.

"Joe," I said, "think it over. Charlie Wilson, Mundt, Dirksen and I agree that Cohn has to go. I think Charlie would agree to eliminating John Adams too and we can, perhaps, make this a one-day sensation with a cleanup on both sides. We can get together tonight or in the morning, the four of us and Cohn, too, if you want, and wipe it up. Otherwise, it's disaster."

"All right," he said. "We'll get together in the morning. I'll get the answers together. There's plenty to be said for this side. It's blackmail. Want a drink?"

I shook my head and smiled at him. Beyond his shoulder on the wall there was a framed motto:

> Oh God, don't let me weaken. Help me to continue on. And when I go down, let me go down like an oak tree felled by a woodsman's ax.

I wondered if he read this to himself when he was alone, very much alone. I wondered if he knew that the woodsman's ax was already taking aim at his head and that his personal devils would bring him crashing down very soon.

Through the warm serenity of the marble corridors, down the elevator and to the subway platform, I thought about the inevitability of the days that lay ahead. I knew there was little chance that he would agree to a sane defense of the situation, that it would be impossible for Joseph Raymond McCarthy in any of his many postures to realize or, perhaps, to admit that Roy Cohn had arrogantly and selfishly led him into the arena with his hands tied and his eyes blinded. Now the wolves would devour him.

There was only one subway car running from the Old Senate Building to the Capitol in those days, a rickety old car that reminded me of the open trolleys I could remember in Milwaukee when I was a youngster. The new subway with its breezy, faster, bigger cars was still a plan for the future in 1954 and it was quite a job to get a seat on the old Toonerville line unless you were a Senator.

My own personal Senate office was in the Capitol Building, an office, incidentally, that was later occupied by one Bobby Baker, who became a fairly well-known figure in 1964. The Republican party had insisted that I use these facilities because they thought it would be easier for me to get to the floor of the Senate. There wasn't any use protesting that I could make better speed than many of them, even with my store-bought legs and canes.

The subway that morning was a squirming mass of visiting schoolchildren. At the other end the elevators were working up and down as quickly as they could but it was another 10 minutes before I could get up to my office. There must be some better way, I thought. American ingenuity should be able to get a U. S. Senator delivered from one office to another in less than 20 minutes.

I put in a call to the Secretary of Defense. When he was on the line, I said, "It's no go, Charlie. He refuses to fire Cohn. He says the Army is blackmailing him."

The answer was lucid and profane.

CHAPTER **3**

Cohn Claims Double Cross

CHARLIE Wilson had alerted me the
night before about the Army's report. We had been close
friends for a long time. He had been one of my supporters in
my campaigns in Michigan and I was delighted when he left his
General Motors presidency to join Eisenhower's Cabinet. I
knew that it would have been difficult to find a better man for
the job.

He had called me about seven o'clock the night before during
that quiet period of the day when it was sometimes possible to
dictate the correspondence that could not be turned over to the
staff, to try to unscramble the mass of details that shower down
on a Senator's office every day of every week.

The Army had compiled a report, Wilson said, which listed a
long campaign of heckling and harassment of the Army by
Joe McCarthy, Roy Cohn and other members of his staff. It
had been going on since the previous July, and it was the appalling history of eight months of Cohn's determination to
arrange a pleasant, and short, Army career for G. David Schine.

Wilson said that the Army, already ruffled by McCarthy's
previous forays against it, had monitored all telephone calls
from Joe's office and had now gathered together 44 specific
instances of "unusual activity" in the Schine case.

31

This was not entirely news to me nor to anyone else on Capitol Hill. The rumor had come to me time and again that Bob Stevens, Secretary of the Army, and John Adams, Counselor of the Army, had been spending a shocking amount of time with both Cohn and Schine in Washington, in New York and elsewhere. I had been part of one such meeting myself.

Dick Russell, the highly respected Georgia Democrat who was a ranking member of the Armed Services Committee of the Senate, was on the trail, Wilson said. Russell had heard the rumor strongly enough to ask the Pentagon for a copy of the report, if there was such a report.

There wasn't any doubt in Wilson's mind, nor in mine, that the Democrats would make explosive use of it.

But perhaps, Wilson said, if I got a copy of the report first, the committee would be able to take action to clean up the mess and muffle the firepower of whatever move Russell might choose to make. He suggested I write a covering letter requesting the report and said he would send it by messenger at once.

It was in my office in less than 30 minutes.

I went through it quickly the first time. "The Department of the Army alleges . . ." and then 34 pages of dates and names, of requests, of threats, of worrying, of tormenting, of promises of reprisals and behind it all the incredible arrogance of Roy Cohn.

It had started in early July when Major General Miles Reber, Chief of Army Legislative Liaison, was summoned to McCarthy's office. David Schine was about to be drafted and McCarthy urged General Reber to arrange a direct commission for him. Roy Cohn was there and told Reber that maximum speed was desired. He also informed Reber that Schine had once held a commission in the Army Transport Command, which was not entirely accurate since he was a ship's purser not an army officer.

McCarthy's request for a commission for Schine was not in itself unusual. Any Congressman is willing to expedite a similar plea and that is one reason why there are Army, Navy, and Air Force staffs for legislative liaison. If the recruit is qualified for a commission, he usually gets it and valuable time has been saved. The service gets the best possible value out of the man and the man avoids the frustration of wasting his abilities in the wrong job.

That is a clean-cut operation. The Senator says here is a young man who has this experience, this education, these special talents; the Army says it can use him in a certain position.

Cohn's demands for Schine were something else. According to the Army report, Cohn wanted Schine to be given a commission within a few days without even bothering to fill out forms and establish his qualifications. McCarthy emphasized, particularly when Roy Cohn was in the room, that David Schine was the greatest expert on Communism he had on the staff and that his short experience—as a civilian—with the Army Transport Service qualified him for a commission.

A week later, the Army report said, Schine called Reber's office and asked if he could go over to the Pentagon that afternoon to "hold up his hand." He had not yet filled out any application forms nor taken a physical examination. That afternoon he did go to the Pentagon, filled out the forms and took the physical.

I skipped through the rest of the report, blinking now and then at some of the allegations. It was nearly eight-thirty and I had been in the office for twelve hours. I wondered why a Senator should need 96 hours a day just to stay even. I asked my administrative assistant to drive me home and I took the Army report.

Washington was moving into springtime. There had been a gusty northwest wind all day and the first flock of summer cumulus clouds had been flying south over the city since morning. As we drove down Independence Avenue toward the 14th Street bridge, the sky was scrubbed clean. A half-moon hung low in the west and seemed to be impaled on the spike of the Washington Monument. We went on around the Bureau of Engraving and down the slope to the edge of the Tidal Basin. Jefferson's Monument splashed its shadow into the choppy water in the moonlight and I wondered if there was any building anywhere that had more simple beauty.

There was no traffic to fight at this hour and we zipped around the Pentagon in seconds to Arlington Towers, where I lived. I took a bath and ate my dinner.

All through it I thought about David Schine and the strange patterns of a man's life. I thought about Roy Cohn. I thought about Joe McCarthy. Here at last, it seemed, the three main characters in the monstrous farce were joined together and the curtain was about to go up.

McCarthy had successfully defied two Presidents, the United States Constitution, the U. S. Senate (including Senators of his own party), the Army and several of its generals as well as its Secretary, the Department of State, newspapers, educators, most of the top-level political writers, a large section of the Protestant clergy, but particularly the Army recently. Now, with this report in my hand, I thought I knew why the Army had been the target for the past six months.

I thought about Roy Cohn and Dave Schine and I couldn't remember the exact quote nor who had said it first, but I could look out my living room window across the roof of the Pentagon to the white, lighted dome of the Capitol and I could say: Joe, you could always outslug your enemies but who will protect you from your friends? There was no one closer to Joe than Roy Cohn.

Perhaps success came too early to Cohn. He had earned his law degree at Columbia University before he was twenty-one. He was tremendously gifted, shrewd and ambitious. Even though he was only twenty-five when he joined our staff, I heard him say one day that he expected soon to be Mayor of New York. When McCarthy became chairman of the committee in January of 1953, one of his first moves was to put Cohn on the staff as Chief Counsel to the subcommittee.

At the time it seemed like a strong addition. Cohn had already demonstrated his anti-Communism in many ways. He had been one of the prosecuting staff in the case of Julius and Ethel Rosenberg, who were executed for delivering atomic secrets to Russia; he had worked as a staff lawyer for the U. S. Attorney of the Southern District of New York in the William Remington perjury trial and the trial of thirteen top Communists.

Somewhere along the line Roy had sipped the heady brew of newspaper publicity. He became a pet of Walter Winchell and George Sokolsky, Hearst columnists who were surfboarding the high waves of anti-Communism. He understood publicity, but shrewdly, not compulsively as McCarthy knew it. He could make it work for McCarthy.

He had come to Washington in the fall of 1952 to work as a special assistant to James McGranery, Truman's last Attorney General. Cohn prepared the indictment of Owen Lattimore on perjury charges after Lattimore's clash with McCarthy when Joe had made his disastrous attempt to prove that Lattimore was the "top Russian espionage agent in the United States." The perjury charge was thrown out of court.

Later, Cohn chopped his way to prominence in a House subcommittee study of the State and Justice Departments' handling of alleged U. S. Communists on the staff of the United Nations. Cohn stayed with Justice until the Eisenhower majority took over, and joined our staff through the suggestion of Walter Winchell, an admirer of both McCarthy and Cohn.

David Schine was, I shall always believe, the unknowing catalyst that brought Joe McCarthy crashing down. Had there been no Schine, there would have been no Army hearings nor the censure resolution of Joe McCarthy in the U. S. Senate.

David Schine himself could not possibly have created a situation which would lead to the Army publishing this anguished

35

34-page report of transgressions with its 44 blasts, each carrying the implied demand of the United States Senate that Schine be given royal treatment. I had not known Schine well and saw him only during committee meetings. I was impressed with his good looks and quiet behavior.

He was, even then, "President and General Manager" of Schine Hotels, owned by his father, J. Meyer Schine, who also controlled a chain of motion picture theaters. He had attended Harvard, equipped with a valet and a Cadillac, and somewhere along the road had decided to become an expert on Communism. He was carried on the subcommittee roll as "Chief Consultant" at no salary and as an aide to Roy Cohn.

He had produced (at least his name was signed as author) a monograph entitled "Definition of Communism," published, according to the inscription, by the Schine Hotels and distributed within the hotels.

The booklet was described by one political reviewer:

> In a couple of thousand deplorably chosen words, Schine managed to put the Russian Revolution, the founding of the Communist party and the start of the first Five-Year Plan in years when these events did not occur; he gave Lenin the wrong first name, hopelessly confused Stalin with Trotsky, Marx with Lenin, Alexander Kerensky with Prince Lvov, and fifteenth-century Utopianism with twentieth-century Communism.

It was perhaps just as well that David was carried on a no-salary basis as an expert on Communism.

I made myself a long, cool drink and studied the Army report. As Joe McCarthy once said in a moment of stress, "It was the most unheard-of thing I ever heard of."

The report outlined a disquieting series of events. Within two weeks after David Schine had made his application for a commission, it had been considered and turned down by the Chief of Transportation, the Provost Marshal General and the Commanding General of the First Army despite continued heckling by members of the committee staff. Roy Cohn then asked that a Reserve commission for Schine might be arranged in the Air Force or Navy. Neither of these services was eager to employ Schine as an officer.

August and September drifted by before Cohn telephoned Bob Stevens, Secretary of the Army, and made an appointment for a conference. Stevens, a gentle gentleman if there ever was one, the head of a huge family textile empire, obviously didn't suspect what was going to happen to him when he agreed to that appointment with Roy Cohn on October 2, 1953, but this was the starting bell for a brutal mauling of this man who was too docile to beat off such a savage attack.

Roy Cohn had two matters to discuss, he told Stevens, the coming investigation of Communist infiltration at Fort Monmouth and the Army career of David Schine. There was no reason for Stevens to think that it was, perhaps, only one matter. Had he known, even then, I doubt if he would have been able to follow any path but the one he chose, to believe what his ears were hearing, to accept each maneuver on his own terms of honesty, decency and kindness. Bob Stevens was a middle-aged lamb suddenly shoved into an arena full of young tigers.

Cohn took Francis Carr with him to confront Stevens. Carr had joined the staff after Cohn. He had a background of service with the Federal Bureau of Investigation and was signed on as executive director of the subcommittee. Technically, Carr was Cohn's boss but it never seemed to work that way.

Cohn complained to Stevens that a blackout order by Major General Kirke Lawton, Commandant of Fort Monmouth, was preventing anyone at Monmouth from talking with members of McCarthy's staff. Could Bob Stevens do anything about that? Stevens could. He telephoned General Lawton and the order was rescinded then and there. Stevens said it was his policy to cooperate with the committee.

The pending induction of David Schine was the next item, Cohn said. It seemed to him that the Army could assign Dave to the New York City area so that he could complete his extremely valuable work for the committee; Cohn said he needed Schine for consultation on many matters pertaining to Communism; he would appreciate the Army's cooperation.

At that moment Bob Stevens made his tragic error. He dithered, he stalled, he appeased. Not able to grasp the far-reaching effects of his indecision, not suspecting that Schine and Monmouth might be linked together, he told Cohn and Carr that after Schine had completed his basic training he would be able to use Schine to great advantage in the Army. Dave could go to some security-type school within the Army, for example, and report his observations to Stevens.

Cohn must have had difficulty stifling a victory cheer over that. He knew now that he could take Bob Stevens' scalp whenever he needed it. The basic training? Well, Dave could stand eight weeks of basic and they could demand plenty of special passes. Committee work and all that. "Executive sessions" for the two of them at the penthouse apartment of Dave's family at the Waldorf-Astoria.

Apparently in October the Army failed to discharge its responsibility to David Schine in a manner acceptable to Roy Cohn. D-day was now known to be November 3, and again Cohn suggested to Bob Stevens that Schine be assigned to temporary duty in New York. Again Stevens appeased, agreeing that Schine might have 15 days of temporary duty between his induction and his basic training. Once again Cohn had won a round from the Army, but he was far from satisfied.

Then, in mid-October, a strange distraction entered the case. Joe McCarthy, it developed, would have been tickled to death if the Army had done what it should in the first place—drafted David Schine, given him a number instead of a name, and handled him the same way it did 300,000 other men that year. In New York, at a time when Roy Cohn couldn't hear him, Joe told John Adams that he considered Schine no help to the committee, a "pest" who was interested mainly in getting his picture in the papers. Delighted, Adams asked Joe's permission to report this thought to Bob Stevens and Joe said go ahead— "But don't tell Roy."

However, Roy was telling John Adams. Time was getting short now and, as Joe McCarthy once said to Bob Stevens, Cohn thought that David Schine should be a general and work from the penthouse of the Waldorf. He turned on the pressure. During one phone call, Adams reminded Cohn that the Army was drafting 300,000 men a year and that David Schine was not the only college graduate who might become a private. He added that it would best serve the national interest if Schine were given no preferential treatment.

This apparently infuriated Cohn, who told Adams that if the Army wanted some national interest it would get it and in its worst possible light. Cohn said, according to the report, that he would show the country how shabbily the Army was being run.

During that time we were having several executive sessions in New York. I attended one of them and spent the night with other members of the committee at the Schine apartment at the Waldorf-Astoria. Several guests were in and out of the apartment all through the evening including George Sokolsky. John Adams was there, too, as it was during our preliminary investigation of the situation at Fort Monmouth. I noticed that there were several huddles in corners between Adams, Cohn and Schine but I thought nothing of it at the time. However, according to this Army report, Cohn was then keeping up an incessant badgering of John Adams over David Schine.

Finally, David Schine was drafted on November 3, 1953. But because of Cohn's maneuvers, he was immediately assigned to 15 days of temporary duty in New York City. The cover-up for this special privilege was that he was needed by the committee to complete certain work in New York although it was never clear to me, a member of the committee, just what work David Schine did.

The committee office, Room 101 in the Old Senate Building, was far from my normal area of activity, far from Joe's office too, so that I would see the committee staff men only during the hearings and those were so frequent there was no chance for me to attend them all. Few of the Senators on the committee could, but when we did not go, we would send a staff man to observe and report back whatever of importance might have happened. This cost me considerable embarrassment after General Zwicker's appearance at our executive session in New York.

It was a strange situation. Almost immediately Joe McCarthy got in touch with John Adams at the Pentagon and urged that this temporary duty for David Schine be canceled. McCarthy always showed a sixth sense about newspaper publicity and he was aware of the hazards of this conniving. But once again Roy Cohn stepped in to tell John Adams that since it was the middle of the week anyway, there was no reason why Schine should have to report for duty with the Army until the following Monday. A later section of the Army report indicated that McCarthy and Cohn clashed violently at about this time.

There was a record of a phone call from Joe to Secretary of the Army Bob Stevens which showed that Cohn had won again. It also would make one wonder who was running the committee, Joe McCarthy or Roy Cohn. Now, McCarthy said, he hoped that David Schine would be free for weekends even though he thought Roy was being completely unreasonable. However, he almost went down on his knees to beg Stevens not to assign Schine back to the committee. There was nothing the Left Wingers would like better, he said.

He told Stevens that maybe, for Roy's sake, it would be best to let Schine come back for weekends so that his girls would not get lonesome. He also suggested that maybe if the Army would shave off David's hair he would not want to come back. All through this conversation Bob Stevens again failed to take the one positive step that was needed at this time, to say that somewhere in the world the Army had more important affairs than fun and games for David Schine.

Within the same twenty-four-hour period, Bob Stevens served luncheon at the Pentagon for Senator McCarthy, Roy Cohn, John Adams and Francis Carr of McCarthy's staff. During this luncheon the inevitable discussion of the Schine crisis was brought up by Cohn. And McCarthy, showing one of his rare flashes of unintentional humor, suggested that Schine could be assigned to New York where he could investigate and report to Secretary Bob Stevens any evidence of pro-Communist leanings in West Point textbooks.

Stevens agreed under Cohn's hammering that Schine would be permitted to leave his post on weekends; that if the staff found it necessary to consult with him they could go to Fort Dix and meet with him during any evening; that if a matter of urgency developed, Schine would be given permission to leave the post. It was apparent, and it became more apparent later, that a fantastic amount of energy was being expended at the Pentagon in an effort to keep David Schine happy.

I put the report down for a few minutes and looked out into the night. I watched the beacon twirling over National Airport and the few lights still burning in the Pentagon. I wondered about Joe McCarthy and Roy Cohn. It would have been difficult to make anyone believe, anywhere in the world, that McCarthy could have been dominated by *anyone*, particularly by a member of his own staff. Still, the evidence seemed to be clear that this was what was happening.

McCarthy would have been glad to get rid of David Schine; at least he was aware of the probable rebound, particularly in the unfriendly sections of the press, of making any move to arrange special privileges for Schine. But always, although he made halfhearted attempts to stop the Cohn-Schine operation, Roy was still able to come out on top in any showdown with McCarthy.

41

I wondered, too, what was driving Roy Cohn. He was brilliant and shrewd; he was ambitious to the point of mania; he had, at the extremely early age of twenty-six, established a pattern of life which many lawyers twice his age were still trying to achieve. And yet, his campaign over David Schine bordered on lunacy. Unless he had become completely bemused by his past victories, he must be astute enough to realize that the repercussions of his all-out attack on the Army had to end in the defeat of Roy Cohn.

Why, then, did Roy Cohn forget all about discretion and threaten to "wreck" the Army if it refused to make whatever concessions he thought suitable for David Schine? Surely the immature desires, active to some extent in all men of his age, to romp and play in a Waldorf-Astoria penthouse would have been of much less importance to Cohn than his political ambitions. David Schine, of course, had more money than Cohn and was willing to spend it. However, Cohn himself at this time was drawing $20,000 a year from a law firm connection in New York, was paid some $11,000 a year by the committee, and had an unlimited expense account.

Still, it was obvious from these Army reports that this campaign had become an obsession with Roy Cohn.

Finally, the report said, at a certain moment on November 10, 1953, G. David Schine boarded a bus in New York City and was transported to the reception center of the United States Army at Fort Dix, New Jersey. He was already a week late; at any rate, a week later than all the other young men who had been drafted in his delegation, and during the next 60 days he would be absent 50 percent of the time because the Chief Counsel of the Special Subcommittee on Investigations of the Committee of Government Operations of the United States Senate insisted that his presence, or at least his absence from Fort Dix, was vital to the security of the United States. Had all the other recruits at Fort Dix been given similar privileges the base might have taken on the appearance of an abandoned installation.

After Schine had been at Fort Dix for about a month, the commanding general decided he had had enough of David Schine's special excursions into the night. Naturally it was no secret around the base that David was using Fort Dix mostly as a place to change his clothes before heading out in a Cadillac to the more enchanting facilities of New York. It was reported, too, that David made little effort to erase a growing rumor in the camp that he was someone who was pretty important in Washington.

And so the general telephoned John Adams at the Pentagon and said that unless Secretary Bob Stevens objected, he intended to terminate Private Schine's passes on week-nights. Adams said he thought that would be a fine idea and, as of that moment, Private Schine need no longer be made available for "important committee business" during the week.

On the same day the committee began open hearings in Washington in its investigation of Communist infiltration at Fort Monmouth. And on the next day Roy Cohn, aware now that David Schine was being forced to spend evenings at Fort Dix, confronted Adams before the hearings opened and demanded to know what the Army's intention was about Schine's future. Adams answered that Schine was going to be handled the same as any other private soldier although later events indicated that his confidence was not so strong as his language.

When the morning hearing ended, Adams followed Joe McCarthy to Joe's office on the third floor. There Adams explained the situation and warned McCarthy that the Schine case was becoming too hot to handle. After some discussion, McCarthy agreed to write a letter to Bob Stevens in which he would say that the committee had no further interest in Schine and that he hoped Dave would be treated the same as other soldiers. He also agreed to ask the members of his staff to stop making demands at Fort Dix. Adams asked McCarthy to call Roy Cohn into the office right then and there and to give this order to Cohn personally. McCarthy evaded this demand.

Later that afternoon Cohn telephoned John Adams at the Pentagon and told Adams that he would soon know what it meant to go over Roy Cohn's head.

That was a Tuesday, and the Washington hearings for that week ended at noon on Thursday. McCarthy suggested lunch at the Carroll Arms Hotel and Bob Stevens, John Adams, and Francis Carr accepted the invitation. When they had settled in at McCarthy's favorite table, Carr reported that Roy Cohn had already taken off for New York and that he was having a tantrum over the new Army rules regarding David Schine.

McCarthy had put in three or four days in a row fighting off Cohn's demands and now, McCarthy realized with a shudder, David could no longer have Saturday morning either. During the luncheon McCarthy suggested, almost pleaded, for a New York area assignment for Private Schine. He didn't see why this couldn't be arranged at the end of eight weeks of basic training although the normal period was sixteen weeks. He said he knew of trainees who had been reassigned at the end of eight weeks. This was a radical change from Joe's stand of a few days before when he had wanted Schine to be handled just like any other private.

In New York the next morning Roy Cohn was raging. Several times during the afternoon he phoned John Adams at the Pentagon and gave Adams a tongue-lashing. The Army, Cohn said, had double-crossed him. Not only that, but it had double-crossed David Schine and Joe McCarthy. The Army had promised to give Schine a commission and had double-crossed him on that, Cohn said. And, although Schine had now been in the Army exactly 31 days, he had not yet been assigned to the New York area. This, Cohn said, was another double cross although he did not mention that Schine had received passes for 17 of the 31 days.

And here was another double cross, Cohn said. It was an absolute outrage that David now had to stay at Fort Dix on Saturday morning. However, at ten minutes past noon on that Saturday, David Schine left Fort Dix with a weekend pass.

Adams was aware that his only hope of stopping this mad operation was to try to induce Joe McCarthy personally to lay down the law to Roy Cohn. He could recall a number of instances when the three of them had been together discussing Schine and never had McCarthy made any attempt to stop Cohn's campaign. McCarthy had, on the other hand, indicated often that he wanted it to end. Schine was now becoming a newspaper personality. It had been inevitable that he would be.

Adams knew there would be hearings in New York City during the next week, that he would be there and so would McCarthy and so would Cohn. He knew that Cohn and Schine would be together on this weekend. Perhaps, he thought, during this coming New York excursion he would be able to catch McCarthy and Cohn together at a time when it would be possible for him to bring the whole thing to a climax.

Adams was aware, perhaps more than anyone else, of the tremendous amount of useless effort that was being spent in the Pentagon over the Army career of this spectacular private. It had become a nightmare to him and to Secretary of the Army Robert Stevens and for many members of Pentagon's staffs who might otherwise have been putting their efforts and abilities into some constructive work. Also, Schine's activities at Fort Dix had already shattered the morale of other recruits.

Later, about 200 of these men were quizzed concerning their memories of David Schine. His fellow draftees were quoted as saying that Schine got a pass every weekend and left the post, with a flourish, in a chauffeur-driven Cadillac, avoided all guard duty except on one occasion, goofed off at target practice and dropped a hint here and there that he was really hanging around Fort Dix only to check on morale.

But Adams and Stevens hadn't seen anything yet.

45

On the following Thursday, the investigation activity moved to New York City. Before the morning session started, Adams met Joe McCarthy at the entrance to the United States Court House. McCarthy told Adams at that time that he had learned about the amount of his staff's interference with the Army over David Schine and he wanted Adams to know that from now on nothing would be done by his committee to interfere with Schine's Army duties. Adams was delighted with this but was still convinced that it was nothing but idle chatter unless Joe McCarthy could be forced to say the same thing to Roy Cohn.

After the short hearing that morning, Adams maneuvered so that he would have lunch with McCarthy, Cohn and Francis Carr. When they were seated, he suggested that they discuss thoroughly the problem of David Schine.

As Adams opened the conversation, he was confident that the problem was about to be solved. Less than three hours before, McCarthy had assured him that the harassment of the Army over Dave Schine was finished. There would be no more demands for weekend and midweek passes; there would be no more requests for a New York assignment for Schine. The Army would, perhaps, now be able to get back to its business of concentrating on defending its outposts around the world against Communism.

However, Adams noticed that Roy Cohn was glaring at him from across the table and that Joe McCarthy was strangely silent. He plowed on, outlining all the preposterous demands which had been made during the past five months, pointing out that Schine had received more passes out of Fort Dix than any recruit in Army history that he could recall, and emphasizing that the Secretary of the Army had more important duties and so did he.

He glanced at Joe McCarthy, hoping the Senator would now take the cue and lay down the law to Roy Cohn. And at that moment Roy Cohn exploded.

46

Another double cross, Cohn said, and he wasn't going to stand for it. First the Army had promised a commission for Schine and they had double-crossed him on that. Adams answered that there had never been any commitment by anyone in the Army that Schine would get a commission; that his request for one had gotten most unusual consideration but no one had been able to find that he was qualified in any way for a commission.

The Army had promised to assign him to New York, Cohn added, and again Adams denied that any such promise had been made. He wondered if Cohn himself had made these promises to Schine and was now trying to switch the failure to the Army. And now this business about no Saturday morning passes, Cohn said, this was prejudiced and unfair.

Adams turned to McCarthy and asked him to repeat what he had said earlier that morning about Dave Schine. McCarthy didn't answer and Cohn continued to attack Adams, Secretary of the Army Stevens, and Joe McCarthy himself. During lulls in the firing they finished their lunch and got into Roy Cohn's car. Adams, who had already missed two trains back to Washington, was hoping to get another at 3:30. During the ride uptown, Cohn seemed more violent than ever, and Joe McCarthy, who had been quiet through the entire luncheon, now suggested that the Army could, if it wanted to, assign Schine to its First Army Headquarters in New York and that he could then examine the textbooks at West Point to see if they contained any Communist teachings. Adams was flabbergasted to learn something he had never realized before—that McCarthy was incapable of handling Roy Cohn.

McCarthy repeated this West Point suggestion several times during the short ride. As they neared Pennsylvania Station, Cohn drove on although Adams would now have to sprint to make the 3:30 train. Despite Adams' protest, Cohn continued for several blocks, then stopped the car in the middle of four-lane traffic and told Adams to get out. He did, got into a cab, and made the train only because it was ten minutes late leaving the station.

That weekend David Schine had a two-day pass, and the following week, which was Christmas, he left Fort Dix for three days.

All through this period, the McCarthy committee was investigating the infiltration of Communism at Fort Monmouth but nothing of any particular importance was being announced. At the same time, Army officers at Fort Dix, showing considerably more courage than their superiors at the Pentagon, were steering Schine into the routine pattern of an Army recruit. On top of this, the time had come for the Office of The Adjutant General to assign Schine to his next post of Army duty. Physical examinations at Fort Dix had revealed a defect in his back but he had qualified as an assistant criminal investigator. He was scheduled to go, at the end of his eight weeks of basic training, to the Provost Marshal General School at Camp Gordon, Georgia, for training in the criminal investigators school, an eight-week session.

Adams checked with Secretary Stevens, got his approval and reported this development to Roy Cohn. He was surprised to find Cohn under control and apparently resigned to spending those eight weeks without Schine. However, Cohn repeatedly demanded that when this course was over, Schine must be assigned to New York.

CHAPTER 4

Roy Is Upset

THE next catastrophe in Private Schine's
life took place early in January. He was given a weekend pass
but he had to return to Fort Dix on Sunday afternoon because
he had been assigned to kitchen police duty. Automatically,
Roy Cohn went into a flap. He could not catch up with John
Adams, who was in Amherst, Massachusetts, on a speaking en-
gagement but he did tear up most of the East Coast in an effort
to cancel this outrage against David Schine. But people were
now avoiding telephones which might produce the voice of Roy
Cohn, and he was unable to spring Schine from the KP duty.

Schine returned to Fort Dix on Sunday but somehow another
pass was issued for Monday and Tuesday and he returned to
New York. Cohn now sighted in on Camp Gordon in Georgia.
He wanted to know if David Schine could take his car to the
camp, if it would be necessary for him to live within the post,
and who would be the officer to call when he wanted Dave excused from duty.

Under Cohn's lash, John Adams telephoned the commanding
officer at Camp Gordon and learned some plans about the
future of David Schine that he knew would trigger another

49

explosion. Eight weeks would not be enough at Camp Gordon, the officer said, because Schine had completed only eight weeks out of the sixteen required in basic training. Therefore Schine would have to complete those eight weeks before he could qualify for the criminal investigators school. If he did qualify for the school, it would be necessary for him to stay at the school for ten more weeks.

Adams smiled rather grimly when he added it up to five months at Camp Gordon for David Schine. He then called Roy Cohn and gave him the news and was told, emphatically, that Cohn would not stand for any more Army double crosses.

A few days later Adams visited Cohn at the Capitol and made an observation that because 90 percent of all Army inductees were being assigned to overseas duty, the chances were nine out of ten that this would happen to David Schine. Adams was obviously needling Cohn and he got the expected result. Roy said that he would wreck the Army and that Stevens was through as Secretary of the Army.

On January 16, David Schine completed eight weeks of basic training at Fort Dix and departed for two weeks' leave, a normal reward to all recruits.

Two days later, Secretary of the Army Robert Stevens flew to Korea, and Roy Cohn, keeping up-to-date on the situation by long-distance telephone, hurriedly ended his vacation in Florida and returned to Washington. He was ready to put more pressure on the Army.

On the next day, members of Army's Loyalty-Security Appeals Board were summoned by Cohn and McCarthy to a one-man hearing, McCarthy being the one man. The members of the board were advised by McCarthy that he was not about to question them on the loyalty-security program alone. He also wanted to dig into what he called widespread allegations of fraud, corruption, and personal misconduct in their official doings.

He did not mention David Schine, nor did anyone else, but Adams got the point. He wondered what had happened to McCarthy's previous stand—that the life of David Schine was of no importance whatsoever to the committee. He knew also that Cohn had already lighted the time fuse on a ten-megaton bomb which was inscribed with the name of Major Irving Peress.

I was near the end of the report now and also near the end of my endurance. There was one more important episode that described a visit by John Adams to McCarthy's apartment, at which time Joe insisted again and again that Schine be transferred to New York. It was clear that, at this point, Cohn had McCarthy ready for the knockout over the Schine case. McCarthy told Adams that Cohn would never give up; that even if he should fire Cohn from the staff, the young attorney's war against the Army would continue through the newspapers. He warned Adams that Cohn had very powerful friends in the New York press and elsewhere, that he would carry on a campaign attacking the Army, alleging favoritism in numerous cases. (Cohn's supporters in the press were mainly members of the Hearst papers with George Sokolsky, Walter Winchell and Lee Mortimer devoting much space in their columns to praise of Roy Cohn. A year after Cohn finally left the committee, he wrote a series of articles which were published in the Hearst papers.)

During the meeting at the McCarthy apartment, Joe continued to refer to the "original agreement" with respect to Schine. According to the history as I knew it, and to the Army report, there never had been any original agreement. This had been a catch phrase recently dreamed up by Roy Cohn, and now McCarthy was parroting it. It was clear now that McCarthy was as sick of the Schine case as was the Army, that it had become an obsession with Roy Cohn. McCarthy was looking for peace at any price and, at the same time, was increasing the pressure on the Army with his demands that the members of the Loyalty-

51

Security Appeals Board be made available for interrogation by the committee.

The implied threat was obvious.

McCarthy had recently shocked the world, and particularly the Army, with his savage abuse of General Ralph Zwicker. Fresh in their memory too was McCarthy's activity at Fort Monmouth and, going back a few years, his performance during an investigation of the notorious Malmédy atrocities. The Army was certainly not eager to submit any man in its uniform to a seat in the witness chair during a McCarthy hearing.

In mid-February, the Army made its final notations in this sorry report. At that time Francis Carr, speaking for Cohn, called John Adams at the Pentagon and said that McCarthy wanted another hearing in New York City two days later at which, Carr said, the Army was to produce the commanding general of Camp Kilmer, the G-2 at Camp Kilmer, and the acting G-2 of First Army.

Adams indicated that the Army would not jump for joy at this request and was told by Carr that the committee would be reasonable if the Army would be reasonable. Then, the Army report said, "Mr. Carr answered rather facetiously that if the Army would only do all that had been requested of it, the Army's problems would be at an end."

I tossed the report on the table. All this over an Army private.

I knew that it was hopelessly late to get a proper night of rest after reading this report. My mind was whirling around with thoughts of McCarthy, Cohn, and Schine. I knew that a new period of uproar and tragedy was ahead. I knew it would be foolish to hope that this controversy could be settled sanely and quietly. For months now McCarthy had dominated the news media from coast to coast. No newspaper could go to press without his name on its front page; he was the top item in every news broadcast on radio or television. Chaos trailed him wherever he went and whatever he did.

Now I knew that the situation was certain to get a lot worse before it got better, that we were all being driven by a wave of national hysteria into making decisions that calm, mature men would not make and, to oversimplify a bit, it was all about an Army private.

CHAPTER 5

Make Way for McCarthy

I BELIEVE that a great many factors were involved in the rise to power of Joe McCarthy. For one thing, the atmosphere of the post-World War II years seemed made to order for his particular tactics. He preyed on the fears of a war-weary nation. My generation, the World War II generation, had reached maturity during the depression years. Our earliest teen-age memories were those of hardship in the home and a dispirited feeling of hopelessness in our parents. Then the war had brought prosperity and many millions of us in the Armed Services found our first security as a premium in return for some of the physical dangers we faced.

In uniform we ate well, which had not always been true in the past; we were well clothed, warm and well sheltered except in actual combat; many of us went to a dentist for the first time in our lives because we never had been able to afford it; we traveled all around the earth to places that had been tiny spots in our geography books and we met strange people and watched new customs.

Many died, but those of us who lived could, in honesty, look back on those years and repeat the corny phrase of the time: "We never had it so good." But by 1946, after the war years of privation, or what we liked to think of as privation, we came back looking for a better life for ourselves and our parents. The emotional drive was ending. We had matured from boyhood to manhood too quickly. And when we got home we found things not at all the way we expected them to be.

All of a sudden our Russian allies had become the new enemy, and the Germans and Japanese were being called our good friends. This strange and rapid switch in national thinking took place while we were still learning more and more details of what the Germans had done to the Jews and what the Japanese had done to our own men in their prison camps. Now we were told we must hate the Russians because they were Communists although I could not remember any such complaint about them when they blasted their way out of Stalingrad and started to roll westward over the German armies.

The tendencies toward war still rumbled in Eastern Europe. In 1947, Greece and Turkey were threatened and it was then that the President announced the Truman Doctrine, a sweeping commitment to defend freedom in the Middle East. Later on, President Eisenhower would slap down aggression in the Middle East, but always the trumpet sounded against Communism, ignoring Arab Nationalism.

Joseph Stalin moved against Berlin in 1948, and it was then that President Truman started the famous airlift of supplies into the city which saved our interests there and sent Stalin's hopes scuttling back toward Moscow.

It was a period of extreme unrest in this country and it was not long before politicians, writers, and self-appointed advisers with all possible motives learned that denouncing Communism was a profitable occupation. Many, of course, were sincere, but few gave their message with restraint and, as always, the press poured out the big, black headlines.

Many people had joined groups during the depression years which were later to be put on various lists as Communist fronts. They had joined in despair, and sometimes in the hope that

55

somehow they might make a better world for themselves. There was no reason to believe that every person who joined these groups was an advocate of the violent overthrow of the United States Government. However, many of them were soon to learn that they might be so labeled by the loudest voices of demagoguery.

The American Legion and other veterans' groups added their belligerent shouts to the confusion, and, all over the country, many ethnic groups, through their own publications and communications, spread the new theory that Communism was one hundred percent wrong and that it was safe to call anyone with whom you disagreed a Communist.

Then came the Korean war and with it the license to denounce Communism more loudly than ever and with less concern as to who might be the target.

The stage was set for an opportunist who would be willing and able to take full advantage of the national confusion and frustration and send it ballooning into hysteria.

Another important factor in the creation of the disgraceful situation which absorbed our country in 1954 was the birth and distortion and growth of investigative committees in Congress. Governmental investigating committees for legislative purposes were not new and even predate the founding of our country. Their proper purposes are to investigate the functioning of existing laws and considerations for either amending or drafting new legislation. However, it was never intended that these legislative bodies should conduct quasi trials with power of punishment.

In an honest investigation for legislative purposes, it is the duty of every citizen to cooperate. The refusal to assist Congress in its investigatory process vests in Congress the power to punish for contempt. However, when a witness in his own opinion considers that the answer to a question might tend to incriminate him, he cannot be compelled to be a witness against himself and made to answer.

This protective shield given to a witness under the Fifth Amendment is written in the blood and lives of many people. But by distortion and abuse, the Fifth Amendment became a pair of dirty words. We heard much of Fifth Amendment Communists and Fifth Amendment generals and Fifth Amendment politicians.

The goal of some committees appeared to be the exposure of people in order to destroy the foundation upon which our country was built: namely, nonconformity of thought and action. The fear of being subpoenaed by investigating committees had silenced many people whose unorthodox and controversial views would be healthy elements in a democratic society.

Into this unfortunate situation came a man who had a tremendous need to be the center of attraction, a man who must have hated himself violently for he found it so easy to drench others with hatred. He was a man of strong ambition but his ambitions had no substance, his dreams reached no further than tomorrow's headlines.

In February 1950, he was invited to speak to the Ohio County Women's Republican Club at Wheeling, West Virginia, and it was there that he either did or did not wave a piece of paper—reports were contradictory—and say that it contained the names of 205 Communists in the State Department.

At that moment, a poison pellet was dropped into our society and the fumes would never entirely blow away.

CHAPTER 6

Flanders Speaks Out

On the same morning that I had con-
fronted Joe McCarthy with the request that Roy Cohn be fired
from the committee staff, Senator Ralph Flanders, a Vermont
Republican, asked for recognition on the floor of the Senate.
Flanders was a man who made few speeches during his life in
the Senate, but when he did take the floor, the rest of us were
prepared to listen. He was a thoughtful, conscientious man, as
dignified and reserved as all the legends of New England would
assure that he would be.

"The junior Senator from Wisconsin interests us all. There
can be no doubt about that. And also he puzzles some of us." In
this quiet understatement, Flanders had summed up my own
thinking about Joe McCarthy.

In his short, hard-hitting speech, Flanders questioned Mc-
Carthy's right to wear the label of the Republican party and
suggested that Joe was doing his best to shatter that party. He
had, perhaps, developed this idea from the speech made by
Adlai Stevenson a few days before in which Stevenson had
charged that the Republican party was now divided against itself, half Eisenhower, half McCarthy.

Flanders pointed out that, in his opinion, Joe had become

58

a one-man party and that its name was McCarthyism and that Joe seemed to be proud to accept this description. The United States was being diverted from far more dangerous problems, Flanders said, while McCarthy confused the public with his "headline-grabbing extremes."

In one sardonic passage, delivered in Flanders' clipped, nasal dialect that made me think of a bitter cold night in a New England forest, he said, "Now is the crisis in the age-long warfare between God and the Devil for the souls of men. In this battle, what is the part played by the junior Senator from Wisconsin? He dons his war paint. He goes into his war dance. He emits his war whoops. He goes forth to battle and proudly returns a scalp of a pink Army dentist."

Flanders' speech was not all critical of Joe McCarthy, but I knew at once that Flanders' name would go on "the list" which Joe seemed to keep in the back of his mind of all those who had wounded him. Somewhere, someday, Joe would ambush him.

Flanders ended with praise for whatever effective job Joe had done of cleaning out the cobwebs and spiders left by the previous administration and urged that Joe go on with this type of work without concealing the dangers the United States was facing from external enemies.

It was a moderate, restrained speech. McCarthy was not on the Senate floor when it was delivered, but I knew that word of it would reach him soon and that he would automatically fire a counterattack. Again there would be emotional charges which I was sure Ralph Flanders expected. I was also sure that they would not bother him at all.

However, I had to wonder for a moment what the final result of this relatively unimportant episode might be. Two other New England Senators had questioned Joe's activities; William Benton of Connecticut had infuriated McCarthy by questioning his right to continue to sit in the Senate, and Benton had been defeated in the next election. At least part of this defeat could be directly credited to McCarthy's campaigning through Connecticut for Benton's defeat. Margaret Smith of Maine had also learned what might happen in answer to an outspoken criticism of McCarthy.

The campaign against Margaret Smith would have made a strong episode for *The Untouchables,* a pure gangland plot in which I got involved through one of my staff assistants. I learned a good deal about lying and bribery and character assassination when one of my own staff decided to become one of McCarthy's agents.

All of us in the cast of characters involved in this controversy with the Army went through that day carrying out our normal activities. However, as my sportswriter friends would say it, there was considerable activity in the McCarthy bullpen. His staff, which was really the staff of the entire committee although we seldom knew what it was doing, was preparing an answer to the Army charges. Roy Cohn and Francis Carr, we learned later, drove the staff far into the night, collecting the defense and the counterattack.

CHAPTER 7

Schine's War on Communism

ROY Cohn's reason for demanding special privileges for David Schine was that David was a very important part of the fight against Communism and that his continuing work for our subcommittee was vital to the security of the country. This, at least, was the reason Cohn gave for public consumption.

I decided to look into it and I called Frank Carr, the staff director of the committee.

"What has Schine been doing for us, Frank?"

"He does a lot of investigating. He knows a lot about Communism."

"So I have heard, but *specifically*, what has he done for us?"

Carr seemed to hesitate too long.

"Well, he worked with Roy on the *Voice of America* stuff," he finally said.

"We're in trouble on this, Frank," I told him. "Have you got any reports, any memoranda that Schine produced?"

"I don't think there are any written documents. But he was a big help to Roy."

"What does he do with all these passes from his Army camp? What committee work does he do then?"

"He usually meets Roy in New York. They go over things together."

"Like what?"

"Well, committee work. Investigations of Communists in the Army."

"What Communists in the Army?"

"Well, we turned up that dentist, that Peress."

"Frank," I said, "let's try to make some sense. Peress was not turned up by our committee. His security file was tagged long before your boys ever heard of him. Schine had nothing to do with that and neither did any one else on our committee. I'm trying to do something to help Joe. He's in a mess and so are you and so am I. Cohn has claimed that Schine was so valuable to the committee that he had to be away from his Army post most of the time. I want to know why. I want to know what Schine did for us during all those leaves. Can you tell me that?"

Again a long silence. Then, "I'll have to check it with Roy."

"You're the director, aren't you?"

He got the point.

"Don't bother to check it with Roy," I said. "I don't want any dreamed-up explanation of what Schine has been doing with all this privileged time."

That ended that bit of research and I never did find out anything important that David did for the committee. But the taxpayers were still stuck for the expense money he had cost them, especially during the slapstick trip through Europe that he and Roy Cohn had made the year before.

In fact, the only evidence I could ever find consisted of a few notations by David Schine on the margin of a draft of a report. This was all there was to show that Schine had been fighting Communism for a year.

I had met with Karl Mundt and Everett Dirksen, the two other Republican members of the committee, early that morning in the Senate cloakroom before I went to McCarthy's office.

I gave them a quick synopsis of the Army charges. Our vote was unanimous that Roy Cohn must be eliminated at once.

Dirksen was the first to insist that Cohn's actions in behalf of David Schine had been inexcusable. Mundt was equally insistent that Cohn's actions this time could not be condoned.

This was not a time, we all knew, to put our loyalty to a Republican colleague above everything else. We all knew that the United States Army would not expose itself to counterattack by making irresponsible charges. If it had decided to make these particular charges public, it was more than probable that it was holding even more damaging evidence in reserve.

Through the balance of that day I was busy with the normal flow of action through my office. So were Dirksen and Mundt, but I was able to get to them by telephone to tell them that McCarthy had refused to fire Cohn but promised to meet with the three of us the next morning to discuss the problem further. Neither of them was pleased and both were aware, as I was, that time and quick action were of top importance.

I was also extremely worried about what Joe would do next. His past performance indicated that he would counterattack, shooting from the hip with a salvo of emotional accusations for which the other six members of the committee would be on public trial. I wished for a moment that Everett Dirksen rather than Joe McCarthy could be quarterbacking our strategy in the skirmish which was now inevitable. Dirksen was a peacemaker; McCarthy could not resist a brawl.

I went home early that evening—early by Senate standards, which was about seven o'clock. This night I was determined to get some rest after staying up most of the night before to absorb the Army report. I telephoned Secretary of Defense Charlie Wilson and told him about my meeting with McCarthy. Wilson said that we could not accept McCarthy's refusal to fire Cohn.

He was certain, he said, that the three Democrats would go along with Mundt, Dirksen, and myself and why could not six

63

men overrule one chairman? I reminded him that the committee members had made an agreement with McCarthy several months ago that he and he alone would be permitted to do the hiring and firing on the committee staff. Wilson said he thought this was an insane arrangement. I agreed with him.

"You made the agreement," Wilson said. "Now is the time to change the agreement. The man has gone too far. No one in this world is safe from his slander. And now we have this disgraceful record of Cohn's harassment of the Army for the last nine months. The Senator is involved in it too and it should have been his responsibility to stop it as soon as it started."

I suggested to Wilson that Robert Stevens, Secretary of the Army, also could have stopped it long ago.

"That's right," Wilson said, "but you know Stevens as well as I do. If a gunman held him up in an alley, he would hand over his wallet and then write the man a check to buy a new suit of clothes. But this has gone too far, Chuck, and it must be handled within your committee. You have my full support and the White House too, and I don't much care what methods you use."

Wilson was still fuming over the Zwicker episode. It had started a week before when President Eisenhower, at a news conference, said that he assumed that witnesses would be treated with courtesy and respect when they were called before Congressional committees. Although the President's statement was very mild and never mentioned the name of McCarthy, I cringed in my office when I read it and waited for Joe to come out shooting.

I did not wait long. "If a stupid, arrogant or witless man in a position of power appears before our committee and is found aiding the Communist party, he will be exposed. The fact that he might be a general places him in no special class so far as I am concerned," McCarthy said. I could picture him dictating it, prowling back and forth in his office, the big shoulders rolling like a bear closing in for the kill.

64

"It now appears," the statement continued, "that for some reason he was a sacred cow of some of the Army brass."

Indeed he was. He was Brigadier General Ralph W. Zwicker, at that time the commanding officer of Camp Kilmer in New Jersey.

CHAPTER **8**

This Man Is Not Fit?

D URING an executive session of the committee held in New York City in February 1954, Brigadier General Ralph Zwicker was told by Joe McCarthy that he was not fit to wear the uniform of the United States Army.

General Zwicker was a distinguished military officer during World War II.

In April of 1944, Colonel Ralph Zwicker was sent to Europe to command the 38th Infantry Regiment. He and his regiment landed with the first wave at Normandy. During the furious assault on the cliffs and bluffs above the beach, Zwicker picked up a carbine which lay beside the body of one of his men and he carried this gun for the next thirteen months.

On a beachhead swarming with heroes that morning, Zwicker won the Silver Star for gallantry in action.

For the next few weeks, the Allies smashed into the desperate gunfire of the German defenses which had been constructed and waiting for the past four years. The 38th Regiment with Zwicker in command turned south toward the Brittany Peninsula and, specifically, the fortress city of Brest.

On August 1, Zwicker's regiment was suddenly brought under intense enemy small arms fire from dug-in hedgerow positions

66

near Torigni-sur-Vire in France. For his bravery this day, Ralph Zwicker was to be awarded the Distinguished Service Cross, Great Britain's highest military honor.

Exposing himself to extremely heavy small arms fire from the hostile troops barely seventy-five yards away, the British citation said, Zwicker crawled along the front, noting the enemy positions. Fire from 88 mm guns was directed against the hedgerow at the slightest movement. Calling for tanks, Zwicker personally led them in a reconnaissance of the enemy's flank. Despite heavy enemy fire directed at him, Colonel Zwicker continued to probe the enemy position. In the calm language of the citation, long after the thunder of the guns had died away, Zwicker was saluted for directing other forces around the area and taking the objective with a minimum of casualties.

With Brittany at last under Allied control, Zwicker and his regiment turned northeast. Paris was liberated and the German armies were falling back, contracting into the boundaries of Germany itself. In August, Zwicker was awarded two of his three Bronze Star Medals. One was for his successful capture of a piece of high ground known as Hill 192, the other for his part in the immobilizing of Brest. Later, his third Bronze Star came for meritorious achievement against the armed enemy during his entire period of active duty, from June 1944 to the end of the war in May 1945.

In mid-December of 1944, in a final desperate move, the German Army stabbed into the onrushing Allied forces with a strategy that soon was named the "Battle of the Bulge." It was a daring and brilliantly conceived maneuver which aimed to cut a deep hole in the Allied front, then to send its panzer divisions circling toward the coast of Belgium to the north, somewhere near Antwerp or Liège. Had these German troops, composed of the remnants of the once outstanding First, Fifth and Sixth Panzer Divisions of Storm Troopers, reached the coast, they would have cut off approximately three hundred thousand Allied soldiers in a huge pocket. Although it was too late for even so crushing a counterattack to save Germany, if it had succeeded it might have delayed the end of the war by many months.

Commanding a division in the center of the target area of the German troops was Colonel Ralph Zwicker. As the power of the German thrust raced by south of his position, it became Zwicker's responsibility to hold on a ridge near the town of Elsenborn. This was on the northern shoulder at the base of the Bulge and was less than ten miles from another town called Malmédy.

Zwicker's position was the key to our defense to the north. Had it collapsed, the encirclement of our troops was almost certain.

At Malmédy, a battalion of the First SS Panzer Regiment under the command of Colonel Joachim Peiper captured about 80 American soldiers and also rounded up several Belgian civilians. These storm troopers, nicknamed the "Blowtorch Battalion," had previously burned at least two villages to the ground and killed many of the civilian inhabitants. Under Peiper's orders, they lined up the captured Americans and machine-gunned them all.

Not far away, I was putting in many agonizing hours in the bitter cold in Diekirch, Luxembourg, and was heading for my meeting a few weeks later with a land mine at Colmar.

At the other side of the world, in the Pacific, Captain Joseph Raymond McCarthy was busy resigning from the Marine Corps and the strange dramatics of destiny would, a few years later, gather Zwicker, Peiper, McCarthy and myself to take part in a ghostly review of these terrifying days. Another minor character in the cast, a bit player who was to become the explosive ingredient, was working as a dentist in New York City. His name was Irving Peress.

Zwicker was awarded the Legion of Merit for his defense of Elsenborn.

In July of 1945, Zwicker was transferred to the Naval War

College in Washington, graduated six months later with a rating of Superior. For the next six months he was assistant to the Assistant Chief of Staff, G-3, Army Ground Forces; then to the National War College until the middle of 1947. After two years on the general staff, he was returned to Europe and from mid-1950 to 1952, he was the commanding officer of the 18th Infantry Regiment in Europe.

Six months as a member of the faculty at the National War College ended in January 1953, and he was sent to the Indiantown Gap military reservation until June 1953.

While there, Zwicker was appointed a brigadier general. His official military record over a quarter of a century sparkles with the comments of his commanding officers: exceptionally able—superior—an officer of the highest type—high sense of duty—capacity for leadership—qualified for high command—extremely loyal—mature—possesses integrity.

In July 1953, he was ordered to report to Camp Kilmer in New Jersey as commanding officer. There he would find the security file of Major Irving Peress.

CHAPTER **9**

The Congress Promotes Peress

WHO PROMOTED PERESS?

During the early months of 1954, this battle cry was sprinkled through the newspapers, carried on little cards in men's wallets, plastered across the sides of the delivery trucks of one powerful newspaper chain, sprinkled through the broadcasts of radio and television news experts, and, by endless repetition, it took the place of "Remember Pearl Harbor."

Joe McCarthy developed the slogan first. He tried it out in one speech, found it successful in that it produced a new series of headlines, and from that moment on, it became a national chant—"Who promoted Peress? Who promoted Peress?" Newspapers and their editorial writers and their columnists all seized on the phrase, which had a certain musical quality but had absolutely no basis in fact as a few moments of research would have told any newspaper editor.

The Congress of the United States promoted Peress. And Joe McCarthy voted for the bill that did it.

In 1950, the Army, with a million and a half men scattered all over the world, found itself with a shortage of doctors, dentists and other medical specialists. In September 1950, Congress passed Public Law #779, an amendment to the Selective Serv-

70

ice Act of 1948. This was a unique bit of legislation in the history of the United States. Never before had we drafted medical men and forced them to become officers in peacetime.

However, the relatively few dentists who had been in the Armed Services during World War II and the Korean action had returned to civilian life as quickly as possible, as was to be expected. Now the Army had a frantic need for dentists, and in January 1951, Irving Peress registered with his local draft board in Forest Hills, Long Island.

During the next three years, one might have thought that the Four Marx Brothers had taken over that section of the Army which would control Irving Peress.

As all present or former members of the Armed Forces will remember, Peress, like any soldier, was asked to fill out an endless stream of documents. The first one, which he answered in May 1952, was called the DD Form 390, and requested initial data for classification and commissioning in the medical services. This form contained the question of membership in subversive organizations, as do almost all application forms for federal employment, and Peress, on his 390, denied membership in any such organization.

The statement on the form which he affirmed says:

> I am not, nor have I been, a conscientious objector and I am not now and have not been a member of any foreign or domestic organization, association, movements, group, or combination of persons advocating a subversive policy or seeking to alter the form of government of the United States by unconstitutional means.

On subsequent forms and applications, Peress invoked the Fifth Amendment in response to similar questions. And it was from this switch by Peress that the entire uproar developed. It should be emphasized, however, that at no time in his Army career did Peress do anything at all or sign anything at all that

71

would have made it possible for the Army to sustain a court-martial against him. But by the time Peress was given his honorable discharge in February 1954, McCarthy, with the help of the news media, had convinced a large section of the public that Irving Peress had entered the Army with plans for subversion.

When the inevitable investigation by a Congressional committee took place some eighteen months later, this one by our own Committee on Government Operations but now under the chairmanship of Senator McClellan, the Army was charged with 48 specific blunders in the handling of Irving Peress.

It was a slipshod operation from start to finish but of no importance whatsoever to the security of the country. While in uniform, Peress functioned as a dentist with no complaints and some praise about his work. He made a normal amount of special requests, one for a transfer to duty nearer the New York area, which was granted. Otherwise his career was no different than that of thousands and thousands of other Americans. After he became a public figure of almost worldwide renown as the key to "Who Promoted Peress?" he was under surveillance at all times. No derogatory reports were filed.

After Peress signed his original papers, the 390 form in which he denied membership in any subversive group, Peress drilled teeth in obscurity for four months before he received a letter from the First Army in New York City that told him it would be necessary for him to contact First Army if he desired a commission. Peress telephoned First Army and said that he did.

In early October The Adjutant General, Reserve Forces, received a letter of recommendation from a major of the First Army that Peress be tendered an appointment in the grade of captain in the Dental Corps of the United States Army Reserve. At this point, the only document which the Army had on Peress was that original form in which he had denied the subversive organizations clause. A week later, a civilian member of the First Army draft board forwarded to Peress a letter of appointment in the grade of captain and enclosed three more forms to be filled out. This was routine procedure. There was no reason for the Army to know that Peress was basically any different from any one of thousands of dentists who were receiving similar letters all over the country.

But now Peress switched. He had received three forms. One of them was a list of organizations which had been declared subversive by the Attorney General, another was a loyalty certificate and a third was a statement of personal history. He was already officially a captain in the Officers' Reserve and he had received this appointment before completing these loyalty forms only because he was a medical officer and only because of the Army's extreme need for dentists at the time. All other reserve officers filled out these forms before they received their appointments.

And so Irving Peress, in answer to the question of membership in any of the organizations on the list, wrote "federal constitutional privilege" in the space where he could have written yes or no. At this moment, sanity fled and the spirit of the Four Marx Brothers took charge. It was pure slapstick and had there not been such a grim, confused and fearful pattern of thinking floating like a poisonous cloud over this country, the whole thing would have been laughed off the front pages in a few days. But in those times, sanity and humor stayed far away from anything connected with Joe McCarthy. However, comedy, even slapstick comedy, demands a balance of tragedy and in the Peress case it was General Ralph Zwicker, his wife and family who provided it.

Irving Peress returned his papers to his draft board and they started bouncing around the country like ping-pong balls from one Army office to another. It was a year before they all got together on the desk of General Zwicker at Camp Kilmer, New Jersey.

In early November, the First Army was ordered by The Adjutant General to call Peress to active duty. This was done and he was told to report on January 1, 1953. Sometime in the next seven weeks, the Army was not sure just when, Peress returned his loyalty papers in which he had claimed the constitutional privilege. During that time, someone in the First Army had discovered that on his original application Peress had signed as a witness to his own signature. The Army returned that paper to him and asked him to get someone else to witness it. He did.

And sometime, in the normal confusion that surrounds all Army paper work, the loyalty papers of Peress went sliding by. Similar forms of five other men who had claimed the identical constitutional privilege were caught in the same office and these five officers were separated from the service at once on the recommendation of the Department of the Army. This was the first fumble, the first of forty-eight.

Peress went on active duty and reported to Fort Sam Houston in Texas, on January 3, and was shipped on to Fort Lewis in the State of Washington in late February. He was on his way to Japan. Then he received a letter from a New York psychiatrist which said that Mrs. Elaine Peress, the dentist's wife, who had been suffering from a severe anxiety neurosis for more than three years, had suffered a relapse. Peress was also informed that his daughter was being treated at a hospital in New York City. These letters were attached to a confirmation of the facts written by the Red Cross, and Peress requested and was granted fifteen days of emergency leave.

He returned to New York, but before leaving Fort Lewis, he wrote a letter to The Adjutant General in which he explained the illnesses in his family and requested cancellation of his overseas assignment. His request was granted and in March, he was reassigned to Camp Kilmer in New Jersey.

At about the same time, the papers on which Peress had invoked the Fifth Amendment arrived at the office of G-2, the intelligence division of the First Army in New York. And, although Peress spent the next year at Camp Kilmer, except for occasional leaves to his home in New York, there were times when G-2 could not find him, had no idea where he was.

His security file was now flagged for investigation, but it was only one file in stacks of thousands. Joe McCarthy's staff had not yet discovered Peress and would not for several months.

However, First Army's intelligence did start action on the flagged file. And it is a good thing that Peress was not really a dangerous man because it took them three and a half months to find him although he was only thirty miles away.

A message went to Fort Sam Houston in Texas, and the answer came back that Peress had never been there, although he had been before he was sent on to Fort Lewis in Washington.

First Army then asked the Surgeon General's office where Peress might be and was shaken up a bit when the answer came back that he had actually been at Fort Sam Houston but had been transferred to Camp Stoneman in California. This was the first time Camp Stoneman had been mentioned and actually Peress had never been there. However, First Army, with a wistful faith in the Surgeon General's office, appealed to the intelligence group in the Sixth Army in San Francisco.

Six weeks later, San Francisco advised the First Army in New York that if it would look out the window it might see Major Irving Peress filling a molar in its own backyard where he had been all the time.

Finally in June, with Peress now an "old soldier" of nearly six months' service, the intelligence group at Camp Kilmer discovered the flagged file and wrote a recommendation that Peress be discharged. Before that, the file had been sent to the Disposition Section of G-2 in Washington where it plowed its weary way through a thirty-day backlog of work and had been returned to Camp Kilmer with the notation that existing regulations required that such material be handled through regular channels at the camp.

In early July, three weeks after its first recommendation, G-2 at First Army sent the file back to Washington, repeating "that the retention of Peress in service was not consistent with the interest of national security because the investigation provided sufficient evidence to find that he had subversive tendencies."

Nearly a month later, the Peress file bumbled its way to the top in Washington, and by now Peress had collected four recommendations that he be allowed to return to civilian life where he could make twice as much money. Two of them had come from First Army's G-2, another from the Office of the Surgeon General, and still another from the intelligence officer at Camp Kilmer.

Another month went by and another batch of papers was sent to Peress. These contained a quiz on membership in subversive organizations and again Peress answered with the Fifth Amendment plea. Back bounced the file to G-2 at Camp Kilmer, to G-2 at Washington, to G-2 at First Army, and to the Office of the Surgeon General in Washington, and by now Peress had collected seven recommendations that he become a veteran.

And then, for the next forty-seven days, the Army rested and nothing was done about Capt. Irving Peress.

However, there was news from an entirely different direction which was to add a bucketful of spice to the comedy. The Doctor Draft Act was being amended by Congress to provide that dentists with experience equal to that of Irving Peress should have been commissioned as majors rather than captains in the first place. Doctors and dentists at Camp Kilmer as well as every other Army base were besieging their superiors to find out if this rumor was true, and one of them was Peress. He wrote a letter to The Adjutant General and said: How about me?

He had been in the Army nine months now and had no reason to think he was any different from any other medical officer. There had been nothing illegal about his invoking of the Fifth Amendment on his papers and the organization he belonged to had not been on the Attorney General's list of subversive groups. If someone had told him at that time that he would soon be a nationally famous public figure, that his promotion would be questioned in giant letters on the sides of delivery trucks, he might have suggested the informer needed drastic psychiatric treatment in a hurry.

The Department of Defense next established a committee composed of two officers from each of the services to carry out the adjustment of medical officers. The committee was told to decide whether or not an officer was eligible on his professional qualifications only. On this basis, Peress definitely was eligible and so he became a major. The official letter appointing him was received at Camp Kilmer on October 30, and three days later, he was sworn in as a major.

And so even before it was first asked, the question: "Who Promoted Peress?" had been answered. Congress had promoted Peress. Congress had reappointed him to a rank more commensurate with his professional education, experience, and ability. However, in the wild tornado of planned confusion that was to develop over this case, each person, newspaper, radio, or television station fled far from reality in an almost psychopathic desire to tell a "better story."

CHAPTER 10

Zwicker Discovers Peress

GENERAL Ralph Zwicker first heard of Irving Peress on October 21, ten days before Peress became a major. He learned about the case at a routine briefing on security problems at his new base. The same day he dispatched a letter to the commanding general of the First Army recommending that immediate steps be taken to effect the release of Peress from active duty. He pointed out that there had been several other previous requests dating back through several months.

Because the complex routines of an Army post provide a built-in blockage of efficiency, ten days went by and Irving Peress became a major. He was a hot potato now, and General Zwicker was outraged when he learned of the swearing-in ceremony that had made Peress a major. First Army had suggested that he be discharged six months before, and although Zwicker's twenty-five years of experience had taught him more than he needed to know about the incredible slowness of Army paper work, he went into immediate personal action on this Peress file.

This, incidentally, was long before Joe McCarthy ever heard

of Irving Peress. Later, Joe tried to take credit for the whole operation.

Zwicker telephoned the commanding general of the First Army in New York, expressed his opinion, and followed it up with a letter to the same general on the same day. This started the final lap which resulted in the end of the Army career of Irving Peress, fourteen months after he had claimed the Fifth Amendment on his loyalty form. On February 2, 1954, he was given an honorable discharge and returned to civilian life.

However, his departure was not a quiet one, nor could General Zwicker close the file on Irving Peress and put it away as finished business. Roy Cohn had discovered the Peress case, and Joe McCarthy was busy rewriting history and reaping the benefit in a new crop of headlines. This was not surprising since the Peress files had been bouncing across the country from coast to coast and back and forth between New York and Washington for several months. It was almost inevitable that sooner or later Roy Cohn's troopers would find him.

At first they thought they had discovered a medical doctor who was a "card-carrying Communist." This was a descriptive phrase which had been developed, mostly by the newspapers. I could never understand why anyone would believe that any dedicated and dangerous Communist would walk our streets with a card in his pocket saying that he was one and identifying him to anyone who might look through his wallet. But we were phrasemakers in those days. Again thanks to McCarthy and the press, we had created the "Fifth Amendment Communist" which, when stripped of its emotional distortion, made a dirty word out of one of our most priceless guarantees of freedom.

On the 22nd of January, three weeks after the Army had decided to give Peress an honorable discharge within 90 days, a member of McCarthy's staff telephoned General Zwicker at Camp Kilmer and told Zwicker that the committee was aware that one of the "doctors" at Camp Kilmer was a card-carrying Communist.

Zwicker sensed that the call was about Irving Peress but he did not yet know that a decision had been made to eliminate Peress from the Army. However, he was cautious and advised Cosmos George Anastos, Assistant Counsel of the subcommittee staff, that he would call back. Zwicker had a hunch he would be asked questions by Anastos and other members of the McCarthy committee and that some of the answers would come under security regulations. There is some information in the files of every Army soldier that is available to the public; there are other files which are available only when approved for release from security. The security file of Irving Peress at this time was a fat pile of papers.

Zwicker knew, because he knew what was in the security file, that there was no evidence to support the reckless charge that Peress was a Communist. Peress had invoked the Fifth Amendment. There was reason to believe that he had been a member of a subversive organization, but none of this information had been proven in court and never would be. Zwicker knew that in a previous test case the Army had court-martialed a Brooklyn physician in a case containing evidence similar to that in the Peress file. The Army had lost the case and the man had been acquitted. Nor had Peress violated any civilian law. He had done nothing but invoke his constitutional privilege as Army regulations permitted.

There was no reason for Ralph Zwicker to know, that morning in January 1954, that he was about to step into a world of fantasy. He told one of his staff to call the McCarthy subcommittee in Washington and to get Mr. Anastos on the line. This was a routine precaution to be sure that the man who had called him a few minutes before was actually who he had said he was. The click of the phone when he picked it up was the signal which started a disgraceful and brutal assassination of the reputation of one of the finest general officers this country had ever known.

He would be called a liar, and it would be three years before he would be cleared of a perjury investigation. He would be called a "Fifth Amendment general," a protector of Communists in the U. S. Army. He would be labeled stupid, arrogant, witless. His family would be bombarded with obscene letters and threatening phone calls. His promotion to major general would be delayed for two years. He would be dragged back and forth through the skies between Washington and Japan several times to testify. Every time his name was printed in the paper, even ten years later, it brought another shower of hate-filled mail to his home.

He was told, and it was reprinted many times in the press, that he was not fit to wear the uniform of the United States Army. There might have been many thousands of Americans who were grateful that he was wearing that uniform during those dreadful weeks of the Battle of the Bulge ten years before, when his military brilliance and courage had done more than one man's share to save three hundred thousand Allied soldiers from death or the German prison camps.

"Mr. Anastos, I have the files before me now. The man you are asking about is probably Major Irving Peress."

At the other end of the line were two open extensions. George Anastos held one; a secretary in his office had the other and she was taking notes, or so they testified later. The memoranda which would be written from these notes would haunt General Zwicker for the next three years. Endless hours of investigations and interrogations would revolve around them but they were never produced. Anastos, the secretary, and other members of the committee staff would swear that they had been destroyed. The memorandum would be the basis of charges that Zwicker had committed perjury. He did not have the foresight to put a monitor on the phone at his end and to have notes made of his side of the conversation. He was not yet aware that he had just stepped into a jungle.

The memorandum claimed that Zwicker, during this phone call, gave Anastos considerable information from the security file of Peress in addition to the information from his basic personnel file. Zwicker claimed that he gave Anastos only that part of the information covering such items as Peress' serial number, his home address.

The memorandum reported that Zwicker had said that Elaine Peress, the wife of the dentist, was a Communist party member along with her husband; that the dentist had been an official in the American Labor Party as well as an organizer and lecturer; also that the dentist's mother had been a member of the same party for several years; and that Elaine attended Communist party meetings and held them in her home.

Had Zwicker given out this information, it would, of course, have been a violation of security regulations, and his detractors, by innuendo and distortion, were able to raise a cloud of doubt when he later denied giving this information to Anastos.

Events were racing now, and the red fox named Irving Peress was still a few lengths ahead of the pursuing hounds and was about to escape back into the civilian world.

In one last desperate attempt to capture him, McCarthy and Cohn set up a hearing in New York City and summoned Major Peress by subpoena from Camp Kilmer.

Peress, accompanied by a lawyer, was given a thorough mauling on the witness stand. He answered most of the questions of McCarthy and Roy Cohn by invoking the Fifth Amendment.

McCarthy had obtained testimony from a policewoman, who had been assigned to join the Communist party as an undercover agent, that both Peress and his wife were members of the party. This meant that they, along with many others, had been "named" as Communists. Therefore, so far as McCarthy and his committee were concerned, they were Communists beyond any reasonable doubt although, in the case of Peress and many others, it had never been proven by due process of the law.

During the first questioning of Peress, McCarthy assumed that because he announced that Peress was a Communist, everyone else should know it and be equally convinced. His questions

82

indicated that he believed it to be a part of a great conspiracy
that a dentist, whose wife and daughter were ill, would be given
a break by the Army and permitted to serve near his home.

McCarthy said he wanted to find out how Peress was stopped
at the port of embarkation when he was on his way to Japan.

He wanted to know who stopped Peress, "knowing that he
was a Communist."

This was a typical distortion of time and facts. At the moment Peress was granted his emergency leave to return from
the State of Washington, there was no testimony by anyone
that he was a Communist. The only shadow of evidence at that
moment was that he had invoked the Fifth Amendment on his
loyalty papers and those papers were bouncing along far behind
him.

Peress invoked the Fifth Amendment thirty-two times during
that first personal tussle with McCarthy, and this was considered a pretty high score. It made larger newspaper headlines
than if he had used his constitutional privilege only twenty-
two times, but not quite so large as fifty-two might have provided.

Near the end of the hearing, he was told that he would be
summoned again to a public hearing three weeks later. In the
final moments of the hearing Peress said, under questioning,
that he had been asked to resign from the Army. He told the
committee that his date of resignation was to be no later than
the 31st of March, but that he could move it up if he so desired.

McCarthy attempted to imply that he was surprised by this
news although he had known it for a week. He tried to get
Peress to admit that he had been asked to resign only after he
had been ordered to appear before the committee. This attempt
to distort the time sequence failed when Peress was able to
show that he had been ordered to appear before the committee
only twenty-four hours previously.

Peress knew now that the fuse was short and that the laws of
self-preservation indicated that the civilian world would be a

safer place. In that world, due process of law was still in control and he had little confidence in what might happen with Joe McCarthy trying to scalp an Army dentist.

He went back to Camp Kilmer and requested an immediate discharge. It was granted.

At the same time, McCarthy's staff prepared and dispatched a letter to Army Secretary Stevens demanding that the discharge be held up. At Camp Kilmer, General Zwicker continued his daily life as commander of several thousand soldiers. The storm clouds were climbing into his personal sky, and the rumble of thunder was beginning.

CHAPTER 11

His Mischief Shall Return

IT was a bad day for everyone the next time Irving Peress faced Joe McCarthy. It was two weeks after Peress had been discharged honorably from the Army and McCarthy was steaming. General Zwicker had also been summoned to testify at a closed hearing that afternoon in the courthouse at Foley Square in New York City. I was not able to attend myself and sent one of my assistants, Robert Jones.

Before the day was over, McCarthy had permitted his accusations to go beyond all bounds of decency, particularly in his questioning of Zwicker. Doctor Peress had been put through the wringer again and slandered over and over as a "Fifth Amendment Communist" as McCarthy abused him.

I also took a wild punch that day when my aide, Jones, saw fit to make a public statement in my name in which he said I backed up McCarthy in his flogging of General Zwicker. This was the beginning of the end of Jones' career on my staff, and he would soon leave me in a storm of unpleasantness generated by his association with McCarthy.

There were two statements made that day that should go down in history. One of them came from Joe McCarthy when he told Zwicker, after a pointless badgering of a hypothetical

85

question concerning the honorable discharge of a Communist, "Then, General, you should be removed from any command. Any man who has been given the honor of being promoted to general and who says 'I will protect another general who protected Communists' is not fit to wear that uniform, General. I think it is a tremendous disgrace to the Army to have this sort of thing given to the public but I intend to give it to them. I have a duty to do that. I intend to repeat to the press exactly what you said. So you know that you will be back here, General."

At that point, it seems to me, the whole pattern of government by investigation hit bottom.

There was no legislation involved here. The basic purpose of any investigation is to provide factual information in the proposal of necessary, remedial legislation. This is the only reason for the existence of any committee of this sort. It is not a court of law, it is not a punitive expedition. The rules and regulations for such committees are loose, too loose, and the witnesses have little defense against irresponsible and reckless attacks. The badgering of witnesses would make any man of law shudder. It was barbaric, obscene.

Here, facing each other, supposedly to find a way to remedy laxness about security matters in the Armed Forces, were a senator and a general, two gentlemen who had risen to positions of top responsibility. There was no reason why the dispute could not be discussed quietly, informally and with mutual respect, without the ever-present desire to make headlines.

Unfortunately Joe McCarthy liked to assume the role of judge, perhaps from some deep-seated dream that had developed as he studied law. He was not the slightest bit interested in legislation. To him the witness was a "bad guy" no matter what witness he might be, and Joe was ready to try him, convict him, and hang him.

The other statement which is worthy of recall was made that day by Irving Peress. He asked and was granted permission to read a short paper before his hearing began and it ended with these words: "His mischief shall return upon his own head and his violence shall come down upon his own pate." It was from the Seventh Book of Psalms, and Peress said that he had learned it as a young man and that he highly recommended it to Senator McCarthy. No one bothered to mention the foresight of Peress when the censure by the U. S. Senate brought McCarthy down less than a year later.

McCarthy was bursting with frustration that morning. Here was the "Communist" who got away. It mattered not to Joe that Peress, if he were a Communist, as an undercover policewoman had testified, was not much of a prize.

He had been "named" like dozens and dozens of others were named during those days. Even Senator Robert Taft was so "named" by a political opponent because Taft favored federal aid for public housing. The professional Communist-hunters of the time were able to summon a stream of professional witnesses who seemed always ready, willing and able to testify that they had known so-and-so at Communist meetings in the past. Their testimony was as suspect as their claims that although they might have once been fooled by the Communist doctrines, they had suddenly seen the light and were now blessed with total recall.

There was on file by now specific testimony that Peress had associated with the American Labor party, which was not on the list of the U. S. Attorney General as a Communist front organization. But it must be emphasized, and it should have been emphasized again and again in 1954, that it was not illegal to belong to any organization whatsoever and there was no charge on which Peress could be tried in a civilian court, nor any other court.

And so Joe McCarthy confronted his frustration that morning. He had not uncovered Peress; the Army had. And finally the Army, after more than a year of floundering, had arranged for the discharge of Peress. It had no sane choice but to give

87

him an honorable discharge under its own rules and regulations. It had been a pretty shoddy performance by the Army, but there had never been any question of a dangerous situation developing because Peress had been under surveillance. To the men in service he was no more, no less, than a dentist.

The opening statement by Peress was based on a sound understanding of law and the constitutional rights of every citizen. He said that he had been subpoenaed to appear before the committee to answer questions concerning his political beliefs, both past and present. He said that he would decline to answer any such questions under the protection of the Fifth Amendment.

At this point, McCarthy interrupted him and told him he was not being called to answer in regard to his political beliefs, but rather in regard to the part he played while an officer in the United States Army in the conspiracy designed to destroy the nation. "You will not be asked about any political belief," Joe said.

Peress then pressed the point that from his earliest schooling he had been taught that the United States Constitution is the highest law of our land and that one of its strongest provisions is the protection afforded to all persons of the privilege of the Fifth Amendment. He said he had been taught that anyone, even a United States Senator, who would deny this protection to any individual or who, under his cloak of immunity, would draw inferences therefrom, would be subversive.

This was a fine legal point, and when the day was over, it might have been surprising if an unbiased judge had decided which of the cast of characters came closest to subversion that day.

Peress explained that by subversive he meant anyone who would undermine the strength of the Constitution and thereby weaken our form of government. He reminded McCarthy that during their previous session, McCarthy had made certain charges concerning his promotion in rank and his honorable

88

discharge. He repeated for the record that he was promoted and discharged under Public Law 84 of the 83rd Congress, and bore down a bit to remind McCarthy that he had been a member of the Senate at that time. He ended with his quote from the Book of Psalms, sat back and waited for the attack. He didn't wait long.

McCarthy's opening question centered on the testimony of the policewoman who had said that Peress had attended a Communist leadership school. Was that true or false? Peress declined to answer under the Fifth Amendment and reminded McCarthy that he was no longer a major but was now "Dr. Peress."

For some reason this seemed to infuriate McCarthy. "Let me make this very clear," he said. "You have been accused, Major, of the most dishonest, the worst conduct that anyone in the Army can be guilty of. You have been accused under oath of being a member of a conspiracy designed to destroy this nation by force and violence. You are here this morning, you are given an opportunity under oath, to tell us whether or not these charges are true or false. If you are a part of this treasonous conspiracy, if you have attended leadership schools of the Communist conspiracy, obviously you will take the protection of the Fifth Amendment. If you are innocent you will tell us that. Now let us ask you this question: Is it true that as of this moment and during all the time that you were an officer in the United States Army, you were an active member of the Communist conspiracy?"

McCarthy opened up with a series of questions on the activities of Peress in the Communist conspiracy. Each one was answered with the Fifth Amendment plea. McCarthy was fuming, and the reason for his anger came pouring out.

McCARTHY: Who signed your honorable discharge?
PERESS: John J. McManus, Major, Infantry.
McCARTHY: Where is John J. McManus located?

PERESS: I have no idea.

MCCARTHY: Let us have the record show that this was signed and handed to this Fifth Amendment Communist, Major Peress, after I had written the Secretary of the Army suggesting that he be court-martialed, suggesting that everyone having anything to do with his promotion, with his change of orders, be court-martialed. I did that feeling that this would be one way to notify all the officers in the Army that there has been a new day in the Army, that the 20 years of treason have ended, and that no officer in the Army can protect traitors, can protect Communists.

This sounded and read, later, when I was able to get a transcript of this session, like a bad play written for television by some hack completely out of touch with reality. First, was Peress a Communist? It has never been proven that he was any more of a Communist than Joe McCarthy himself.

Court-martial for Peress might have been good for more sensationalism in the press but there was the certainty that he would beat the charge in court.

Court-martialing "everyone having anything to do with his promotion" meant court-martialing the Congress of the United States, including Joe McCarthy.

The 20 years of treason slander against the previous administration was pure sedition and was an irresponsible smear of thousands of good people.

It was an infamous statement, full of slander and a total lack of respect for everything decent. And it wasn't really Joe McCarthy. He was playacting again—Big Joe, the Hanging Judge.

McCarthy, recalling the name of the major Peress said had signed the honorable discharge, noticed John Adams, legal counsel to the Army, sitting in the back of the room. He whirled on Adams and demanded that the major be produced that afternoon at 2:30.

Near Adams, General Zwicker waited, accompanied by his aide and a medical officer. Zwicker was recovering from a severe case of flu and he was beginning to wonder what it would be like to face the inquisition which was waiting for him that afternoon. He listened to Peress trying to explain to McCarthy that on the day before his discharge he had personally asked General Zwicker that an Army inquiry be made into the charges which the newspapers had printed after the previous discussion.

The dropping of Zwicker's name into the conversation seemed to stir up a new firepot of anger in McCarthy, who chose to believe that somehow Zwicker had blocked him from capturing his Communist.

At one point, after McCarthy had pounded on Peress to answer a certain question, he was interrupted by Roy Cohn who reminded him that Peress had already answered that one. As Peress calmly gave the Fifth Amendment answer to almost every question, McCarthy was exploding in a series of minor rages. Finally Roy Cohn took over and led Peress through the same general attack. But the calmness of Cohn's approach seemed to irritate McCarthy again and he now introduced Robert Jones, my administrative assistant, and Harold Rainville, who held the same position on the staff of Senator Dirksen. He said that these two men could have the same right to ask questions which any Senator would have, although I have never before or since heard of such a privilege being given to members of Senatorial staffs.

This was the signal for "come on, boys, I've knocked him down, now let's kick him to death."

Robert Jones then decided to get into the act and asked Peress several questions which produced Fifth Amendment answers. McCarthy soon became bored with this and whirled on John Adams. This part of the testimony is a classic of distortion and confusion:

McCARTHY: While the witness [Peress] is examining that [a document], may I ask a question of Mr. Adams, the legal counsel of the Army?

The information we have is that this man signed affidavits as to nonmembership in the Communist party and subversive groups. Is it the position of the Army that by the honorable discharge which he received after he was before this committee, that he had been removed from the court-martial jurisdiction of the Army; or does the Army take the position they have jurisdiction to court-martial this Fifth Amendment Communist for false-swearing, of which he is obviously guilty?

ADAMS: I am not quite sure that I know the question.

McCARTHY: The question is—you are the legal counsel for the Army and I assumed you discussed this. I know you are aware of the fact that I have been discussing it now since he got the honorable discharge. The question is, has he been removed from the court-martial jurisdiction of the Army or does the Army take the position that even though he received his honorable discharge, he can still be court-martialed for false-swearing or any other crime of which he is guilty? [Joe, as a lawyer, had to know that this was an absurd question.]

ADAMS: Mr. Chairman, a separation such as Major Peress received on February 2, is a final action. Under the Uniform Code of Military Justice there is a section in the law which permits the Army to court-martial an individual for offenses which call for penalties in excess of 5 years, provided the offenses are known.

I submitted the questions raised in your letter to the Judge Advocate General of the Army who has the responsibility, by statute, in the Army for military justice, and he gave me an opinion that probably a court-martial against the individual could not be sustained on the facts now before the Army.

McCARTHY: In other words, on the grounds that this would not call for a penalty in excess of 5 years, he has been removed from the jurisdiction of the Army?

ADAMS: He has been removed from the jurisdiction of the Army, and the Army is not aware of any offenses which have been brought officially to its attention under which he could be tried.

McCARTHY: You say the Army is not aware of any offenses, Mr. Adams?

ADAMS: That is correct, sir.

McCARTHY: I do not pretend to cross-examine the legal counsel for the Army. You are here as a guest of the committee. But this matter disturbs me greatly. I have heard that statement before. You have the evidence, the sworn testimony, that this man was part of the Communist conspiracy. You have that from a policewoman of the city of New York. It has been available to the Army for years, ever since she has been filing her reports. You have the information that he took a false oath when he swore that he was not a member of the Communist party. [Peress had never taken such an oath.] You have his refusal to answer questions before a Senate committee. [There was nothing actionable about that.] His refusal to answer questions by the Army would certainly constitute conduct unbecoming an officer. [It wouldn't, but Joe was groping now.]

I do not think you want the record to stand, John, as saying that you were not aware of any offense. You said that it was not brought officially to your attention. May I say that you are here in an official capacity? [A moment before, Joe had said Adams was a guest.] Everything that this committee develops, including what we develop in an executive session, is your official knowledge.

As I say, I do not want to put you on the stand here and cross-examine you [a guest on the stand?], but I am just curious about this fantastic procedure where we have this man before us and have invited the legal counsel for the Army to sit in and listen to all of his testimony. He refused to answer, invoking the Fifth Amendment, so I wrote to the Secretary of the Army

93

and asked for his court-martial. Before Secretary Stevens could get back to the United States, somebody in the Army—and I cannot believe they were acting in good faith—gave him a hurry-up honorable discharge. My letter was made public on Monday, February 1; and Tuesday morning, February 2, this man—about whom you have so much testimony engaging in organizing Communist cells, holding Communist meetings in his home, attending Communist leadership schools, his refusal to answer—was given an honorable discharge.

As you know, John, every Senator receives dozens of letters every month from young men who have good reason for not wanting to serve. They want honorable discharges. If this is the pattern to be followed, if all you need to do is join the conspiracy against this nation to receive the stamp of honor from your country, to get an honorable discharge, then the Communist party perhaps should go out and recruit all the—well, although I do not think they would have much success, go out and try to recruit the young men who would like to get out of the Army.

I am going to ask you this, but I am not going to ask you to answer it now; I am going to ask that you give us the names of every officer, every member of the military personnel or any civilian who had anything to do with this man's promotion, knowing he was a Communist, anything to do with his change of orders, knowing he was a Communist; anything to do with his honorable discharge, knowing he was a Communist, knowing I have suggested a court-martial for him.

[This was Joe at his most irrational. He now threatened to court-martial the Congress, including himself, the Red Cross, all the Army people who handled the routine of Peress' family difficulties "knowing he was a Communist." None of them knew he was a Communist, and neither did Joe.]

I am curious to know whether or not that information will be forthcoming without a subpoena. If not, this is something that will not be allowed to drop. I want to assure everyone concerned, if it's humanly possible, I intend to get to the bottom of it.

I think you have here the key to the deliberate Communist infiltration of our Armed Forces, the most dangerous thing. [Peress had been drafted, he had not enlisted.] And the men responsible for the honorable discharge of a Communist are just as guilty as the man who belongs to the conspiracy himself. [This was certainly a vicious slander of the integrity of the Army.]

So, may I ask you, will the information be forthcoming without subpoena? If not, I intend to take this right to the very limit to get the names of all those individuals, John. If you are not in a position to answer today, I want to know when you can answer it.

ADAMS: Mr. Chairman, the Secretary has given you a letter, which you received yesterday, which discussed the facts of this case as he knows them. He is investigating to determine such additional facts as he can.

If there can be developed any indication of conspiracy of a subversive nature with reference to the handling of this or any other officer assignment, those matters will be prosecuted by the Army.

[This, of course, was a sane, sensible answer. It was the Army's problem and the Army's duty to clean up its own troubles. But Joe would have none of that.]

McCARTHY: John, I will not take any double-talk, any evasion on this. Either the Army is going to give me the names of the individuals responsible for coddling and honorably discharging a known Communist—not only a run-of-the-mill, but an important member of the Communist conspiracy [Peress had been promoted?]—or the Army is going to refuse.

I may say now, for the benefit of everyone concerned, if the Army refuses, I intend to take this to the floor of the Senate, and I intend to try to have cited for contempt any man in the military—and I do not care whether he is a civilian or an officer

—who tries to cover up those responsible for this most shameful, most fantastic situation. [He thus threatens Adams with a contempt charge.]

If you cannot answer that today [answer what? That was a speech, not a question], I would like to know when I can get an answer. It is a simple decision. I want to know whether or not there is a new day in the Army or not. I have a lot of respect for Secretary Stevens and I received a letter which I cannot conceive of Secretary Stevens having written. He may have. [Forgery, now?]

Complete double-talk does not answer any of our questions. We are not going to take this, John, in any case. We are going to make an example here and see if we cannot set a pattern for a clean-out of those who have been invited into the military. [Now he fires Stevens.]

If the new Secretary wants to do that himself, very good. I think he will. [Or his head will roll too?] But I will want to know within 24 hours whether or not the Army is going to give us the names of those whom I just indicated. We will ask for that information by tomorrow night.

If that period of time is unreasonable, we will give you additional time. I will be in Albany holding hearings tomorrow and I will want that information there.

Mr. Peress, just one or two more questions. While you were an officer in the Army, did you ever have access to any decoding or encoding machines?

PERESS: I don't even know what they are.

Did he ever see any messages either before or after they were decoded? Peress answered that the only messages he ever saw were his orders and he thought they had been mimeographed. McCarthy pushed on, attempting to insert the belief that Peress was a sinister character. Peress said that he had occasionally filled out a dental form on which he listed the name of the patient, his serial number, and what he had done for him.

Senator Charles Potter tells newsmen that Chief Counsel Roy Cohn should be fired immediately if it is true that he sought to force the Army to give special treatment to David Schine.

Secretary of the Army Robert T. Stevens (*left*) and Senator Joseph McCarthy leaving closed hearing of Senate Permanent Subcommittee on Investigation at Federal Courthouse in New York City.

Senator Dirksen (*second from right*) discusses the resignation of Roy Cohn and the transfer of Donald Surine. At table (*from left*) are Senators Mundt, McCarthy, Dirksen, Jackson (proxy for McClellan and Symington). *Standing left:* Senator Potter.

A major figure in controversy, Brig. Gen. Ralph W. Zwicker, commanding officer of Camp Kilmer, N.J. The general was a much-decorated hero of World War II who took part in the D-Day invasion.

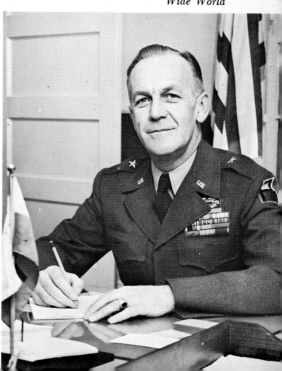

Wide World

The scene from the back of the hearing room during the first session of the McCarthy-Army inquiry, April 22, 1954.

Senator Symington (*left*) talks to McCarthy and Committee Counsel Robert Kennedy after a clash. McCarthy had accused Jackson of misrepresenting facts on TV. Symington had demanded that charges be withheld until the accused was present to defend himself. McCarthy had banged on the table with an ashtray in an attempt to silence Symington.

Wide World

McCarthy covers the microphones in front of him as he confers with Roy Cohn. An almost continuous whispering was a side feature of the Hearings.

The three democratic members of the Subcommittee: (*from left*) Senators McClellan of Arkansas, Symington of Missouri and Jackson of Washington.

Principals in hearing room. *Left to right:* Army Secretary Robert Stevens, Major General Robert Young, Roy Cohn and McCarthy.

McCarthy and his aides, Cohn and Surine.

McCarthy looking at two photos which figured in a wrangle at the hearing on April 27. The Army said the smaller of the photos was a doctored version of the larger one. McCarthy denounced the accusation as "untrue."

McCarthy then turned to Zwicker and said that the file on Peress contained a reference that he had been considered for sensitive work in May of 1953, after, Joe said, it was "fully known" that he was a Communist and that the file did not show whether he was rejected or not. Would Zwicker know what that sensitive work would be? Zwicker said he did not know and even if he did, he would not be privileged to tell McCarthy under the executive order which forbade him to discuss matters of that nature.

This lit another explosion, and McCarthy threatened that Zwicker would be in difficulty if he refused to tell what sensitive work a Communist was being considered for. Peress then interrupted and offered the information that the sensitive work was that he had been needed as a prosthodontist, that he had been transferred to that section and had worked there for a few months.

That ended the questioning on the question of sensitivity but it left General Zwicker with something to consider during the lunch hour. He had now been told that McCarthy was prepared to defy the executive order of the President under which Zwicker could not give confidential file information to anyone under any circumstance.

There were only a few more questions for Peress. When was he married? Did he have brothers, sisters, a father? Did any of them work for the government or in a defense plant? He declined to answer all of them. Finally, McCarthy unwound one final question which summed up his whole gnawing frustration and synthesized the confusion which had been created over this former Army dentist. It was a long rambling wail about a commission, a discharge, and records which disclosed, Joe said, that Peress was a "Communist party leader." At the end of it, McCarthy wearily said, "What is your answer?" And Peress, with what might have been a flash of bitter humor, answered, "I really couldn't make a question out of it. Would you repeat it please?"

That ended the morning hearing.

Through it all, Joe had shown his unusual ability to confuse and distort by ignoring the time sequence of past events. He had accused dozens of officers, the Red Cross, the United States Senate and General Zwicker of being part of some incredible conspiracy directed, he implied, by the Russian Secret Service which was using a dentist as its secret weapon.

A few nights later, some "persons unknown" manifested their patriotism by throwing rocks through the windows of the Peress home in Brooklyn. This, at least, Joe could add to his list of triumphs in his fight to "wake up America."

CHAPTER **12**

I Am Not Their Judge

RALPH Zwicker stepped into the witness chair as the afternoon session opened, and Roy Cohn asked the first few questions. He suggested that Zwicker might like to tell what steps he and others had taken against Peress before "action was finally forced by the committee." This was a curious statement by Cohn. The action to separate Peress from the Army had been totally an Army operation, and now that it was completed, McCarthy seemed to be furious because Peress had been discharged.

Cohn was questioning Zwicker calmly concerning what had happened at Camp Kilmer. He suggested that whatever it was, it would not reflect unfavorably on Zwicker nor on a number of other people at Kilmer and in the First Army. Zwicker said that he did not think it would.

Then McCarthy jumped in. "It would reflect unfavorably upon some of them of course?" he asked. Zwicker said he could not answer that.

But didn't Zwicker know that somebody had kept this man on knowing that he was a Communist? Zwicker said he did not know that.

McCarthy backed up a little bit. But Zwicker did know,

didn't he, that someone had kept him on knowing that he had refused to tell whether or not he was a Communist? Zwicker said he could not answer that question under the executive order.

Here again was the twisting of the record. The whole problem of Peress was not that of someone keeping him *in* the Army but of no one getting him *out* of it within a reasonable time.

Zwicker's answer, perhaps his cold dignity and the symbolism of everything he represented, seemed to infuriate McCarthy. Zwicker was "the Army" and it was the Army or the mere fact that there was an Army through the last harrowing eight months which had brought on most of Joe's troubles. The Army, which had drafted David Schine, had "double-crossed" Roy Cohn, had been the subject of a growing storm of protest from the press against Joe, had, he thought, tried to block him at every turn. Now here it was, sitting in the witness chair, tall, confident, unshakable, the direct opposite of the many witnesses of the past who had been fearful, rattled and easy to knock apart.

In moments like this, Joe McCarthy seemed to assume automatically another of his many roles. He was back at Marquette again, the heavyweight boxing champion, whirling out of his corner against a cool, scientific craftsman who was stabbing him with sharp jabs, not hurting him but piling up points. Joe knew the answer for that. Wade in, chin tucked between his huge shoulders, and start punching. To the jaw, to the belly, to the groin, it didn't matter, just keep on punching. It had always worked before, but it wouldn't work this time.

Did Zwicker know that somebody had kept Peress in the Army knowing he had refused to tell whether he was a Communist? McCarthy had put aside the essential fact—that the somebody who had the authority to discharge Peress did not know that he had invoked the Fifth Amendment on his loyalty papers thanks to those forty-eight recorded fumbles by dozens of different Army people. Zwicker said he could not answer that question under the Presidential order.

McCarthy started to hammer on Zwicker with his contention that somebody, that mysterious "somebody," had given Peress an honorable discharge although he knew that the dentist was a "Fifth Amendment Communist." Again and again this meaningless phrase was thrown into the arena. Zwicker said that he had read the news stories about the previous appearance of Peress but that was all he knew about it.

Within a few minutes, Zwicker was accused of being coy, of hedging and hemming, and of being untruthful. The low punching was beginning to bruise the general and he snapped back that he didn't like to have anyone impugn his honesty. McCarthy said that it had to be either honesty or intelligence, that he couldn't help impugning one or the other "when you tell us that a major in your command who was known to you to have been before a Senate committee, and of whom you read the press releases very carefully—to now have you sit there and tell us that you did not know whether he refused to answer questions about Communist activities."

McCarthy then attempted to blame Zwicker for letting Peress out of the Army. Although this had seemed to be the goal of everyone involved with the case, Joe now took off in a different direction—Zwicker should have held Peress for court-martial because Joe had written a letter to the Secretary of the Army demanding it. The general, of course, had no authority to do anything of the kind and McCarthy knew it.

Harold Rainville, administrative assistant to Senator Dirksen, then offered a strange suggestion. He had a theory that Peress could have been detained for 90 days by a medical officer who might have found that he was not physically qualified for separation.

This was too incongruous even for this hearing, and McCarthy interrupted. It was his new theory that if a soldier had stolen $50 just before his discharge, Zwicker would have been required to delay his discharge and therefore, since being a "traitor" as part of the Communist conspiracy was just as bad as stealing $50, Zwicker should have retained Peress. It was a rambling, unrealistic proposition with its own built-in denial. Irving Peress was innocent until proven guilty and, ten years later, he was still innocent.

They moved into the final round then, and McCarthy threw the rule book out the window. The hearing, if it could be dignified with this description, was turned into a disgraceful brawl, with a senator of the United States insulting and vilifying a general of the Army as if he were a member of the crime syndicate.

Then McCarthy began a long rambling hypothetical question about a mythical Major John Jones who had refused to testify on his connection with the Communist conspiracy, and a General Smith who was responsible for Jones receiving an honorable discharge. Did General Zwicker think General Smith should be removed from the military or kept on in it? Zwicker answered that he should be kept if he were acting under competent orders. But what if General Smith originated the order? McCarthy asked, now trying to split Zwicker into two people with the double responsibility of approving the discharge of Peress and then directing his separation.

McCarthy: You said if you learned that he stole $50 you would have prevented his discharge. You did learn something much more serious than that. You learned that he had refused to tell whether he was a Communist. You learned that the chairman of a Senate committee suggested that he be court-martialed. And you say that if he had stolen $50 he would not have gotten the honorable discharge. But merely being part of the Communist conspiracy, and the chairman of the committee asking that he be court-martialed, would not give you grounds for holding up his discharge. Is that correct?

Zwicker: Under the terms of this letter, that is correct, Mr. Chairman.

McCarthy: That letter says nothing about stealing $50, and

it does not say anything about being a Communist. It does not say anything about his appearance before our committee. He appeared before our committee after that order was made out.

Do you think you sound a bit ridiculous, General, when you say that for $50 you would prevent his being discharged, but for being part of the conspiracy to destroy this country you could not prevent his discharge?

ZWICKER: I did not say that, sir.

[Things went from bad to worse for the next several minutes with McCarthy becoming obsessed with the imaginary theft of $50. Why, why, why could Zwicker not hold Peress?]

ZWICKER: Because, Mr. Senator, any information that appeared or any releases were well known to me and well known to plenty of other people long prior to the time that you ever called this man for investigation, and there were no facts or allegations, nothing presented from the time that he appeared before your first investigation that was not apparent prior to that time.

This was the heart of it. The Army, in a time-consuming, blundering way, had handled the "security problem" of Irving Peress long before McCarthy and his boys had ever heard of him. And Peress had not been the only officer released for identical reasons during that time and before and since. Had there been reason to prosecute him, either as an officer or a civilian, it would have been done under due process of law, not to provide a circus for a publicity-mad Senator.

Zwicker said that was not a question for him to decide, but was ordered to answer the question because McCarthy wanted to know how he felt about getting rid of Communists.

Zwicker said he was all for getting rid of Communists. McCarthy again demanded that Zwicker answer the question unless he wanted to take the Fifth Amendment. He stormed that anyone with the brains of a five-year-old child could understand the question although by now the original hypothetical snarl had been further confused. Finally, Zwicker was permitted to say that he did not think such an officer should be removed from the military, that an officer or any other military man obeys orders without question.

It was then that McCarthy committed his most regrettable foul. "Then, General," he said, "you should be removed from any command. Any man who has been given the honor of being promoted to general and says 'I will protect another general who protected Communists' is not fit to wear that uniform, General."

It was not over yet. Did Zwicker think it was proper to give an honorable discharge to a man known to be a Communist? Zwicker said he did not. Why did he think it was proper in this case? Because he was ordered to do so. And "anything that I am ordered to do by higher authority, I must accept." Did he think the higher authority guilty of improper conduct in this case?

"I am not their judge, sir," Zwicker said, and here was the difference. McCarthy had appointed himself judge.

Roy Cohn moved in then in an attempt to sweep up the mess and put the whole thing in proper perspective. Was it not correct, he asked, that Zwicker had received an order signed by The Adjutant General telling him to give Peress an honorable discharge within 90 days and that Zwicker had no choice but to carry out that order? Yes, said Zwicker, that's the way it was.

McCarthy was silent for several minutes while Harold Rainville asked a few questions, followed by Robert Jones who wanted to know Zwicker's "considered opinion" of the order forbidding him to give confidential information to the committee. "Sir, I cannot answer that," Zwicker said, "because it is signed by the President. The President says don't do it and therefore, I don't."

Jones was still not satisfied. Again he asked for Zwicker's considered opinion and seemed to sum up the muddled confusion of the whole episode by saying that here was a perfectly good example of a Communist being promoted, all because of the executive order. This was one of the most inane remarks of the whole affair. According to Jones' theory, Peress had been promoted because President Eisenhower had issued a directive forbidding Army officers from revealing confidential information. Zwicker said he would not answer because he would not criticize his Commander in Chief.

It was over now, or almost. McCarthy had one more shot to fire. He told Zwicker that he would be called back for a public hearing on the following Tuesday and ordered him to contact the proper authority who could give him permission to tell the committee "the truth." Zwicker said it was not his prerogative, meaning that he could not go to Dwight Eisenhower and say, "Mr. President, I want to be relieved of my obligations as an officer in your Army so that I may give confidential information to the McCarthy committee."

McCarthy shouted that he would be ordered to do it. Zwicker repeated that he would not do it.

And the disgraceful session ended.

Zwicker would not appear again the following Tuesday. By then, the story of McCarthy's attack would be thundering from coast to coast. We were all heading for the climax now, the Army-McCarthy hearings. It had all started eight months ago when an Army draft board had listed the name of G. David Schine.

But Ralph Zwicker was not through yet. It would be three years before he reached the end of his affair with Joe McCarthy.

As the hearing room emptied that day, there was an echo from the opening statement of Irving Peress—"His mischief shall return upon his own head and his violence shall come down upon his own pate."

CHAPTER **13**

Like a Battle Royal

I HAVE never seen a real old-fashioned battle royal. But some of my older friends from the South have told me that it used to be a status-establishing event to stage one at social gatherings. As I understand it, a half-dozen or more husky young fellows were put together in a ring with boxing gloves and told to go ahead and start punching. The last man on his feet was the winner and received a prize which was supposed to make it all worth while.

I thought of this the day after I received a copy of the Army report. For this was a day when Joe was punching blindly and wildly in all directions.

It would seem that a normal man would have suspended all other operations during that day of grace and prepared a defense. It was too late now for McCarthy to go back eight months and undo all the damage that had been done by Roy Cohn and himself over the drafting of David Schine. Now was the time for rational soul-searching and, if necessary, for paying the penalty and for being grateful that this might be no more expensive than losing the services of Roy Cohn.

I wondered then, and I wonder now, why this price was too high for Joe to accept. He was definitely not a man of little knowledge, he was a cynical realist insofar as political maneuvering was concerned, and I cannot believe that he could have believed he could be the winner in a head-knocking contest in an open arena with the Army of the United States.

However, like one of the warriors in a battle royal, he spent most of that day and most of that night punching groggily and with increasingly poor aim at other targets.

First, in the morning, it was Annie Lee Moss who appeared before the committee. She had once been employed by the Army Signal Corps but had been suspended from her job when called to a previous hearing by McCarthy and branded a Communist. She was being brought in now, McCarthy said, as an example of how the Army "coddled" Communists.

As the hearing opened, McCarthy told Mrs. Moss that he was curious to know why she had been shifted from working in the cafeteria in the Pentagon to Army code work when, Joe said, her superiors knew she had a Communist record. Here again was the routine distortion—the Army had no such record then nor at any other time. Mrs. Moss testified that she had not at any time been a member of the Communist party and that she didn't even know what the Communist party was until she had been called to the previous hearing. Stuart Symington told her that he believed she was telling the truth, and I think that summed up the feelings of all of us including Joe McCarthy.

Mrs. Moss faced him with dignity from the witness chair, and her all-out honesty and bewilderment at the charges, her grief at losing her government job, and Joe's realization that once again another of his balloons was about to be pricked, caused him to make up his mind to leave the room and the further questioning to Roy Cohn. Before he left, he was further humiliated by the loud applause of the audience after Symington told Mrs. Moss that he thought she was telling the truth.

Cohn tried to save something from this fiasco by saying that the subcommittee had substantiating testimony from an unidentified witness that Mrs. Moss had been a Communist in 1943. This was, of course, an underhanded and vicious attempt to use hearsay evidence, and Senator McClellan protested vigorously.

This time McClellan got the cheers from the spectators and Karl Mundt, sitting as chairman after McCarthy left, ordered Cohn's remarks stricken from the record.

It turned out that the "evidence" against Mrs. Moss was that a former undercover agent had testified that her name was one of many listed as members of Communist front organizations. It was also brought out that there were three Annie Lee Mosses in Washington alone.

If any one of the three women named Annie Lee Moss who lived in Washington at that time was a Communist, research could certainly have determined which one it was; the hearsay evidence of a corroborating witness could have been produced by bringing in the witness to confront the suspect. Then, if this Annie Lee Moss who had been called in (or whichever one) might have been the true suspect, McCarthy would have had a case.

As it was done, this woman who did appear had been suspended from her job—and what person at her low-level income can afford to be out of work for even one day?—and the pattern of her life had been permanently damaged.

However, the day was not yet over for Joe. That night he was on the radio with Fulton Lewis, Jr., over a local Washington station. This was the best outlet he could arrange despite his demand that he be given coast-to-coast television and radio time to answer the speech made by Adlai Stevenson a few days before, an address in which Stevenson accused the Republican party of being half McCarthy, half Eisenhower. The President and his advisers had decided that Richard Nixon should answer Stevenson and had ignored McCarthy's demands.

During the radio broadcast with Fulton Lewis, McCarthy lashed out at just about everybody, his enemies and his friends.

Many Republicans, even at this late date, were standing by, willing to help Joe solve his problems. Because they may have believed that he was sincere in his efforts to attack Communism, because they were aware of the serious damage being done to party unity, or even because of fear of his attack against themselves, there were many powerful men who would have given him their strength through these difficult days.

He wanted none of them. At least, it seemed on the surface that he wanted none of them, but when he was not performing in the public arena, I knew that he was deeply hurt because he thought they had deserted him, and he could never understand why.

That night on the Lewis program he again defied President Eisenhower and everyone else within the Republican party. He made an emphatic declaration that he would continue on his own independent way and would disagree, as he had before, with members of his own party when he felt they were mistaken. If Joe had gathered together all the policy makers within the Senate and had asked them to create the worst possible statement to make at that time, they could not have topped this one. It helped, along with all the rest of his irresponsible activities, to end his political career.

He claimed that night that he could go on indefinitely naming Communists that he and his committee had exposed, but this list has never been found. He did name three former government employees, two of them women, without quite naming them, but these were more of his "Fifth Amendment Communists" who had refused to answer questions and had resigned or been removed from government service even as was Annie Lee Moss. They were of trivial importance, and certainly failed to make his record impressive.

He swung wildly again at Edward Murrow. He had discovered that in 1935, Murrow had been on the National Advisory Council of the Institute of International Education, an agency which had helped to bring three hundred professors to safety from Axis countries and which administered student exchange programs between the United States and seventy-four other countries. Here, Joe pointed out, on a booklet printed nineteen years before, was the dreadful truth about Murrow. The word "Moscow" was printed right on the same book.

Unfortunately for all of us, thousands of American citizens gulped down this irrational smear and quickly translated it to an unshakable belief that Ed Murrow was indeed a Communist.

Moscow University, Joe said, taught the violent overthrow of the entire traditional social order. This might explain, he added, why Ed Murrow felt that, week after week, he had to smear McCarthy.

Actually, Murrow had devoted one broadcast hour to showing filmed records of McCarthy in action. Any smearing that had been done had been done by Joe himself.

The next night Murrow answered this preposterous charge with the information that the Institute of International Education was financed by the Carnegie Institute and the Rockefeller Foundation and that on its board of trustees were John Foster Dulles and a long list of prominent American educators including many presidents of universities. Furthermore, the summer session of the University of Moscow never took place. It had been canceled by Russian authorities, and the council had been dissolved. It had been the belief of the council, Murrow reported, that an exchange of cultural ideas was possible between men of intelligence although their basic beliefs might differ, and that the representatives of democracy would not necessarily become contaminated nor converted through discussions with Communists.

"To deny this would be to admit that in the realm of ideas, faith and conviction, the Communist cause, dogma and doctrine is stronger than our own," Murrow said.

He was certainly right on this. If people of different beliefs cannot mingle on a rational level with mutual respect, nothing lies ahead for the world but endless chaos and baseless hatred.

As the years go by, only the intermingling makes progress. Self-righteous oratory never convinced anyone of anything, but the mixing, particularly in the world of sports, does more to promote harmony than anything else. The hope for world peace moves a tiny inch forward each time an American track team competes with the Russians. The same progress can be made through cultural discussions.

This debate, Murrow must have known, could never reach a satisfactory solution. Facts and rational statements are never an answer to the type of attack he faced.

And so Joe McCarthy had finally maneuvered himself into an untenable position, alone except for the support of the lunatic fringes of our society, gravely wounded by Roy Cohn and David Schine. From now on the script would read as the tragedy of a man who had plunged too boldly and alone into the dangerous jungle.

CHAPTER **14**

Anything a Senator
Says Is News

M$_c$CARTHY'S answer to the Army charges was no surprise. It was blackmail, he said. The Army was holding David Schine as a hostage in an attempt to stop McCarthy's exposure of the coddling of Communists in the Army.

The Army report, he said, was twisted, distorted and untrue. And, as usual, Joe had a handful of documents to prove it. He claimed they were copies of notes and memoranda written by his staff during the previous months, and they told an entirely different version of the maneuverings and discussions that had gone on between Roy Cohn, Francis Carr, John Adams and Secretary Stevens. Whether these papers were authentic or had been prepared during the past few hours was never established to my satisfaction.

McCarthy had set up a news conference to make his countercharge, and in doing so had run out on his agreement with me to meet with Dirksen, Mundt and myself to discuss the Army report. I had told him to bring Roy Cohn along and I had believed that he would honor this obligation. However, instead of that, he informed us that he was canceling the meeting and leaving town to make a speech in Wisconsin. Actually, he did go to Wisconsin later that evening but first he had the news conference.

I have never seen Everett Dirksen angrier than he was that afternoon. A man of honor himself, he was incensed by McCarthy's crude tactics. He told the press that Cohn would have been questioned under oath at the meeting of the four Republican members and that he now intended to see to it that this questioning took place. Karl Mundt also demanded a showdown. The three Democrats on our committee were delighted.

McCarthy had seen me at the Annie Lee Moss hearing that morning. We had said hello, but he had mentioned nothing about canceling the "executive session" with Mundt, Dirksen and myself. Nor did he mention it to either of them. Then came the phone call to my office.

"Charlie, I am postponing the meeting."

"Oh?" I said.

"I have to go to Wisconsin for a speech."

"We haven't any time, Joe. Every minute is important on this thing. I'd like to clean it up this afternoon."

"I'll take it up with you fellows in a few days," he said, and that strange giggle of his came through the phone. "The Army can't get away with this, Charlie. It's blackmail."

"Joe, you've got to make sense on this. It won't do any good to throw out a lot of wild countercharges. Get rid of Cohn. The Army will sacrifice Adams, and the whole thing will be forgotten in a week. Let Schine serve his time like anyone else."

"Charlie, I'll get together with you next week."

He giggled again and hung up the phone.

A few minutes later he and Cohn were busy telling the press that it was all nonsense, that the Army was holding David Schine as a hostage to stop the exposure of Communists in the Armed Forces. And while the press and radio and television

113

were splashing this preposterous charge around the world that night, Joe McCarthy was flying to Wisconsin to repeat it.

A study of the newspapers published on Saturday, March 13, 1954, would convince anyone that nothing of any importance happened any place in the world that was not involved with Joe McCarthy. The Washington *Post,* on page one, used an overline, two screaming banner headlines, a four-column picture of McCarthy and Cohn, another picture of David Schine, a side story listing three Congressional committees that were trying to get in the act, another side story on Ed Murrow's answer to McCarthy's radio attack, and guides to five more McCarthy stories inside the paper.

Almost apologetically, the *Post* used a small section of page one to report that two U. S. Navy airplanes had been attacked by Soviet jets on the German-Czech frontier. All through the paper one could find Joe's footprints.

One Southern Senator, for example, had told the Senate that he was opposed to statehood for Hawaii because of Communism in the islands. He said that the Communists planned to use Hawaii as a base for assaults on our democratic way of life.

There was a story from Camp Gordon in Georgia, in which the commanding officer stated piously that Private Schine was, indeed, leading a rugged life. There was a long rundown of the leading characters who would play the parts in the Army-McCarthy hearings, their biographies and some of the things they had been doing in the past several months.

Another story told of Joe McCarthy's wavering policies about David Schine. It ran for nearly a column on an inside page and listed Joe's switches from one extreme to another.

Drew Pearson, in his column, wrote that revenge was McCarthy's strongest motivating force. Still another inside story said that Nixon would go on the air that night and would "not dodge the issue of McCarthyism."

In still another story, Ed Murrow was hailed by a radio-television industry magazine for his "indictment" of Senator Mc-Carthy.

Senator William Jenner announced that the Senate Internal Security Subcommittee would launch an investigation into the handling of Communist files by the Armed Services. This seemed to be stepping into McCarthy's territory, and I wondered what Joe would have to say to that.

The application for a renewal of a television station license at Erie, Pennsylvania, was being held up because one of its officers had been "named" as a member of the Communist party.

Dr. Louis B. Wright, director of Washington's Folger Shakespeare Library, in a speech at Richmond, said that America was in danger of being turned into a land of intellectual illiterates because of demagogues railing at our traditional liberties under the name of patriotism.

On the editorial page, Roy Cohn and McCarthy had scored in the top editorial, and McCarthy alone was the only figure in the editorial cartoon of the day drawn by Fitzpatrick of the St. Louis *Post-Dispatch.* It showed Joe storming at the door of a TV studio but ignoring another door labeled "court of law" and carrying a sign which read McCARTHY-BENTON LIBEL CASE.

Another short story reported that a Connecticut housewife's anti-McCarthy campaign was being pressed in Maryland.

Still on the editorial page, a letter signed and dated in England wanted to advise America that Anglo-American relations were deteriorating—and blamed Joe McCarthy. The writer said he thought the time had come when President Eisenhower must speak up.

Far back in the sports pages I found a story that Queen Mother Elizabeth of England was being urged to scratch her jumper from the "shameful grueling" of the Grand National steeplechase. I was surprised that no one had seen fit to describe the Grand National as part of the Communist conspiracy.

In Caracas, Venezuela, Secretary of State Dulles was assured by Brazilian officials that the United States could depend on their unconditional support in the fight against Communism.

And finally, down amongst the moving picture ads on page twenty, the *Post* devoted six inches to the report that the battle for Dienbienphu in Indochina was near the end. Red troops were bombarding the airstrip, and the French fortress, after seven long years, was about to fall. This, one of the great defeats of the freedom forces since World War II, was of much less importance to the editors than the activities of an Army private in Georgia, and was of about equal importance to a story that Barbara Hutton Rubirosa, the Woolworth heiress, and her fourth husband had separated after ten long, grueling weeks of marriage.

And so the climactic clash was upon us. After several years of hearing that "this time Joe had gone too far," I knew now that he finally had. And I knew that the public thinking of the time, stirred by the endless sensationalism of the newspapers, radio and television, would not permit a rational simmering down of the tempest that had been created.

It was too late now to second-guess. It would have been easy to say that none of this would have happened had not David Schine been picked in the lottery of his draft board at a moment in his life when he was involved with Roy Cohn. It was certainly true that from that moment the whole weird pattern had developed.

It would have been easy to say that there would have been no Army-McCarthy hearings if the basic character of Roy Cohn had been different from what it was. His brilliant successes, granted to him so early in life, had made him arrogant, over-ambitious and determined to have his own way at all costs. His campaign to direct the Army career of David Schine had become an obsession and his usual shrewd judgment had vanished whenever he involved himself with Schine.

I know now that none of us on the committee had done what

we should have done and that all of us would have liked to reverse the clock, to make a more courageous record and to have
arrested, at any expense, this madness.

All six of us who served under McCarthy's chairmanship
must carry on our records forever a great share of the responsibility for the whole disgraceful performance, particularly we
Republicans.

Looking back at that time in March 1954, I know that some
of Joe McCarthy's excesses could have been controlled. When
I had demanded that McCarthy fire J. B. Matthews, who had
written an absurd and vicious magazine article accusing the
Protestant clergy of being loaded with Communists, Joe had
surrendered and Matthews had been fired. But this one surge
of boldness on my part should have been followed with a continuing vigilance. None of us on the committee could say hon-
estly that we were not aware of a long series of excesses in the
handling of witnesses called by the subcommittee. Although
Joe McCarthy was the chairman and the dominating force because of his position, there were six more of us who had a
responsibility that we had let slide.

It is difficult, after several years, to re-create one's own thinking in times of stress without rationalizing to give one's self the
best of it. I think now that I was, perhaps, unable to believe
in 1954 that there could be great weaknesses in our government.
Not in the structure, perhaps, but in the weaknesses of men who
would misuse their powers.

Our system of checks and balances is splendid on paper. Our
Bill of Rights is the top level, until now at least, of civilized law.
But somewhere the theory of restriction of abuses breaks down
when a maverick is loose. It was not only McCarthy. It was
never only McCarthy. And, in the years since Joe died, the
same abuses have gone on, many of them without ever being
spotlighted in the press.

Others, too, must share the blame for these days of shame.
Bob Stevens, an honorable and decent man, had shown an un-

117

believable lack of awareness of the consequences all through the Schine affair. As Secretary of the Army, he could have slapped down Roy Cohn at the first realization that Cohn wanted special privileges for David Schine. Stevens had proven time and again that appeasement is always disastrous.

President Eisenhower also had dithered, depending much too much on the advice of the strategy wing of the Republican party that hoped to retain the votes of the thousands who blindly supported McCarthy. The President suppressed his natural instincts of disgust and refrained from using the power that was his to maintain discipline in his government.

Then there was the world of communications. Radio, television and the newspapers "sold" McCarthy to the public with a remarkable lack of responsibility. No matter how loudly the editorial trumpets sing the claim of objective reporting, the strongest sales factor any newspaper has is, unfortunately, sensationalism. Violence, tragedy, and scandal sell more newspapers and air time than any other stories, and even the most piously restrained newspapers are well aware of this. The airplane disaster, the suicide of a prominent Hollywood star, murder, war, sex crimes, grand larceny, adultery and all the other less attractive factors of life on this planet have been, and probably always will be, the top news.

So, too, is the propagation and spreading of slander, if the slanderer or slanderee is a prominent person. If Senator A, craftily crouching behind his Senatorial immunity, announces that the United States Ambassador to the United Nations is a former bank robber, every newspaper in the country will report this in a banner headline the next day. On the day after that they will follow up with an editorial stating that if these charges are true, somebody ought to do something. The Ambassador will "categorically" deny the charge and challenge Senator A to repeat it out in the open where he is not under the protection of his constitutional immunity. On the following day, deep in the inside pages, there may be a story that Senator A claims that he was misquoted.

This is the classic pattern of Senatorial slander, aided and abetted by the American press. Few of those who read the original charge are convinced by the Senator's weaseling retraction. So many of us prefer to believe the bad things about others. The editorial excuse of the newspaper which has spread and made a permanent record of the public smear is that "anything said by a Senator of the United States is news," and that their objectivity demands that they report only what he said without comment. They also claim that they pick up the pieces in editorials which follow sometime later. They do not admit, however, that very few people read the editorials, although many studies of public reading habits indicate that this is the *least read page in the paper.*

And so the object of any irresponsible slander is permanently smeared in print. He has no legal counterattack because of the immunity of his attacker and because any libel suit against the newspaper could be successfully defended with the claim of objective reporting. This is a completely unethical situation and will continue to be so as long as irresponsible men of government take unfair advantage of their own constitutional rights.

Then too, there really is no such thing as objectivity. Every reporter has his own prejudices either for or against every subject. He can be enthusiastic, cynical, bored, facetious, cold or warm. He can be knowledgeable or ignorant of the background material involved in any story. Whatever he is, he turns in his report to his editor and here another personality factor with all the same characteristics processes the story. By positioning, by display and by the tricky language of headlines, it is given prominence on the level that the editor himself decides.

If Senator A has become prominent in our national life, his charge that the UN Ambassador is a bank robber will get the full treatment on page one; if he is a Senator of no prominence,

119

the sensational nature of his charge will upgrade his standing instantly. If he has issued a long statement in which he says nothing more than that the Ambassador is a fine fellow, the story will be dropped in a convenient wastebasket.

As the McCarthy story ballooned to its climax in 1954, I am sure most newspaper editors were aware that they had permitted it to get out of control. Through their own excesses, through habit, through the highly emotional response of the public, they had created a nightmare from which there appeared to be no awakening. Joe McCarthy had become the automatic lead story each day no matter what was going on anywhere in the world. He had scored with more inches of type than had ever been given any other single man in the history of the American press. He had dominated the news month after month and, in the summing up, he could not possibly have been that important. Through the earlier days he had been exciting and his charges had been strong. He had sold many millions of extra newspapers.

But where was the integrity? Where was the balanced judgment that newspaper editors claim? It was obvious by 1954 that the newspapers, at least some of them, were becoming self-conscious about the role they had assumed.

The Washington *Evening Star* wrote an editorial about it in early 1954, and confessed that the press must be credited with a very substantial and entirely unnecessary assist in McCarthy's rise to national fame. It listed in a deft, humorous essay three familiar methods the press had used time and again during the past few years.

One, it said, was the "he didn't mention McCarthy but we knew he meant to do so, so we'll do it for him." This method, the *Star* said, is used when Senator X makes some passing reference to divisive influences or disruptive forces. And then the news stories begin with "In an obvious reference to Senator McCarthy."

Another method, the *Star* said, was when the speaker said

five thousand words on something else and fifteen on McCarthy, and "it's up to us to put it in the proper perspective." These stories begin "The Reverand So-And-So made a slashing attack on Senator McCarthy tonight." The Reverend's topic was actually "The Need for Better Choirs in Rural Churches." At the end of his hour-long address, the Reverend said, "That goes for Senator McCarthy too."

The third method, said the *Star*, is the "nobody even thought about McCarthy and we just can't conceal our surprise" gambit. One of the best examples had occurred recently in Washington: "Meeting in the midst of widespread controversy over the activities of Senator Joseph McCarthy," one story began, "the Daughters of the American Revolution completely ignored the Wisconsin Republican." The headline said: DAUGHTERS IGNORE MCCARTHY.

One of my own favorite souvenirs of the time was a banner headline in tremendous type which said: MCCARTHY SAYS PUSEY IS NOT A COMMUNIST. Nathan Pusey, President of Harvard University, had been one of the sponsors of a booklet published by a group of citizens in Wisconsin exploring the legislative record of their junior Senator. After tentatively jabbing at Pusey, McCarthy, for reasons unknown, refrained from an all-out smear attack on Pusey, who was also a native of Wisconsin.

Although much of the performances of newspapers in that period could be described as incongruous nonsense and some as deliberate mischief, none, to my knowledge, failed to make the most of McCarthy's preposterous charge that the Army was guilty of blackmail.

The few which did maintain a rational editorial approach to Joe McCarthy were attacked as members of the Left Wing press and part of the Communist apparatus. "Left Wing" in those days had become a dirty word.

My office mail increased to several thousand letters a day as soon as it had been reported in the press that I had been the first one to get the report from the Army and that I had demanded that McCarthy get rid of Cohn. It had been necessary for me to go to Detroit that first weekend on personal business, and I had told some reporters there that it was obvious someone was lying about the story of David Schine and that I thought our subcommittee could get the facts.

This brought on a flood of letters denouncing me as a lover of Communism and accusing me of calling Joe McCarthy a liar. They all followed the same pattern, full of profanity, obscenity, and signed, if at all, by "patriotic American" or "100% American." Each one of these pitiful scrawls indicated that the writer was dominated by hatred and fear and a determination to avoid facts.

Facts are more to be avoided than cancer germs to a fanatic, and the letter-writing followers of Joe McCarthy wanted none of them. They had gotten fat on a daily diet of lies, distortions, wild accusations, and their hate-filled minds had now found a Messiah.

Any man, or woman, as Senator Margaret Smith and many others could testify, who said, "But look, this just is not true," and could prove it, was immediately put on the list as a Commie-lover.

I got my share of it. If they were rational and signed, we acknowledged them, but most were like this:

A writer from Hazel Park said: "Our Civic Improvement Association believes you [Potter] are either a Communist, a fellow traveler, or a man sympathetic to the Communist party."

A Detroiter, in apparent sympathy with McCarthy's rough handling of Brigadier General Ralph Zwicker, wrote: "You weren't elected on the coat-tails of Eisenhower, but your war record and sympathy for your disability and as a protest against Truman got you in. Now you seem to forget who put you there. If you want to defend the Army brass, I wish to assure you we shall be happy to make you a one-termer." (And they did!)

"Why back those hidden Communists?" queried another

angry writer from Birmingham, Michigan. "Why not back loyal Americans who are trying to uncover them?"

Another Detroiter: "I'm sorry you felt you had to get in a dispute with Senator McCarthy. Again I must call your attention to the Protestant attacks on Senator McCarthy. I was in hopes you would keep out of it."

Two messages typified a large proportion of anti-McCarthyites, angered by his and Cohn's alleged intervention to win special favor for Army Private G. David Schine.

"I have four sons. One of whom was killed in Germany," wrote one Birmingham man. "None of them were given special preferment."

A Detroit telegram read: A MOTHER OF A DRAFTED COLLEGE MAN DEMANDS THAT COHN BE THROWN OUT.

An Army major's anti-McCarthy approach was different. "A week ago," he wrote, "I submitted a letter asking to get out of the Army because I've had a bellyful of the pussyfooting and fear and trepidation of the Eisenhower Administration at the mere mention of the word McCarthy."

More general were complaints about McCarthy's methods.

"The only Red we know," wrote an Ann Arbor man, "is what we see as we listen to the reports of McCarthy's apelike antics."

Said a businessman in Standish: "The early Romans threw their victims to the beasts. This man destroys by slander and intimidation."

All Senators receive mail now and then from the organized hate groups. Any action or public statement by any man in government which can be distorted into being a gesture helpful to minorities, Negro, Jewish, or Catholic, seems automatically to turn on a flood of psychopathic letter writing. McCarthy, somehow, was supported by a coalition of honest people who were seriously concerned about Communism in America and also by a shabby parade of all the hate groups that infest this country.

Trailing along were the Isolationists, the politically ignorant who believe that all liberal thinking is part of Socialism and that Socialism is part of Communism; the kind of people who join organizations like the Ku-Klux Klan and the John Birch Society.

These people were afraid to think because it is hard work and afraid to let other people think because it might turn out that what they themselves have always thought is wrong. They were dominated by an appalling ignorance and a basic fear that the principles of freedom on which this republic was founded will not stand examination, that it will crumble in any direct contact with another doctrine.

McCarthy had made no effort to recruit these neurotics. They had always been here, the ultraconservatives, the racial bigots, the anti-Liberals, the native Fascists, but now they had a national leader and they had a cause. Joe had convinced them that something terrifying was going on in our own country, in our State Department, in our Army, in many other branches of government. It was Communist infiltration, he said, and it was here and now. He told them that the President of the United States was soft on Communism, and they believed it. He told them that the Army had many Communists high in its ranks and that they were not only protecting Communists but promoting them into the higher ranks. He told them that he could go on indefinitely listing the names of Communists he had exposed.

They believed all this although there was not one single fact to support his statements.

To these people, Communism was something that had been invented in this country in the late 1940's. Had they been asked to name the most dangerous Communist of the time, they might have answered that it was Alger Hiss and sometimes Dean Acheson and sometimes Eleanor Roosevelt and sometimes Adlai Stevenson. It would not have been Joseph Stalin nor Malenkov and certainly not Marx, Engels, Lenin, Trotzky or any of the other philosophers who had founded the Communist party. They did not want to be told that Karl Marx himself always preached against violence.

I have no doubt that many of the people who wrote me letters in those days really believed that Communism was strictly a part of America and that a Communist was any person with whom one disagreed. I have letters in my files which, if accepted as rational thinking by an American citizen, tell me that I was a coddler of Communism because I did not attack any belief in equal rights for all races; if I did not oppose federal funds for schooling, for housing, for highways, for electric power; that Social Security was part of the Communist conspiracy; that fluoridation of public water supply was also part of the theory of Karl Marx.

It finally became a national pattern, and it was still evident ten years later, that a Communist in the United States is anyone with whom you do not agree.

This, however, was not the only powerful public support behind Joe McCarthy. The conservative editorialists of the press, the ones I had hoped would have been my supporters too because I certainly was a Conservative, seemed to have slipped out of focus. It was only a few days after the Army released its charges against Joe McCarthy that David Lawrence and Westbrook Pegler started firing.

"The Left Wing has achieved a number of significant victories in Washington in the last two weeks," Lawrence wrote. The most notable of these, he said, was to bring influence to bear on President Eisenhower to use the headline power of his press conference to carry on an open war with Senator McCarthy.

It was hard for me to believe that Lawrence could have been referring to Eisenhower's gentle slap at McCarthy in which the President hadn't even pointed at Joe by name. It was rather a surprise to find myself listed now as a "Left Winger," but here again was the automatic distortion of the day—a Left Winger was a bad guy—anyone who opposed Joe McCarthy was a bad guy—therefore, my demand that Joe fire Roy Cohn, if Cohn was actually guilty of the Army charges, made me a bad guy and therefore, a Left Winger. This was a perfect example of what had happened to the thinking processes of some of our finest writers.

Pegler, who described me as a "Republican but a greenhorn of frail political fortitude," reported that I had done the most decisive dirty work in temporarily stopping Joe McCarthy and his young assistant, Roy Cohn. His column spent several inches praising Roy and also "reporting" that David Schine had been responsible for discovering that the United States was about to spend ten million dollars on a radio station to fight the enemy with propaganda, a station planted in a spot where it could not even peep because of metals in the ground.

David had not "discovered" it, and the charge was completely false. Pegler then wrote that David's reward was a call from his draft board, as if asking him to serve his country was some dirty trick, and that other members of the press had joined in a foul, dirty deal to stop the McCarthy inquiries. He dropped in a vague accusation that the Communists had penetrated into the administrative circles of the Vatican and ended with a statement that I had voted with the Democrats to hamper the pursuit of Communists.

At the same time, I began to get telephone calls at my apartment at all hours of the day and night. These followed the pattern of the unsigned letters that came to my office, full of obscene abuse, the male and female voices telling me that I was a traitor to my country, a Communist, a foul fiend who had dared to "oppose" Joe McCarthy.

Two o'clock in the morning seemed to be their favorite time to call, and the dialogue followed a pattern.

"Potter, are you for or against McCarthy?"

"I'm for him when I think he's right and I'm against him when I think he's wrong."

"You're a no-good son of a bitch, Potter. You're a Communist."

After about a week of it I asked for and got an unlisted number.

CHAPTER 15

Communist Hero

IT is strange but true that in the years be-
fore Joe McCarthy discovered the headline possibilities in ranting against Communism in the United States, he had joyfully
accepted their support during one campaign in Wisconsin and,
in 1949, had become the American hero of the strong combina-
tion of Communists and ex-Nazis in Germany.

During this unpleasant episode he had helped save the lives
of 43 Nazi murderers who had been sentenced to hang for
slaughtering American prisoners of war; he had driven out of
government one of our finest Senators, Raymond Baldwin of
Connecticut; he had described American Army activities as
"worse than the Russians, worse than the Germans."

It started with Hitler's final military thrust in the fall of 1944.
The maneuver was planned as a smashing, concentrated attack
to the west through parts of Belgium in an effort to encircle
several hundred thousand Allied troops in a pocket against the
North Sea. Part of Hitler's strategy was that a reputation of
horror must precede his troops with the hope that the Allied
forces would panic.

"Sepp" Dietrich, a long-time close friend of Hitler, was at

the strategy meeting and added the condition that no prisoners of war were to be taken alive. The key group in the German attack was the First SS Panzer Division under the command of Colonel Joachim Peiper, formerly an adjutant to Heinrich Himmler, the leader of Hitler's secret police who was to commit suicide when captured by the British.

The attack began and, for awhile, it was successful. I was in the area at the time, and everything was going for the Germans. The weather, bitter cold, brought a series of heavy snowstorms sandwiched between fog, and there was no way for our Air Force to fly in supplies and ammunition. The American people began to read about the Ardennes Forest, about Bastogne where General Macauliffe gave his famous answer of "Nuts" to a German commander who demanded his surrender. Here, too, in the area of the Bulge, Colonel Ralph Zwicker was fighting desperately and brilliantly to hold a key point, and, on the opposite side of the world in the Pacific Theater, Joe McCarthy was resigning from the Marines to hurry back to Wisconsin for a political campaign.

In the Bulge area in Belgium, Colonel Peiper's storm troopers ripped through a fifty-mile area northward through Honsfeld, Bullengin, where they burned the tiny villages, killed many civilians and on to a tiny dot on the map called Malmédy. It was here that Colonel Peiper's storm troopers gathered about 150 American prisoners of war, who had been overwhelmed and surrendered, into a field by the Malmédy crossroads and machine-gunned the entire group. There were twelve survivors, all wounded who had lain on the ground making believe they were dead until nightfall and then had escaped into a nearby forest.

After the war, 74 of the murdering storm troopers had been brought to trial after months of interrogation, and 43 of them had been sentenced to hang by a U. S. military court. There was a long delay before the dates of execution and, gradually, the

Malmédy massacre dropped out of the newspapers, overshadowed by the shocking testimony that was coming out of the Nuremberg trials of the top Nazi war criminals.

Sixteen months went by and then dozens of affidavits began appearing from the death cells where the Malmédy killers were confined. The convicted men now claimed that they had confessed after being tortured by American prosecutors; that lighted matches had been forced under their fingernails; that they had been terrified in mock trials during which American interrogators had supposedly threatened reprisals against their families; that they had been beaten about the sex organs and tortured until they signed confessions.

The Communist press in Germany seized on these affidavits, and a new wave of anti-American feelings swept through Germany, seriously damaging efforts of the United States to win the defeated country over to a reversal of the goals of Adolf Hitler. Eventually, the unpleasant charges of the convicted men reached such a volume that the United States Supreme Court reviewed the case and upheld the sentences. This, the German Communist newspapers screamed, was proof that the United States was incapable of justice.

And so, in April of 1949, a three-man investigating subcommittee, consisting of Senators Baldwin, Estes Kefauver and Lester Hunt, opened a study of the case, and sitting at Baldwin's side was Senator Joseph McCarthy, who had demanded the right to attend the hearings although he was not a committee member. He also demanded the right to call witnesses and to cross-examine, and Baldwin would soon regret that he agreed to these conditions.

Attorney Joseph McCarthy had some very important clients now—the Malmédy murderers—and his performance during the next few days indicated that they could not have found a more ardent supporter.

No one on the American side of the controversy escaped McCarthy's attack. Kenneth Ahrens, one of the survivors, testified at the hearing. He was an American soldier who had been wounded three times during the massacre and had survived the terrifying ordeal. When he testified that the storm troopers had been laughing and seeming to enjoy the slaughter, McCarthy jumped to his feet and roared at Ahrens that he was trying to inflame the public and start a "Roman holiday" by his testimony.

Doctor William A. Perl, the chief interrogator for the Army, told the committee of his experiences with the captured Germans. He explained that they had been thoroughly indoctrinated to believe that, if captured, they would be tortured by the American Army, that they were tough, hardened professional soldiers. He explained that the case had finally been broken through the psychological approach, denied that there had been any physical torture of the prisoners. McCarthy had an answer for that—"I think you are lying. You may be able to fool us. I have been told you are very very smart. I am convinced you cannot fool the lie detector."

At one point Joe howled that the American judges who had convicted the Nazis were morons and demanded that all the U. S. officers involved be given lie detector tests. Although evidence obtained by lie detectors is usually not admissible in court, McCarthy continued to use the inflammatory word in a series of public statements denouncing the U. S. Army. He kept it up for several weeks and, in Germany, the Communist press was reprinting most of his statements, inflaming the German people to the point where they threatened riots all over the country if the convicted murderers were executed.

He heckled and insulted Senator Baldwin into taking his ridiculous lie detector suggestion before the full Senate Arms Services Committee where it was voted down. Joe then walked out on the hearings, where he never should have been in the first place, with a statement that they were a shameful farce and were deliberately attempting to whitewash the American military. Senator Baldwin, he announced, was "criminally responsible." However, Colonel Joachim Peiper, commander of the storm troopers, signed an affidavit in which he denied that any of his men had been tortured by the American interrogators. The United States expediently commuted the sentence of the 43 convicted killers and by 1957, those who were still living were free to lead a normal life wherever they might be.

Probing later through the wreckage of American justice, it was learned that McCarthy obtained his "evidence" from Rudolf Aschenauer of Frankfort, Germany, a member of a Communist spy ring. Although McCarthy later gave a series of slippery answers about his association with Aschenauer, the spy himself testified that he had been transmitting the information to Joe.

Also involved in the case was the shadowy figure of one of McCarthy's best friends and financial backers, a Milwaukee manufacturer who had previously been ordered by the Fair Employment Practice Commission to stop discriminating against workers because of race and religion in refusing to employ Jewish or Negro help. This man had been openly criticizing the war crimes trials and urging that Germany's prewar colonies be restored.

McCarthy's performance not only saved the lives of 43 brutal killers but finished the Senatorial career of Raymond Baldwin, a decent gentleman who had not expected to meet a brawling hoodlum in the U. S. Senate. Baldwin retired before his term was over and returned to Connecticut where he became a federal judge.

At this point Joe McCarthy was a Communist hero, not only in Germany but in Wisconsin where many followers of the Marxian theories infested the trade unions along with thousands of fellow admirers who secretly said, "Hitler was right." Little did they suspect that a year later he would be screaming from the other side of the fence.

CHAPTER 16

Pre-Hearing Hoopla

IT was five weeks after the Army charges were published before we finally got down to business and started the hearing. It should have been five days, and even five hours would have been better. We continued to drift and dawdle and to permit Joe McCarthy to get away with his evasive tactics and his continuing attacks on his old and new adversaries.

However, there was some benefit to the public during those five weeks. Newspaper readers, as if awakening from a nightmare, learned that there were other events taking place in the world and that they could be found now on page one, not after a scratching search through the inside pages.

Early in the week, after the Army charges became known, Joe announced that he was taking off on a speaking tour through the West despite the demand by Senate Republican Leader William F. Knowland that an immediate investigation of the charges should take priority over all other matters. Knowland said there should be no delay, it should be cleaned up that week. However, Joe was still making his own rules and off he went.

At the same time it was announced that the United States Information Agency had rejected Joe's offer to supply copies of two of his books for distribution in its overseas libraries. One of them was called *McCarthyism, the Fight for America,* and the other was a reprint of Joe's attack on General George Marshall. And the title for that little gem was *America's Retreat from Victory.*

And so Joe left town but before he departed, he took another halfhearted swing at Secretary Bob Stevens, "reminding" Stevens that he had promised to produce for questioning all Army officers concerned in the promotion and discharge of Irving Peress. But even the newspapers were getting tired of that one.

As normal news floated back to the surface, we all learned that life had been going on elsewhere in the world and that nothing had really changed much. Hollywood stars were still consuming overdoses of sleeping pills; the Washington Senators continued to "boot away" baseball games in the late innings; auto racing drivers were dying on schedule; and Drew Pearson was chortling that statistics indicated that the Republicans under Eisenhower were outdrinking the Democrats under Truman by ninety-six thousand gallons of whiskey per year.

Another explosion had taken place in early March. Our second test of a hydrogen bomb, which had been held under total security, had proved to be three or four times more powerful than the scientists had expected.

A long synopsis of European and British editorial comment was printed with the conclusion that Europe considered Uncle Sam to be the sick man of the world. Until recently, it reported, Europeans had thought that McCarthy was just a crank and a political hoodlum who would soon shut up because no sane American could possibly have any sympathy for him. Then they read that public opinion polls showed that more Americans favored him than were unfavorable to him. Thus the McCarthy problem, in Europe, passed from the slightly ludicrous to the deadly serious.

One European commentator said that they would have been

happier if the American controversy over Irving Peress had concerned the right of an Army dentist, or any other man, to hold whatever political views he pleased. This certainly made sense. I remembered that one of Thomas Jefferson's finest statements was: "I have sworn upon the altar of God eternal hostility against every form of tyranny over the mind of man." If Jefferson had reappeared in the United States in the early 1950's and tried to follow that principle, he would soon have become a "Commie Coddler."

It was during this period of early April that Bishop Bernard J. Sheil of Chicago dropped a bomb on Joe McCarthy, a most unexpected counterattack. Joe had always been able to depend on the open or silent support of the Roman Catholic Church and its basic ideological dispute with Communism. Many priests had openly cheered Joe and a few had criticized him gently but none, however, of the stature of Bishop Sheil, often described as Chicago's most beloved man, founder of the Catholic Youth Organization and always a courageous fighter for social justice.

Speaking before 2,500 members of the United Auto Workers-CIO, the Bishop said the time had come "to cry out against the phony anti-Communism that mocks our way of life, flouts our traditions and democratic procedures and our sense of fair play. You cannot fight tyranny with tyranny."

The Bishop told the audience that Adolf Hitler had been one of the noisiest anti-Communists but had been a dismal failure at it, and half of Hitler's own country was now living under Communism.

"I take a pretty dim view of some noisy anti-Communists," Sheil said, "particularly the junior Senator from Wisconsin. I do not take a dim view of them because they are anti-Communists, but because they are such pitifully ineffective anti-Communists."

The Bishop made it clear that he was speaking as a citizen and not for the Church.

135

"Excitement galore there is but precious few results as Communists, supposed Communists, phantom traitors and innocent people alike are pursued from headline to headline," he said. "Combating Communism is a serious business and not a game to be played so that publicity-mad politicos can build fame for themselves. Are we any more to be feared by the Communists because of the hundreds of headlines the Senator from Wisconsin has piled up? I don't believe so. The large-type charges always peter out to a back-page item after they have served their purpose—to gain a headline. But by then our man on horseback is charging off in another direction—tomorrow is another day, another edition, there is need for another headline."

Bishop Sheil added that the nation is faced with the job of protecting itself from subversion within and from aggression from without. He said that the first task of a true anti-Communist is to see that conditions are such that Communism won't take root, that people have decent homes and enough to eat, and to remove class, religious, and nationality barriers.

The Bishop was making only one tactical mistake—he was making sense in a country that was living on hysteria.

As we all got ready for the opening of the baseball season in mid-April, Herblock, the brilliant political cartoonist, seemed to sum up the whole atmosphere of Washington, D.C., at that moment. His cartoon showed a baseball player making one of the routine errors we had learned to expect from our Washington Nats. In a box at the edge of the field a Congressional-type man is shaking his fist at the ballplayer and shouting, "You disloyal American. You Communist."

Finally, the date for the Army-McCarthy hearings was set for April 22. There had been an incredible amount of maneuvering. Several different Senate committees had toyed with the idea of trying to take over the hearings. Some had wanted them, some had scrambled to avoid them, depending on the courage and political obligations of each chairman. Joe McCarthy had made himself scarce around the Capitol for a month, rampaging through the Midwest and elsewhere and roaring his routine charges against his familiar targets.

But there was a new factor developing—he was losing his hold on the newspapers all across the country. He made few banner lines on the front pages except in some of the smaller cities where he was performing at the moment. And there were even days when he did not make the front page at all.

CHAPTER 17

The Hearings Begin

ABOUT a week before the Army-McCarthy hearings began on April 22, 1954, there was a story from Dakar, French West Africa, in a local paper. It reported that a witch doctor and three other Ivory Coast natives had been sentenced to life at hard labor for eating the wife of Barou Komere, the headman of one of their districts.

All through the next ten weeks, I could not get that story out of my mind. Was the spectacle of the trial of these four African natives any more sordid and disgraceful than the one beamed all over America from the Senate Caucus Room?

I was forced to believe that perhaps the African court might have been conducted with more dignity than ours . . . even though our hearings opened with a statement by Karl Mundt, Acting Chairman, that we had been convened in open session for the purpose of investigating charges made by Secretary Stevens and his counsel, John Adams, that Senator Joseph R. McCarthy as Chairman of the Permanent Subcommittee on Investigations of the United States Senate and its chief counsel, Roy M. Cohn, as well as other members of its staff, had sought by improper means to obtain preferential treatment for Private G. David Schine.

Also, Mundt said, to investigate countercharges made by Senator McCarthy, Cohn, and other members of the staff against Stevens, Adams, and Assistant Defense Secretary H. Struve Hensel. Hensel had become a last-minute added starter following some wild charges by McCarthy which he later admitted had no basis in fact.

Mundt said it was the purpose of the investigation to "make a full and impartial effort to reveal that which is true and to expose that which is false with respect to the charges and the countercharges." Unfortunately, these goals were forgotten that first day. In fact, within a very few minutes.

The reputations, actions, and integrity of responsible public officials were being challenged, Mundt said, and added, "Under these circumstances, it is right and proper that each of us at this end of the committee room considers himself, in a sense, to be on trial and that all of us have the obligation to do our best to enable justice and equity to prevail."

This, I thought at the time, is like singing the National Anthem before the start of the wrestling matches. After a few minutes of dignity and a solemn pledge to decent principles, the eye-gouging, hair-pulling, and pie-in-the-face would start. Mundt ended his opening statement by saying he was confident that each of us on this subcommittee would zealously and earnestly strive to fulfill the solemn obligation. I noticed that as he said these words his eyes flicked to Joe McCarthy in almost piteous hopefulness. But McCarthy was whispering with Roy Cohn and paying no attention to Mundt.

Senator McClellan then made a short statement in behalf of the minority Democrats, saying that they too would cooperate to make the hearings impartial, fair and thorough, and Mundt quickly asked that the first witness be called.

"A point of order, Mr. Chairman."

That was the first time we heard it, the first time many millions of Americans, their eyes glued to the other end of the television apparatus, would hear and see Joe McCarthy bring

139

up his endless points of order. His puffed eyelids, his tight upper lip that never moved when he talked, the stone cold eyes and the front hair grown long and slicked back over his balding head would dominate these hearings for the next ten weeks.

He knew where the cameras were located and he was always certain to be facing one as he made his endless points of order. Most of them were improper.

McCarthy's point of order was his objection that the specifications in the Army charges were entitled, "Filed by the Department of the Army." It wasn't the Army, he said, but Stevens, Adams, and Hensel who were bringing the charges, not the Army. These three were not the Army but were "Pentagon politicians" attempting to disrupt his investigations. He said that it was a disgrace and a reflection upon a million outstanding men in the Army to let a few civilians, who were "trying to hold up an investigation of Communists," label themselves the Department of the Army.

I began to feel sorry for Karl Mundt. He just was not capable of controlling McCarthy. But—who was?

Joe was on camera now; he had the audience and he was certain that out there many millions of people were believing him, were nodding their heads over the ludicrous charge that Stevens and the others were, indeed, coddling Communists.

The "Pentagon politicians" were the highest officials, appointed by Eisenhower to head the Army. They always acted for the Army. They were the ones who could have given in to McCarthy's early demands, made David Schine an officer and assigned him to West Point "to review the Army textbooks for traces of Communist teachings."

Had this been done, I am sure that McCarthy would have said that the Army, not Pentagon politicians, had been responsible.

The first witness was Major General Miles Reber, at that time the Commanding General of the United States Army in Europe. He had been flown to Washington from his headquarters in Kaiserslautern, Germany, to appear at the hearing. Flying General Reber back and forth to Europe so that he might testify for a few minutes at this hearing was just a small fraction of the idiotic expenses with which the public of the United States was charged.

But once again before the hearings could move on in an orderly way, Joe McCarthy decided to cause another commotion. Struve Hensel, Assistant Secretary of Defense, was sitting next to Miles Reber. Two days before, McCarthy had suddenly taken a wild swing at Hensel, accusing him of launching the Army report to block, Joe said, exposure of Hensel's "misconduct and possible law violation which was being investigated by his subcommittee." Once again, this was news to all us other six members of the subcommittee. Hensel, McCarthy charged, had helped organize a ships' supply firm which sold goods in an illegal way to the U. S. Navy during World War II when Hensel was a Navy official.

Hensel answered that the charge was a "barefaced lie." McCarthy, Hensel said, "is cornered and is pursuing his usual tactics. If he cares to repeat the charges against me without his Senate immunity, I will sue him."

McCarthy was in Houston that day for a speech and was asked by United Press if he would repeat the charge openly. He refused.

A long time later Joe admitted that his charges against Hensel were as phony as a three-dollar bill and that he had learned this type of strategy from an old friend whom he called Indian Charlie. Whenever Charlie was in a tight spot, Joe said, he would first kick his adversary in the genitals and then go on to more normal discussions.

Now, at the hearing, Joe demanded that Reber identify his "counsel" sitting next to him. This, as Joe knew it would, infuriated Hensel who said that he was not Reber's counsel and that McCarthy knew well who he was.

Joe's nervous giggle spread through the microphone to the

far walls of the Caucus Room. His eyes flicked to the TV cameras like a burlesque comedian who has scored with a laugh.

Reber told the hearings that he had been called to Joe's office in July where both Joe and Roy Cohn had urged that a commission be obtained for David Schine. And that during that first conversation Cohn had told him that Schine had been a junior ship's officer in the Army Transport Service and had served in that capacity for approximately a year in 1946, on the U. S. Army transport *General Widner*.

This was not true. Schine had been a purser and a civilian.

Reber said that he had been urged by both McCarthy and Cohn to go into full-speed-ahead action because Schine was now on the ready list to be drafted.

The Pentagon guessed rightly, and Reber did testify, that never before had he been under such pressure to obtain a commission for a rookie soldier although his office processed an average of a thousand a week.

In less than a week, David Schine called the Pentagon and asked if he could come over that afternoon and "hold up his hand" and thus be sworn in as a reserve officer. The colonel who took his call told him that before that could be done certain papers had to be filled out and approval obtained from some branch of the Army which might find him eligible. Schine went to the Pentagon that afternoon and reluctantly filled out some of the necessary papers, leaving out a lot of answers.

The next day Reber personally took the application back to Schine at the committee office and explained to him that he would have to answer ALL the questions before the processing could proceed. He left the papers with Schine, who again failed to complete them, and once again Reber took them back. This time David got it done.

Reber then started to search for a commission for David Schine. The Transportation Corps said that David was not qualified by his previous experience as purser. Reber tried the office of the Provost Marshal General because of Schine's investigating background. They said sorry, not qualified. The Office of the Chief of Psychological Warfare also gave Reber a turndown and so did the Commanding General of the First Army in New York.

Reber reported this to Roy Cohn, who suggested that he try the Air Force and the Navy. This Reber did and again was a loser. Through all this time, Reber testified, he and his staff were bombarded with telephone calls from Roy Cohn or members of Cohn's staff.

In the ten minutes allotted to me for questioning, it went like this:

POTTER: General Reber, how long did you serve as Chief of the Liaison Division for the Army on Capitol Hill?

REBER: I served as Chief, Senator Potter, for three years and four months. I served as Deputy for approximately seven years prior to that.

POTTER: So you have been here for ten years in the Liaison Division, is that correct?

REBER: Approximately; yes, sir.

POTTER: Can you tell the committee approximately how many members of Congress have asked or made similar requests for commissions for persons, either constituents or friends that they might have?

REBER: Senator Potter, I couldn't possibly estimate the number of cases that I have been asked to look into with references to things like commissions over the past ten years. It would be just a very rough guess. It is a sizable number.

POTTER: It is a sizable number?

REBER: A sizable number.

POTTER: It was a part of your duties and responsibilities to service such requests, whether they came from a member of Congress or from a citizen from the hometown or from parents?

REBER: Yes, sir.

POTTER: Or the individual himself, is that correct?

REBER: This is correct, sir.

POTTER: Now, General Reber, I believe you touched on this question; you stated that neither Senator McCarthy nor Roy Cohn intimidated you or threatened you in any way, is that correct?

REBER: That is correct, Senator Potter.

POTTER: Neither by word or by action, is that correct?

REBER: That is correct, sir.

POTTER: You stated, however, that the frequency of Mr. Cohn's calls, you felt, was unusual pressure, is that correct?

REBER: I do, sir. I base that on my ten years' experience.

POTTER: It wasn't the normal action?

REBER: It was more than normal.

POTTER: Did you report that activity to any superior officer or to the Secretary of the Army?

REBER: I reported the request for a commission, as I stated, to both General Hull and to the Secretary of the Army. I made no report on the number of telephone calls or various things like that. That is something that I personally was responsible for.

POTTER: General Reber, isn't it a normal procedure for a person who is seeking a commission to appear before a board of officers?

REBER: That is correct, Senator Potter.

POTTER: Did Mr. Schine appear before such a board?

REBER: He appeared before a board of officers in New York. He did not appear before a board of officers here in Washington because, as I understand it, there was no necessity for appearing before that board as he did not possess the necessary qualifications of experience and background to be commissioned here in Washington.

POTTER: In other words, he was deemed ineligible because of lack of qualifications without the necessity of going before a board.

REBER: That is correct, Senator Potter.

POTTER: I think it might be well if you would explain to the committee just what is the United States Army Transportation Service. Is that a part of our military branch?

REBER: Yes, sir. That is one of the seven technical services of the Department of Army that is charged with the mission of providing the necessary transportation of all kinds that the Army needs to conduct its missions both in peacetime and wartime, in the course of acquiring the necessary supplies, training the necessary personnel, and carrying on the necessary research and development in the transportation field.

POTTER: Did Mr. Schine, serving with that service, serve as a military man?

REBER: I am afraid I didn't quite understand the question.

POTTER: Did Mr. Schine, when he served, as I understand, with the United States Army Transportation Service, serve as a military man?

REBER: No, sir, he did not. He was not in the Army.

POTTER: And that was one of the bases on which he was not qualified, is that correct?

REBER: I believe the basis was more; that he was not what I would call a junior ship's officer, and, in other words, a ship's officer who has gone through the necessary schooling to permit him to navigate ships. I believe that was it. I am not an expert in that field, Senator Potter, but that is my understanding.

POTTER: That is all.

Joseph Welch, special counsel for the Army, wasted no time with Reber in his first active part in the hearing.

WELCH: General Reber, I think I have about three questions for you. Were you acutely aware of Mr. Cohn's position as counsel for this committee in the course of your conversation and contacts with him?

REBER: I was, Mr. Welch.

WELCH: Did that position occupied by Mr. Cohn increase or diminish the interest with which you pursued the problem?

REBER: To the best of my ability, I feel that it increased the interest.

WELCH: One more question, sir. Disregarding the word "improper" influence or pressure, do you recall any instance comparable to this in which you were put under greater pressure?

REBER: To the best of my recollection, I recall of no instance under which I was put under greater pressure.

Then the fireworks began.

There was nothing startling or defamatory about Reber's testimony. He had performed with the efficiency and dignity that we had learned to expect from West Point officers appearing before committees. But there must have been something about an Army officer, and particularly this type of Army officer, that infuriated McCarthy. After the questioning had gone around the committee twice and there seemed to be nothing more needed from this witness, Joe gave the hearings another injection of Indian Charlie.

"Is Sam Reber your brother?"

General Reber was startled as was everyone else in the room. Did anything about Sam Reber's activities make the general acutely aware of the fact that Mr. Cohn was chief counsel of the committee? Joe wanted to know. General Reber, wary now, said no.

McCarthy then asked: "Do you know that Mr. Sam Reber was the superior to Mr. Kaghan, that Mr. Cohn and Mr. Schine were sent by me to Europe to inspect the libraries, that your brother, Mr. Sam Reber, repeatedly made attacks upon them, and that your brother, Mr. Sam Reber, appointed a man to shadow them throughout Europe and keep the press informed as to where they were going and where they were stopping?

Were you aware of that at the time you were making this great effort to get consideration, as you say, for Mr. Schine?"

(Samuel Reber had been Acting High Commissioner for the State Department in Germany at the time of the Cohn-Schine trip. The "shadow" appointed by Reber had been an official of the Visitors Bureau who arranged, at the request of Cohn and Schine, the details of their plane schedules, appointments and hotel rooms. The "attacks" had been Sam Reber's refusal to denounce Ted Kaghan as a "Communist sympathizer." Kaghan had been respected as one of the most effective organizers of anti-Communist propaganda in Germany.)

The storm simmered down for a minute and McCarthy asked Reber if, at the time he was processing the application of David Schine, he was aware of the fact that Schine had had a very unpleasant experience with Reber's brother, who was then Acting High Commissioner for the United States in Germany. Reber answered that he had known of no such episode although he was aware that Cohn and Schine had had specific difficulties with the Department of State.

McCarthy backed away from Sam Reber for a few minutes and made the mistake of referring to the original meeting between himself, Reber and Cohn, and emphasizing the point that Reber had said he had thought Schine would be entitled to a commission. This gave Reber the opportunity to testify that he had thought so too because Roy Cohn had told him that Schine had served as a junior ship's officer. If that had been true, Reber now testified, Schine might have been commissioned.

Joe was groping now. "General, you were before this committee a number of times, is that right, when I was chairman?"

"I actually only testified, Senator McCarthy, once—on the 8th of September, 1953," Reber replied.

Then Joe seemed to fly off into outer space.

McCarthy: At that time I asked you—as I recall—I repeated the question a number of times—asked you whether or not you felt that the committee should be entitled to the names of individuals in the Pentagon who had protected and covered up Communists. At that time I had difficulty getting an answer from you on that. I ask you this question today because I am firmly convinced the reason we are spending our time on the question of whether or not Private Schine received special consideration is because we are getting close to the nerve center in the Pentagon of the old civilian politicians over the past ten or twenty years who have covered up. I want to ask you today whether or not you feel that this committee, when we get through with this television show, should be entitled to get the names of those, for example, who received the cases of individuals who had been suspended from Fort Monmouth. I am not speaking of the 33 suspensions during our investigations. I am speaking of investigations made long before that, over the past five, six, or seven years by competent commanding officers— I believe the figure was 35, I am not sure—by different commanding officers, who were found unfit by the First Army Loyalty Board because of Communist background. They applied to a screening board or an appeal board or a loyalty board, I don't know what you would call it, in the Pentagon; and of the 35, 33 . . .

Mundt rescued him. "The Senator's time has expired."

I had watched Reber and Cohn through this droning, pointless monologue, delivered in that strange, tight-upper-lipped, overdramatic voice that Joe never used unless there was an audience or a camera in range. They were both trying to follow what he was saying, but first puzzlement, then apprehension, then a shadow of pity seemed to hit them both. There was something of disgust, too, evident in Cohn, a literate man being forced to listen to a pretty terrible script.

Mundt then asked for further questions from the six of us. Only Symington accepted the offer to bring out testimony that General Reber, under his oath of office, would have acted entirely in accordance with that oath no matter what might have happened to his brother or anyone else. We adjourned then until after lunch, and I was happy for a few moments that McCarthy's ugly punch at Sam Reber was apparently ended. I soon learned that this was only the beginning.

Roy Cohn took over the questioning as the afternoon session opened. He made a minor attempt to score a point by bringing out that no Army report similar to the one charging him and McCarthy had been filed by the Army after Captain Irving Peress had asked to have his overseas orders canceled because his wife and daughter were ill. Cohn was off side on the play, and he knew it and did not press it.

Henry Jackson brought out from Reber that at no time during the long negotiations over the commissioning of David Schine had Roy Cohn, or anyone else, complained to him about any alleged bias connected with his brother. The general said that the first time he had ever heard either McCarthy or Cohn mention his brother was at this hearing.

Then it was McCarthy's turn again and he had apparently been refueling at the Carroll Arms Hotel during the lunch period. Out the window went all the rules of this particular hearing, of any hearing.

"Are you aware," Joe demanded, "of the fact that your brother was allowed to resign when charges that he was a bad security risk were made against him as a result of the investigations of this committee?"

This was news to the other six members of the committee, and, I am sure, news to Joe until this moment.

Ray Jenkins jumped in with an objection on the grounds that the question was wholly irrelevant, which it certainly was.

McCarthy, totally washed free of any courtesy now, interrupted to say that if Reber's brother was forced to resign as a bad security risk, it should be on the record as a possible motive for his testimony.

McClellan objected, pointing out that there was no testi-

149

mony that the statements McCarthy was making were true and until they were proved true, McCarthy's question to Reber was incompetent. Ray Jenkins said McCarthy was entitled to ask Reber whether or not the statements were true.

Finally, having made his point over radio and television, McCarthy dismissed the entire question as unimportant and pompously said he would withdraw it.

This time it was the witness, General Reber, who objected and asked for permission to answer the serious charge against his brother. The squabbling continued for two hours with Ray Jenkins contributing the strange observation that he thought General Reber was in error in saying that a serious attack had been made on his brother because no proof had been introduced by McCarthy. Jenkins did not mention that upwards of twenty million Americans had heard the serious slander of Samuel Reber. That was the McCarthy technique.

Henry Jackson recognized this and said that McCarthy's distorted charges against Samuel Reber could be stricken from the record but could not be stricken from the newspapers, the television audience and the radio audience. He thought Miles Reber should be given the opportunity to answer.

McCarthy snarled at Jackson, made a wild statement that he and Roy Cohn had been accused of everything except "murdering our great-great-grandmother" and said that he had a duty, not a right but a duty, to show the motive of the witness.

Stuart Symington interrupted to say that he did not understand what General Reber's brother had to do with General Reber with respect to telephone calls that may have been made, properly or improperly, because his brother may or may not have been a security risk. This was a cold dash of logic and sanity squirted into the hurricane that McCarthy was attempting to create, and we heard no more about it.

Finally General Reber was allowed to speak. "I merely wanted to say that, as I understand my brother's case, he retired as he is entitled to do by law upon reaching the age of fifty. That is all I wanted to say. I know nothing about any security case involving him."

There was, of course, no security investigation against Samuel Reber. This senseless slander of his name had resulted from the seventeen-day tour of Europe by Roy Cohn and David Schine, an episode that had made the United States the laughingstock of the world. Several thousand dollars which belonged to the public had been poured down the drain, and the pouring had been approved by Joe McCarthy without mentioning a word of it to any other member of the committee that was supposed to be sponsoring the tour.

As soon as Reber was able to get his statement on the record, Karl Mundt hastily dismissed him from the witness stand, and McCarthy turned to a snapping debate with Jackson over the date on which Francis Carr had been appointed to the staff. It was a minor squabble but it did put on the record another instance of perjury. There would be many many more in the ten weeks to come.

As I left the Caucus Room and went back to my office in the Capitol, I found myself thinking again of Mrs. Komere, who had been served for lunch in French West Africa. She and Samuel Reber now belonged to the same club.

CHAPTER 18

Target: Margaret Smith

I FINALLY scuffled my way through the crowds and back to my office that first afternoon of the hearings. There was mail to be checked, information to be absorbed, and staff plans to be made. I knew I would not be much use to my constituents for the next several weeks.

I thought back to a few months before when Senator Margaret Chase Smith and I were visiting on the Senate floor one morning and she told me that my press secretary, Robert Jones, was planning to run against her in the Maine primary. I had put Jones on my staff a few months before that when it was brought to my attention that he was a pleasant young man with a wife and three or four children and that he was out of work and desperately in need of a job. He seemed to know his way around Capitol Hill, and, until now, I had no reason to doubt his loyalty.

"I just can't believe it, Margaret," I said. "He has no qualifications to be a Senator, and he hasn't the money to mount a campaign."

"You're probably right about the qualifications," she answered, "but I think he is going to have plenty of money from Joe McCarthy's friends in Texas."

"McCarthy? Where does he come into it?"

"I guess it all started nearly four years ago," she said. "Ever since I gave that Declaration of Conscience speech, I have been having my troubles with our friend."

I couldn't believe it. Perhaps I just didn't want to believe it. But there was no way to avoid it. In June 1950, shortly after McCarthy had discovered there was power in attacking Communism, Margaret Smith had prepared a statement to be delivered in the Senate. Among other things, it had said that "certain elements of the Republican party have materially added to this national confusion through the selfish political exploitation of fear, bigotry, ignorance and intolerance. It is high time that we all stop being tools and victims of totalitarian techniques—techniques that if continued here unchecked, will surely end what we have come to cherish as the American way of life."

Nowhere in the speech was Joe McCarthy named but he got the point and from that moment on life became more difficult for Margaret Chase Smith.

First, McCarthy had used his seniority and dumped her off the Senate Investigating Committee. They had clashed again when the Senate Subcommittee on Privileges and Elections under the chairmanship of Senator Guy Gillette attempted, in 1951, to determine whether expulsion proceedings should be instituted against Joe, an episode which I shall discuss later. Margaret Smith had objected vigorously as a member of the committee when McCarthy had charged it with being guilty of "stealing from the taxpayers" and of being "completely dishonest" because it was trying to investigate his financial record.

"But why Robert Jones?" I asked Mrs. Smith. "I remember now that he is from Maine, but certainly he would have no chance whatsoever to beat you in a primary."

"Apparently McCarthy couldn't find anyone else. I know he tried Owen Brewster, who was beaten out by Fred Payne, and Brewster turned him down, told him he believed my reelection was pretty certain. However, I think he is planning another campaign in Maine similar to those he put on against Tydings in Maryland and Benton in Connecticut. We know what he is capable of doing. It could become rather unpleasant, Charlie."

"Could he possibly be doing this because of that speech of yours four years ago?"

"Perhaps you don't know him as well as I do, Charlie," she said. "It seems inevitable that every year or so he finds me objecting to something he is doing, and it seems to add to his determination for revenge. The Declaration of Conscience speech was just the beginning. You may remember that after that—it was before you were in the Senate—I protested again after his attack on General Marshall. Then I voted in favor of the Benton resolution which started the whole mess with the Gillette Committee. That request of Benton's seemed very reasonable to me. Then you may remember that last summer Bill Knowland and McCarthy tried to push through a resolution which would have permitted McCarthy to file committee reports on hearings he had held as a one-man committee. This would have given him the chance to make a permanent record of all those sordid little episodes, and I was against it and I blocked it. That is when he started to look for a candidate to knock me out of the Maine primary."

"You are not the only one who opposed him on these things, Margaret," I said. "Why does he make you his special target?"

"I'm not a psychiatrist, Charlie. I could tell you some things you might not believe," she said. "Do you remember a shabby little book called *USA Confidential* that was written by two Hearst writers, Lee Mortimer and Jack Lait? It was published a couple of years ago. In it, I was described as being pro-Communist, among other things, and I am sure that this translated to anti-McCarthy. As you know, McCarthy has always been the particular hero of Winchell, Sokolsky, and the Hearst press in general, and Lee Mortimer used his column to support the theory that Joe McCarthy could do no wrong.

154

"Naturally, I immediately filed legal action against Lait and Mortimer and the Crown Publishing Company, which put out the book. The idea that I am pro-Communist is just too much. But that was just the beginning. In the course of the litigation, which, incidentally, is still going on and is being delayed by every possible legal maneuver, I have been accused of murder. Not one murder, but three."

"Margaret, you must be teasing me. I haven't heard anything about this."

"Mortimer was the source of this pretty phrase. Jack Lait has died, and so have both of Mortimer's parents and, in his deposition concerning my suit for slander, he claims that all three of them died from worry over my 'vicious attack,' as he calls it. So, since Joe McCarthy is the only person in the world who has ever called me pro-Communist, the whole thing traces back."

"Incredible, unbelievable," I said. "But just what has happened with Robert Jones?"

"Well, you have been sending Jones to represent you at several of these one-man headline raids by McCarthy," she said. "As I mentioned, Joe first approached Owen Brewster and, incidentally, he told Brewster that he had three goals so far as I was concerned. First, he intended to drain me financially. Second, to harass me and make life as miserable as possible. And third, which bothers me most of all, to force me to break my voting attendance record. I haven't missed a vote since 1952, and I am rather proud of that record.

"Owen would have nothing to do with it and so McCarthy turned to Jones. Haven't you noticed, Charlie, that Jones is picking up McCarthy's mannerisms? He imitates McCarthy. That tight upper lip that never moves when he talks. The same gestures with the hands and the same habit of repeating the first three or four words of each sentence. There was a hearing in Schenectady a few days ago. Jones was there, representing you. McCarthy took Jones after the hearing to Portland, Maine, where they picked up a Congressional Medal of Honor winner, a Captain Millett, and they put on a show. That seems to be the pattern these days, to drag along some war hero, which is supposed to indicate that the candidate is a great patriot, I suppose."

"Margaret, I'll call Jones over as soon as I return to my office. I don't doubt what you're telling me, but it's so fantastic." She smiled and we talked for a few more minutes. I asked my secretary to summon Jones from the office he occupied in the Senate Building as soon as I got back to my office.

"Bob, I hear you are thinking of going into politics as a career," I said.

"I don't understand, Senator," he answered.

"I have a report that you were thinking about running against Margaret Smith in Maine." I could see that he had not been expecting that and there was a long hesitation.

"It's not true, Senator. How could I possibly run against Mrs. Smith?"

I decided to let it go at that for the moment. I had his denial, which I was pretty sure was a lie, and there was no reason to press it further. If I told him the source of my information, McCarthy would know it in a few minutes. If Margaret Smith's theory was correct, Jones would have to make his move soon.

The final showdown with Robert Jones happened sooner than I expected, and Margaret Smith had been right. After my first talk with Jones about his political career in Maine, I had found that the rumor about it was pretty strong around the Capitol. And, at my suggestion, he had issued a public statement saying that it was untrue.

There were two reasons why I fired Robert Jones in late February 1954. First, I sent him to represent me, a move I shall always regret, at the hearings in New York when Senator McCarthy put on his dreadful performance against General Ralph Zwicker. Jones, after questioning Zwicker, issued a statement to the press indicating my approval of McCarthy's performance at the hearing. During the same day, before I knew about Jones' doings in New York, I happened to meet Bill Lewis, Mrs. Smith's administrative assistant, in the Capitol.

"Senator, your boy Jones is going to make his big announcement in a few days."

I still didn't quite believe it and I said so.

"Bill, it makes no sense. Campaigns cost money. His wife and children don't have groceries."

"I'll make you a little bet, Senator," he said. "Jones will make his announcement on Washington's birthday, next week. There will be a ringing, flag-waving statement about saving the nation from Communism. He will have plenty of money."

"Where is he going to get it?"

"McCarthy was in Texas this week," Lewis said. "He talked with some of his Texas oil friends. He convinced them that Senator Smith is soft on Communism, and an international Left Winger. Jones got a letter from them this week urging him to announce on Washington's birthday and promising all the financial help he needs. They told him that McCarthy has two men shadowing me and the Senator. They hope to get some ammunition to use against us. Nice, isn't it?"

"Shadowing you and Margaret?"

"Yes, and that isn't all. We are receiving reports from home that a story is being spread that the Senator is dying of cancer. You can have one guess as to the source of that one."

I went back to my office and waited for Jones to return from New York, but he did not appear until the next morning.

I was in my office early the next day and I had time to read the newspaper reports of the McCarthy-Zwicker affair before Jones showed up. I was shocked by Joe's ill-mannered abuse of General Zwicker and appalled that he had seen fit to give his side of it to the newspapers. He had told them that he thought it was his duty. Duty for what? To destroy the reputation of a dedicated, honest military man? And all over a distorted, twisted

157

circus performance in which he was trying to get credit for maul-ing a no-account dentist whose transgressions had already been settled by the Army. Then there was Jones' statement, "my" statement, supporting McCarthy in this episode. It was not a healthy moment for Robert Jones to appear in my office.

"Jones, are you responsible for these statements credited to me?" I asked.

"Yes, sir, I thought you would want to be covered."

"When I want to make statements about Joe McCarthy and his hearings, I will make them myself."

"I'm sorry. I thought, well, Zwicker was very evasive, es-pecially when I was questioning him."

"*You* questioned him?"

"Yes. McCarthy said that since I was representing you, and Harold Rainville was representing Senator Dirksen, we could question him too."

There was no answer for that. McCarthy had always made his own rules.

"Jones," I said, "I am firing you. For two reasons. First is that you lied to me about your plans to run against Margaret Smith. I know now that you have been making this plan all along and your denial was a complete lie. I know why you are doing it and who is backing you. I'd suggest that you think back a few months to the time when you were out of work and I put you on the staff. Who will take care of your wife and children after your primary campaign against Mrs. Smith is over? Will Mc-Carthy find you another job?"

He didn't seem to have anything to say. I called my secretary and told her to cut off his salary at the next payday and to get me a full transcript of the McCarthy-Zwicker hearing. I also asked her to get me copies of certain hearings in which Margaret Smith and Joe McCarthy had been involved. I was hoping to find out how she alone had managed to survive while openly standing up for what she thought was right against Joe McCarthy.

Within a few hours, Jones sent me his note of gratitude for the several well-paid months he had spent on my staff. He announced to the press that he had not been fired, he had quit, and gave them this formal statement:

> It is obvious that very powerful sources were determined that I should not oppose Mrs. Smith in the Maine Republican primaries. I am thoroughly convinced that this is the handiwork of devious Left Wing elements who are fearful of a bitter political showdown in Maine between the forces of Americanism and international Liberalism. My only regret is that Senator Potter, a great American with whom I shared a most happy relationship, was innocently involved in these vicious maneuverings to keep me out of the Senate race.

My only answer to that was "no comment." Things were getting a little too weird.

CHAPTER **19**

Picking the Taxpayers' Pockets

MARGARET CHASE SMITH survived although several other fine Senators were destroyed by Joe McCarthy. She had no difficulty turning back the competition of Robert Jones in her 1954 primary campaign. McCarthy, tied down in Washington by the Army hearing, was unable to make more than a few hit-and-run raids into Maine to support Jones and attempt to torpedo Mrs. Smith.

Jones, supplied with a trailer truck fitted out with sound equipment and a liberal allowance, left his family in Washington and worked the campaign trail. I was informed that he had now adopted many of the speaking mannerisms of Joe McCarthy and was spewing out the same senseless charge that Margaret Smith was a fuzzy-minded, pro-Communist Left Winger. It would have been impossible to think of any description further from the truth.

I knew that the life of Joseph McCarthy was racing to a climax and that Robert Jones might provide the spark that would make me the next target. It seemed like a good time to check through the career of Margaret Smith, especially at those times McCarthy had been bombing her.

I had not been in the Senate, but in the House, in 1950, when

Margaret issued her famous "Declaration of Conscience" statement.

I was still in the House in 1951, when Margaret Smith publicly deplored McCarthy's sixty-thousand-word attack on General George Marshall; and when Senator William Benton of Connecticut introduced a resolution to impeach McCarthy in August of the same year. Benton's courage caused a sensation, even over in the House. The memory of McCarthy's assassination of Senator Tydings in Maryland was still fresh and clear. It was during this campaign that Joe used the infamous faked photograph supposedly showing Tydings in intimate conversation with Communist Earl Browder. Although the two men had never met face to face, it had been easy for McCarthy's staff to obtain separate pictures and paste them together.

Many Senators secretly saluted Benton for his courage, but none of them wanted to be involved with any resolution seeking to impeach Joe McCarthy. Benton listed ten specific charges:

1. That Senator McCarthy had perjured himself with respect to statements he had made on the radio concerning Communists in the State Department;

2. That Senator McCarthy had been highly unethical in accepting a $10,000 fee from the Lustron Corporation;

3. That Senator McCarthy had alleged that General Marshall was a member of a "conspiracy to aid Russia";

4. That Senator McCarthy had engaged in calculated deceits in his statements that he had been forced to make public the names of persons with Communist affiliations in the State Department;

5. That Senator McCarthy engaged in fraud and deceit in the Maryland Senatorial election of 1950;

6. That Senator McCarthy allegedly stated that he would not claim Senatorial immunity;

7. Dealt with an alleged FBI chart referred to by Senator McCarthy and described as a hoax by Senator Benton;

8. That Senator McCarthy repeatedly stated that he would

161

name the names of Communists in the State Department when subsequent statements by him disclosed that he had no names;

9. Dealt with Senator McCarthy's intervention on behalf of the defendants in the Malmédy Massacre case;

10. Dealt with persons Senator McCarthy employed—particularly Don Surine's false statements concerning the circumstances under which he had left the employment of the FBI, and the employment of an alleged Communist, Charles Davis, for investigation work in Europe.

This was a hot one, all right, and the Senators fled to their hiding places as if an angry polecat had suddenly appeared on the Senate floor. After considerable bobbing and weaving, the resolution was tossed to the Subcommittee on Privileges and Elections of the Senate Committee on Rules and Administration. Senator Guy Gillette of Iowa was the chairman of the subcommittee.

McCarthy's first reaction was completely predictable—it was a "Communist smear." He was too busy, he said, to "even bother reading or answering the tripe put out by Connecticut's odd little mental midget." It was difficult to recognize Benton as a mental midget, whether you agree with his politics or not. A graduate of Yale, he had created an explosively successful advertising agency with Chester Bowles, had served as Vice-President of the University of Chicago, as Assistant Secretary of State in charge of public affairs and was Chairman of the Board of the Encyclopaedia Britannica.

Then, although Joe had just finished saying that he was too busy to answer Benton, he spent the next several months publicly insulting Benton and Guy Gillette, who, even from McCarthy's side, was guilty only of taking on a messy job that no other Senator would touch.

Benton, McCarthy said, had established himself as the hero of every Communist and crook in and out of government. "I call the attention of all honest, loyal Democrats to how men of little minds are destroying a once great party," he added. "While Benton was Assistant Secretary of State, he worked hand in glove with the Crimson clique which have been so bad for America and so good for Communist Russia. The exact number that he personally brought into government is not fully known at this time. No wonder he squeals and screams in panic as the McCarran Committee starts to uncover some of them."

Benton repeated his ten-point bill of particulars in his resolution and said, "I regard Senator McCarthy as a menace to our American way of life." And, here was what I was looking for, he mentioned that Senator Margaret Chase Smith, as well as Robert Hendrickson, had joined him in denouncing McCarthy's performance.

McCarthy circled around the outskirts of the Senate, and particularly the Gillette Committee, throwing his filth from a safe distance. In a speech at Savannah, Georgia, aware that he was talking outside his Senate immunity, he carefully avoided mentioning Benton by name but said that several United States Representatives and Senators had known Communists on their staffs.

Benton said, All right, prove it. "McCarthy should hand over to the United States District Attorney any evidence he has to support his charge that several members of the Congress have known Communists on their staffs. If he doesn't turn over the evidence, he is derelict in his duty as a citizen and as a United States Senator. It is time that we put a stop to these reckless charges. He has never proved one of them."

McCarthy ignored this challenge and several invitations from Gillette to appear before the committee to answer Benton's resolution. McCarthy's reply, in a letter to Gillette, was:

The Benton-type material can be found in the *Daily Worker* almost any day of the week and will continue to flow from the mouths and pens of camp followers as long as I continue to fight against Communists in government. Frankly, Guy, I have not and do not intend to read, much less answer, Benton's smear attack.

It seemed that Joe was becoming fairly vitriolic over nothing if he had not read "Benton's smear attack." All through McCarthy's career, he used the device of yelling "smear" before the evidence was in and of claiming that any disagreement with him was instigated to defeat his hunt for Communists. It was not a particularly clever maneuver, but in those times, in this country, it worked. His first few punches at Guy Gillette were fairly gentle taps but when this brought on no panic in the Senator from Iowa, Joe reached down into his bag of poison and let go.

In another letter to Gillette he said:

> Over the past few months it has repeatedly been brought to my attention that a horde of investigators, hired by your committee at a cost of tens of thousands of dollars of taxpayers' money, has been engaged exclusively in trying to dig up on McCarthy material covering periods of time long before he was even old enough to be a candidate for the Senate. . . . This is being done in complete disregard of the limited power of your Election Subcommittee. The obvious purpose is to dig up campaign material for the Democratic party for the coming campaign against McCarthy.
>
> When your Election Subcommittee, without Senate authorization, spends tens of thousands of taxpayers' dollars for the sole purpose of digging up campaign material against McCarthy, then the committee is guilty of stealing just as clearly as though the members engaged in picking the pockets of the taxpayers and turning the loot over to the Democratic National Committee. . . . While the actions of Benton and some of the committee members do not surprise me, I cannot understand your being willing to label Guy Gillette as a man who will head a committee which is stealing from the pockets of the American taxpayer tens of thousands of dollars and then using this money

to protect the Democratic party from the political effect of the exposure of Communists in government. To take it upon yourself to hire a horde of investigators and spend tens of thousands of dollars without any authorization to do so from the Senate, is labeling your Election Subcommittee as even more dishonest than was the Tydings Committee.

As was his custom, McCarthy gave copies of these and other attacks to the press before they were delivered to Gillette. And the press, as was its custom, gave them prominent display without making any particular effort to show the absurdity of them.

Finally, Senator Mike Monroney, of Oklahoma, had had enough of McCarthy's antics. Monroney was basically a gentle man who could tolerate an unusual amount of the sometimes peculiar antics of his fellow Senators. He was, however, capable of boiling over. He demanded a showdown in the Senate. Senator Herman Welker, of Idaho, voted against it, but the other subcommittee members went along with Monroney. The question was offered to the full Senate Rules Committee, and this time the vote was 8 to 3 with only Dirksen, Welker and William Jenner voting for McCarthy.

Technically, the Senate would be asked to vote whether or not the subcommittee was qualified to investigate Benton's charges against Joe (a vote of confidence), and Joe knew now that he was trapped, that he could no longer hit and run. And so he reversed everything he had said in his blistering letters to Gillette and announced that he had full confidence in the subcommittee because now he had a resolution calling for the investigation of—guess who—Senator William Benton.

On the Senate floor, Benton said: "I spent much time studying Soviet propaganda. I pointed out the tactics; the tactics of hitting and running, of never standing still, of never answering charges, of hitting, of hitting again, of running again—tactics which have so brilliantly been illustrated on the floor of the Senate this afternoon. It was the Senator from Wisconsin, the skillful propagandist which all of us know him to be, who today had the floor of the Senate. It is what he said then that will appear in the newspaper headlines this afternoon."

He was right. Joe's demand for an investigation of Benton took over the headlines. There was very little to be found on the Senate debate of McCarthy's hit-and-run history with the Gillette Committee. But Joe had not entirely escaped, and Mike Monroney had waited a long time. He was indignant about McCarthy's charges that the subcommittee had been "spending tens of thousands of dollars to hire hordes of investigators and picking the taxpayers' pockets."

"The payroll showed," Monroney said, "that we had two stenographers, one assistant counsel, and three special investigators. These three investigators were employed a period of approximately forty-five days. They were investigating also the Senatorial campaign in Ohio. So where are the tens of thousands of dollars? Where are the hordes of investigators? The record shows that $3,200 was spent for forty-five days of work by three investigators who were working on the Senatorial campaigns in three of the largest states in the Union. The junior Senator from Wisconsin had that information, although he did not appear to want to use it."

Joe had also charged that the Gillette Subcommittee had no authority to investigate him. And now Senator Carl Hayden of Arizona, who, in later years, would be only two steps from the Presidency when Vice-President Lyndon Johnson replaced President Kennedy, told the Senate: "The precedents clearly show that the jurisdiction of the former Committee of Privileges and Elections . . . extended to expulsion, exclusion, censure and other matters totally unconnected with the conduct of Senators and elections."

Now McCarthy switched again. A few minutes before, when he wanted it to investigate Senator Benton, he had indicated full confidence in the committee. He regained the floor now and the following remarks were recorded:

McCARTHY: I hope the Senator will not misunderstand my vote against the discharge of the subcommittee as a vote of confidence in the subcommittee. I have absolutely no confidence in the majority members of the subcommittee.

MONRONEY: It has been well established for seventy-five years that the Privileges and Elections Subcommittee has the jurisdiction. It is so well settled, Mr. President, that even the junior Senator from Wisconsin, after traveling across the country and broadcasting and telling the country over the Associated Press and United Press wires that the committee had no jurisdiction and that it was usurping your jurisdiction, finally admitted in a press release that the committee had jurisdiction. . . .

Mr. President, let us not delude ourselves as to what this issue is all about. The issue is whether Senators have confidence in their committee and believe that it is not stealing taxpayers' money or whether we are to have a continuation of the performance to which I have referred. . . . If the junior Senator from Wisconsin believes what he has written and what he has said across the land on every Associated Press and United Press wire, he should vote to discharge the committee.

McCARTHY: After the fantastic activities of the subcommittee in the Maryland elections case, I can have no confidence in it. However, I shall vote against a discharge of the subcommittee because I feel, now that a precedent has been set in the McCarthy case, the subcommittee should follow the same precedent in the Benton case and in every other one.

(Margaret Smith had listened to all this with growing indignation and now she took the floor.)

MRS. SMITH: Mr. President, I was a member of the Subcommittee on Privileges and Elections when Senator McCarthy charged on December 5, 1951, that the members of that subcommittee were "guilty of stealing" and accused them of complete dishonesty. I say to the members of the Senate that Senator McCarthy has made false accusations which he cannot and has not had the courage even to try to back up with proof. . . .

Regardless of the face-saving attempts and words of Senator McCarthy at this time in trying to soften the rebuff and to confuse the issue, any Senator who votes "yea" for this resolution is saying unequivocally to the people of his state and the people of the nation that he believes that Senator McCarthy's charges are truthful and that Senators Gillette, Monroney, Hennings, Hendrickson, and Smith of Maine are guilty of complete dishonesty and of stealing. Any Senator who votes "nay" and against the resolution is voting to repudiate the McCarthy charges against Senators Gillette, Monroney, Hennings, Hendrickson, and Smith of Maine.

(There was some more scuffling back and forth, and then Senator Bourke Hickenlooper of Iowa rose to make his contribution. He was mystified by it all, he said. He couldn't understand why Margaret Smith was objecting so vigorously. She told him.)

MRS. SMITH: Will the Senator from Iowa tell me whether he was ever accused of being a thief?

HICKENLOOPER: I may say to the Senator from Maine that I am utterly sympathetic with the umbrage and justifiable objection which the Senator from Maine may entertain from a generalized statement of McCarthy's kind. I am utterly in sympathy with her feelings.

MRS. SMITH: I would like to ask the Senator if he thinks that McCarthy's "picking the pockets of the taxpayers" charge is a general statement. I would consider it a very specific statement, an accusation. I should like to ask the Senator a specific question. Was he, as a member of that subcommittee, ever accused of stealing taxpayers' money?

HICKENLOOPER: No, I don't believe I have ever been accused as a member of that subcommittee. . . .

MRS. SMITH: Would the Senator ever become callous enough not to mind being called a thief by a fellow member of the Senate?

HICKENLOOPER: I presume no person who is honorable would

ever become callous to charges of that kind. I am not indulging
in any approval or disapproval of the statement by the Senator
from Wisconsin, but I cannot for one minute place myself in
the position of being subjected to an interpretation of what my
vote will be by the statement of the Senator from Maine.

MRS. SMITH: It is not a question of interpretation, it is a
question of fact.

(Finally Mike Monroney had enough of it.)

MONRONEY: I would like to have the Senator from Iowa
[Hickenlooper] say whether even one charge, repeated nine
times, that we are stealing taxpayers' money is a matter of
"casual" criticism which one should lightly brush off. I wonder
whether the Senator from Iowa agrees that we do need a little
confidence in our government. I get worried about democracy
sometimes. I get worried when some forces in this nation try to
shake the very foundation stones of our government and try
to stir up suspicion, distrust, and religious hatred and do other
things that are completely inimical to free and democratic government. We have seen the same pattern overseas, where we
saw many governments fail because of these very attacks on the
foundation of government by people who created doubt.

It is unfortunate that a vote was not taken immediately, because McCarthy arose to prove by his actions that he could perform to perfection the routines used "overseas" that Monroney
had mentioned.

Putting aside everything that had any bearing on the current
discussion, he flew at the throat of Darrell St. Claire, the chief
counsel of the Senate Rules Committee. St. Claire had once
served in the State Department on the Loyalty Board, and Joe
now accused him of casting the deciding vote in a case in which
a subversive suspect had been found loyal. Joe roared that St.
Claire had assisted the staff of the subcommittee in drafting
the Maryland election report which had deplored Joe's actions
during his campaign against Senator Tydings.

It was outrageous; it was absurd; it was effective.

Joe finished it off by accusing St. Claire of writing the present "scurrilous" report against McCarthy and conveniently forgetting that in his previous clash with St. Claire, Joe had produced a forged FBI report.

While other Senators were busy defending St. Claire, including Margaret Smith who swore that "he never sat with the subcommittee, never had anything to do with the typing of the report or anything to do with the Maryland or Benton resolution," McCarthy vanished from the Senate floor. He was in a hurry to catch a plane to make a speech on "Ethics and Honor in Government."

The Senate voted 60–0 in favor of the subcommittee.

CHAPTER 20

Oops, Wrong Woman

I COULD find nothing unique anywhere that would tell me why Margaret Chase Smith survived McCarthy's attack and so many other Senators were torpedoed. Perhaps it was her cool, calm fearlessness, her refusal to panic, her ability to wipe off the mud and the poison as a pet-lover cleans up the mess of a naughty puppy.

She seemed to have handled Joe as if he were no more than a lawless, adult delinquent. She did not instigate an attack of her own but slapped him down with dignity whenever he came brawling into her neighborhood.

Joe made the mistake of attempting to befoul another woman at about the same time as his first clash with Margaret Smith. She was Mrs. Anna Rosenberg, appointed Assistant Secretary of Defense by President Truman. She had had an outstanding career as a lawyer and judge in New York City, specializing in the juvenile court. Her legal background would be valuable in the Pentagon, and, perhaps, her training with delinquents helped her to understand Joe McCarthy. McCarthy got into trouble this time because of his natural laziness and a failure to be automatically suspicious of the anti-Semites who led him up the wrong road in the Rosenberg case.

First came the Reverend Wesley Swift, who is perhaps best remembered for his refusal to concede that Christ was a Jew. Swift delivered "evidence" to McCarthy's office that Mrs. Rosenberg had been a Communist. He said, specifically, that she had been a member of the John Reed Club, a Red front organization. At that moment, as well as every other moment, Joe was in desperate need of a Communist, a real live Communist that he had captured himself. He sent one of his investigators to New York City to dig up further evidence. They carried with them a letter of introduction which read, in part, as follows:

> Congratulations on the terrific job you are doing in helping to keep the Zionist Jew, Anna M. Rosenberg, from becoming the director of the Pentagon. This is to introduce two gentlemen who are helping in this fight. One is the bearer of this note. I understand that he is Mr. Nellor, the chief aide to Mr. Fulton Lewis. Mr. Lewis and Mr. Nellor should be treated very kindly. You should give any information that will help them, because Mr. Lewis is doing a magnificent job in the Rosenberg matter. Please destroy this upon reading it.
>
> Sincerely yours,
>
> GERALD L. K.

This, of course, was Gerald L. K. Smith, a rabble-rousing anti-Semite who had been infecting the United States for many years.

The letter was addressed to a Benjamin Freedman, who put the two investigators in touch with Ralph DeSola, supposedly an ex-Communist who was "going straight."

In the meantime, "back at the ranch," the Reverend Swift had appeared in the office of the Senate Armed Services Committee where he spread the report that Anna Rosenberg was a Communist and said that he had given the information to Senator McCarthy. Panic reigned among certain members of the committee for three reasons: the charge might be true; whether true or not McCarthy, if he followed the past performance chart, would be screaming it from the top of Washington Monument within a few hours; and third, because in those days United States Senators panicked very easily.

Richard Russell of Georgia and Harry Byrd of Virginia huddled quickly and decided they would have a hearing. In the background, Fulton Lewis, Jr., was warming up his radio microphone to burn Anna Rosenberg at the stake.

Ralph DeSola, the alleged ex-Communist, followed the pattern of many others of his kind. He was one of that shoddy group of professional witnesses that we got to know so well in those unhappy days. Their only claim to integrity was their testimony that they had once belonged to a society of liars, the Communist party.

However, McCarthy and Fulton Lewis, Jr., thought they had a live one in Ralph DeSola. He testified that he had been introduced to Mrs. Rosenberg by a James McGraw whom he also identified as an ex-Communist. He said that a William Harris, whom he described as an ex-FBI agent, had reported Mrs. Rosenberg's membership in the John Reed Club to Ted Kirkpatrick, the publisher of a magazine called *Counterattack*. He also swore that he had reported the whole story to George Starr, a retired FBI agent.

Finally, in the hearing room DeSola "positively" identified Anna Rosenberg as a former Communist. McCarthy was delighted, and Fulton Lewis, Jr., told his radio audience that it reminded him of the time when "Alger Hiss was confronted across the table with Whittaker Chambers." On the sidelines, J. B. Matthews, another dedicated trailer of Communists, who would be employed by Joe McCarthy a few months later and who would be immediately fired at my demand, was yipping along the trail and saying, Yes indeed, Anna Rosenberg was a Communist.

Then the lady herself was given a chance to answer DeSola. "He is a liar," she said. "I would like to lay my hands on that man. It is inhuman what he has done to me in the past few days. If he is crazy or a Communist, I want to face him. I have never been a member of the John Reed Club; I have never been a Communist; I have never sympathized with Communists; I have spent my life trying to do something to help my country. How can a human being do this to someone?"

Joe McCarthy sneered; Fulton Lewis stepped up his attack by radio.

Then DeSola's name-dropping backfired. James McGraw denied that he had ever introduced Mrs. Rosenberg to DeSola. William Harris, the "ex-FBI agent," said he wasn't anything of the kind and had never told anything to Ted Kirkpatrick about Mrs. Rosenberg. Kirkpatrick himself said DeSola was a liar. George Starr testified that DeSola had never told him anything at all about Anna Rosenberg. Finally, J. B. Matthews admitted that he too had been wrong.

McCarthy was stricken and his sneer turned into his famous giggle. Gerald L. K. Smith, who had been using a nearby hotel as a command post in his campaign to destroy the "Zionist Jew," scuttled out of town.

Finally, and it seemed almost inevitable, it was discovered that there was a different Anna Rosenberg, living on the West Coast, who actually had been a member of the Communist John Reed Club.

Once again, McCarthy's carelessness and love for the big headline had made a fool out of him, but he never seemed to learn. Mrs. Rosenberg was confirmed as Assistant Secretary of Defense, and, to Joe's credit, it must be reported that he voted in favor of the confirmation.

McCarthy had an uncanny ability to collect unsavory fanatics amongst his loyal followers. These strange, irresponsible people, who live on a diet of hatred, seldom find a leader of national stature. McCarthy was their man, and it is fortunate that he did not have the ambition nor the ability to organize them into a political force. He gave them a loud mouthpiece, they put his name in the big headlines, and that was the end of it.

CHAPTER 21

McCarthy Rides High

For thirteen days after my first report to President Eisenhower, I sat at the committee table in the Senate Caucus Room and watched Joe McCarthy clash with Robert Stevens.

It was no match.

It was a contest between a mild, gentle, and overage Boy Scout who believed in the rules and regulations and a brawling hoodlum who believed in nothing.

The hearing, if such it could be called, was supposed to be a meeting between gentlemen, leaders of our government, to discuss violations of our code. Stevens had been charged with blackmail. There was certain evidence to be produced by both sides, mostly transcripts of monitored telephone calls and memories of certain conversations. There was no need for dramatics or for loud talking or for ill-mannered abuse. Unfortunately, however, there was no referee. Maintaining order and decorum was Karl Mundt's duty, but neither he nor anyone else could do so.

If anyone was running the show, it was Joe McCarthy. And

176

McCarthy, who had respect for no man, ripped and tore at the throat of Stevens, the Secretary of the Army.

Stevens had become involved in this personal disaster in three different ways. One had been his handling of David Schine, which was his own fault. The other two—the Fort Monmouth investigation and the case of Major Peress—were stormed up by Joe McCarthy and Roy Cohn. Joe was, as always, desperately in need of finding a Communist that he could call his own. And in his irrational hunt for a trophy, he and Cohn had made a shambles of Fort Monmouth.

In its four laboratories in New Jersey, the Fort Monmouth complex was staffed by approximately fourteen thousand Army personnel and four thousand civilians. It was the principal research development and training center for the Signal Corps, and its job was to improve and perfect our long-range warning systems. It had been the target of a well-organized spying group led by Julius and Ethel Rosenberg, who were executed in Sing Sing prison in 1953. Naturally, it was probable that some remnants of Rosenberg's team were not caught in the first cleanup and the Army was well aware of this.

In 1947, President Truman had issued a loyalty order which said that present membership in the Communist party was proof of disloyalty and grounds for expulsion from government service. The Army had its own even more powerful statutes, enacted in 1942, by which it had been granted the right to remove any employee at its own discretion, and the Army had satisfied itself that it had cleared the Fort Monmouth operation of all dangerous subversives by early 1953, after keeping them under rigid surveillance for many months.

President Eisenhower revised the standards of security, made them tougher, and it was now the Army's job to review the records of some employees who had been cleared under the milder regulations of the past.

There were suspects then, no doubt about that. There were men and women, civilians, who needed to be trailed and investigated quietly and efficiently. Their names might have appeared in an innocent way during the Rosenberg case; informers might have pointed them out as suspects, possible followers of the Communist party. They were not yet "Communists" although automatically McCarthy stamped that label on them.

J. Edgar Hoover once told a House committee: "Counter-espionage assignments of the FBI require an objective different from the handling of criminal cases. In a criminal case the identification and arrest of the wrongdoer are the ultimate objectives. In an espionage case the identification of the wrongdoer is only the first step. What is more important is to ascertain his contacts, his objectives, his sources of information and his methods of communication. Arrest and public disclosures are steps to be taken only as a matter of last resort. It is better to know who these people are and what they are doing, and to immobilize their efforts, than it is to expose them publicly and then go through the tireless effort of identifying their successors."

This is exactly what the FBI and the Army Intelligence Force were doing in 1953. They were trailing thirty-five suspects. Then, unfortunately, someone in the FBI stole some documents and delivered them to McCarthy. It was confidential information and it was against the law for McCarthy to accept them. But Roy Cohn sensed the possibilities, called Joe back from his honeymoon in the West, and soon we were getting stories leaked by McCarthy, who roared that there was a tremendous spy ring operating at Fort Monmouth—"Bigger than those involving Rosenberg and Hiss."

It was nothing of the kind. It was a collection of fragmentary rumors and distortions which, when reviewed by the Federation of American Scientists, involved 120 charges against nineteen employees. When these charges had been sifted out, six suspects remained. One admitted that he had attended Communist meetings with his mother when he was twelve years old; the other five denied that they had ever been affiliated with any

Communist group and there was no proof to indicate that they were not telling the truth.

This was McCarthy's "spy ring" which he had trumpeted from coast to coast, alerting and driving into hiding any important subversives who might, until then, have been under the complete control of the FBI. He had earned, if anything, a special merit badge from the leader of the Russian espionage apparatus in the United States whoever he might be.

If it had been a matter of prime importance in the Soviet Union to bury us, they missed their best chance in those thirty-six days of our hearing. Members of the Armed Forces went through the motions, but neither their minds nor their hearts were in their work. The Army and its number one man were locked in a slapstick television farce, its morale shattered by the incessant hooligan attacks on its finest officers. Who would have manned the defenses with an all-out effort if the Army had already been surrendered to a publicity-mad politician?

If Bob Stevens had been blessed with just a few drops of the blood of the tiger, he could have blunted McCarthy's claws with a show of courage. Why had he debased himself in the long series of surrenders to the insatiable Roy Cohn? Why had he approved, and demanded that his generals approve, a long series of special privileges for David Schine? This was the time for Stevens to be fearlessly honest—to admit that he had been afraid of Joe McCarthy and what McCarthy might do.

Instead he said, "I had been cooperating right along with the Senator and his committee, and I want it to continue." He said, "Mr. Cohn indicated that Senator McCarthy was very mad and felt that I had double-crossed him." After Cohn had told him this, Stevens flew to New York, took McCarthy to lunch at which the main course was Stevens' appeasement on toast. He used his own Army airplane to fly McCarthy and Cohn down to Fort Dix from New York to visit David Schine and from there to Boston, where McCarthy had a date to make a speech in which he again attacked the Army for coddling Communists.

All through their relationship, McCarthy had treated Stevens with contempt and now, with twenty million Americans watching, he continued to do so. McCarthy was riding high through these first two weeks of the hearing. He moved in, punching and slashing, to prove his contention that all of Stevens' activities had been aimed at stopping Joe's hunt for Commie coddlers in the Army.

MCCARTHY: Now, can you tell us today whether or not you wanted the hearings at Fort Monmouth suspended?

STEVENS: I wanted them suspended in order that the Army could carry out the hearings themselves and stop the panic that was being created in the minds of the public on a basis that was not justified by the facts.

MCCARTHY: How did you finally succeed in getting the hearings suspended?

STEVENS: How did I succeed?

MCCARTHY: Yes, they are suspended as of today. How did you succeed?

STEVENS: They aren't suspended as far as I know.

MCCARTHY: Bob, don't give me that. You know that the hearings were suspended the day you or someone filed your charges against Mr. Cohn, Mr. Carr and myself—let's not be coy.

And so, in the opening act of this obscene drama McCarthy appeared to be the hero, and Bob Stevens was knocked down and kicked to death without ever striking back in the only language McCarthy understood. He was the victim of McCarthy's endless battle cry that the Army for the past twenty years was filled with spies, and of the myth that McCarthy's primary concern was to drive them out and that McCarthy and the dozen members of his staff were capable of doing it.

McCarthy's case was preposterous, a plot fit only for the comic strips or the television dramas in which the good guy always wins over the bad guy. As the author, McCarthy wrote his own part, and millions of Americans tore themselves away from the comic strips long enough to believe him.

But it wasn't over yet.

CHAPTER **22**

A Restricted Oath

I T was the week after Determine won the eightieth running of the Kentucky Derby when I went to see President Eisenhower again. As before, it was the cloak-and-dagger routine, reporting at the north gate of the White House. I knew I was supposed to be some sort of secret agent but I had to smile at the idea of my being able to slink in, blending into the scenery, with my two canes and two artificial legs.

The President was waiting for me on the third floor again.

"When is it going to end, Charlie?"

"I don't know, Mr. President. It may go on for a long time but McCarthy is finished."

He looked up at me in surprise.

"We can be grateful to television," I added. "The public is watching him now and they are seeing him at his worst. He has been telling them for a long time that McCarthyism is Americanism. Now they are beginning to wonder if Americanism means faked photographs and forged documents."

"I was told about the FBI letter and Hoover's answer. But I don't see that this has changed anything," the President said. "I made a statement this week giving Stevens my full support."

It was not for me to tell the President that the support he

had been giving to Stevens was not enough. He had coupled his support for Stevens with support for Secretary of State John Foster Dulles, who had just returned from Geneva and was being attacked for his performance there, or rather, because no clear-cut solution of the growing problems in Asia was possible. The President had said that he considered Dulles the greatest Secretary of State in his memory and that he had picked the Army Secretary for his job with great care. He had said nothing would make him lose confidence in Stevens' administration of the Army. However, when a friend has been knocked to the floor and is being stomped by a hoodlum, it helps him little to announce that he is a fine administrator.

"The fake picture hurt him some," I said. "They brought that in about a week ago. I don't know whether you saw it or not. [I was never sure just how much Dwight Eisenhower knew about the details of the case.] It was supposed to be a chummy picture of Bob Stevens and Private David Schine at Fort Dix, and McCarthy's crew claimed that Stevens had asked that the picture be taken. The next day Joe Welch, the Army attorney, brought in the complete picture. There were two or three other people in the original, and it just happened that Schine and Stevens were facing each other. This is an old McCarthy trick. You may remember that he used it in his campaign to beat Millard Tydings in Maryland, but that time it was a complete fake, a manufactured shot of Tydings supposedly talking to Earl Browder. McCarthy's theory seems to be that if it works once it will always work."

"Who was responsible for it?"

"McCarthy, of course. There was a lot of double-talking testimony by Cohn and Carr and even David Schine. And the Army photographer who took the picture said that the only reason he took it was that there were some big names standing there in the group. But the implication and the use of it and the way it was used was pure McCarthy, and, after all, he is responsible for the actions of his staff."

"Why do you feel so strongly, Charlie, that McCarthy is finished?" the President asked.

"Because the fiasco of the faked picture knocked him off balance. That Joe Welch is far too smart for Joe McCarthy and Cohn together. He doesn't say much and he doesn't do much and sometimes you think he's not even paying attention. But when he shoots, he hits the target and he has wounded them a couple of times. He was questioning one of McCarthy's assistants, James Juliana, trying to find out the truth about the picture. He asked Juliana if he thought the picture came from a pixie. McCarthy couldn't resist getting into the act and made a sarcastic request that Welch define what a pixie is. Welch said it is a close relation of a fairy, and from that moment on McCarthy lost his coolness about Welch.

"Welch's thrust got a big laugh in the Caucus Room, and one thing a man like McCarthy cannot stand is laughter. If Joe ever took the time and had enough honesty to examine an inventory of his performance during the past few years, his statements, his accusations, he would have to know that it has been essentially comic. If you take him seriously, he is dangerous, but if he reveals himself to a national audience as a cheap clown, as he did in that little exchange with Welch, people begin to laugh at him. This he cannot stand. His judgment goes out the window and he is ready to gamble in an attempt to be the hero again."

As I sat there I tried to picture Dwight Eisenhower on coast-to-coast television answering questions about Joe McCarthy with a gusty roar of laughter. In my quick dream scene, he would have been followed by General George Marshall, General MacArthur, General Zwicker; Dean Acheson and John Foster Dulles from the diplomatic ranks; and a long line of ex-Senators—each and all of them laughing hilariously at McCarthy's charges against them. This treatment would have ended the farce.

"He came up with the document late Tuesday afternoon,"

I said. "He described it as part of a series of letters from the FBI, warning of the tremendous danger of a particular man and his associates at Fort Monmouth. He tried to make Bob Stevens read the document, and he said that the warnings in it were disregarded by the Pentagon until his committee started its investigation. He ridiculed Stevens because Bob said that he did not know of the existence of such a letter. I could see that Joe Welch was skeptical about the whole thing. He was probably remembering the fake picture but he held off until the next day, letting it develop."

"And that was a fake too?"

"Yes. It would have been pretty hard for Bob Stevens to know about such a document because there wasn't any. Edgar Hoover denied that he had ever sent or written any such letter, which, incidentally, was two and a quarter pages long. It developed that it was a rewrite of a fifteen-page memorandum Hoover had sent to the Pentagon more than three years ago. All the charges in it had been investigated by G-2 long before McCarthy ever heard of Fort Monmouth. But it wasn't so much the document itself—you learn to expect these things from Joe—it was Mc-Carthy's performance under oath in the witness chair that I think was the turning point in the whole life story of Joseph Raymond McCarthy."

"I don't see that it has made any difference, Charlie," the President said. "The hearings are still going on, and you tell me that you can't even guess when they will stop."

"We haven't heard the echo from it yet," I said. "Joe wrote the script for this episode himself and his worst enemy could not have done a better job in an attempt to destroy him. Bear in mind that it had now been established that Joe had obtained, first, a stolen document. He claimed that it had been delivered to him by a serviceman in G-2. If that part was true, then we have a subversive in G-2, a man who takes it upon himself to give secret information to an unauthorized person. Then, from the stolen document, the phony letter allegedly signed by

J. Edgar Hoover was produced. It was a pretty silly move from
the start, just some more of the old rehash routine, trying to
smear the Army with a mess it had cleaned up long ago. Sometimes I wonder if Joe's judgment doesn't go bad after his liquid
luncheons at the Carroll Arms. He always seems to make his
worst mistakes in the afternoon."

"What is driving this man?"

"I think, Mr. President, he is a lonely rebel who thinks he has
found a cause. I would guess that he has a deep longing to be
important, and he loves the headlines. Outside the Senate, outside the hearing rooms, he is warm, friendly, pathetically so.
I think all this uproar is just a game with him. I don't think he
has any deep feelings about Communism one way or the other.
I would guess that if he could get bigger headlines by being in
favor of it he would switch tomorrow. He's like the bad-guy
wrestlers who put on their show, then leave the arena with the
man they have been assaulting and take a friendly ride to the
next city. I've noticed that he always seems shocked when someone resents his insulting remarks and carries the resentment
outside the Senate. He would be surprised, for example, if he
should bump into General Zwicker on the street and Zwicker
did not give him the big hello. Personally, I am rather fond of
him outside the Senate. Some of my happiest hours are spent
having a few drinks with him when we aren't talking business."

"That's a strange thing for you to say, Charlie. You seem to
be one of the very few people who hasn't gone along with him."

"I'm aware of the other side of him, Mr. President, of his
cruelties and his recklessness and his bad manners and his
ignoring all the rules, but I always seem to think of him as a
sort of juvenile delinquent who has never grown up. I was a
social worker once, and you learn to be tolerant of the emotion-
ally unbalanced. He's about ten years older than I, but I see
him as a kid who needs several good spankings.

"But anyway, he gave himself a spanking yesterday. We had

him on the stand under oath, and he stabbed himself in the back. If you remember, he has taught the whole world to despise the witnesses that he has browbeaten for their refusal to tell what they knew. He has called them Fifth Amendment Communists and traitors because, for one reason or another, they refuse to answer his questions. Forget for a minute that he had no right to ask most of the questions, and the only reason he was asking them was to destroy either the witness or some of his associates. But now he was in the target area, under oath, and the first thing he did was to make a statement that he wanted to notify the people who gave him information that there was no way on earth that any committee or anyone else could get him to violate the confidence of those people. This was his pledge, by television, to the army of malcontents and seditionists who take it upon themselves to give him rumors and hints and stolen documents.

"But Joe Welch had him where he wanted him now, trapped in front of the cameras that McCarthy has always loved. Welch asked for the source of the phony letter, and McCarthy said he wouldn't answer that. I brought along a copy of the testimony because I thought you'd be particularly interested in this part. Let me read you just a page or two."

"Yes, I'd like to hear it."

I read him the following:

MCCARTHY: I won't answer that.

WELCH: Could I have the oath that you took read to us wholly by the reporter?

MUNDT: Mr. Welch, that doesn't seem to be an appropriate question. It's the same oath you took.

WELCH: The oath included a promise, a solemn promise by you to tell the truth and nothing but the truth. Is that correct, sir?

MCCARTHY: Mr. Welch, you are not the first individual that

tried to get me to betray the confidence and give out the names of my informants. You will be no more successful than those who have tried it in the past.

WELCH: I am only asking you, sir, did you realize when you took the oath that you were making a solemn promise to tell the truth to this committee?

McCARTHY: I understand the oath, Mr. Welch.

WELCH: And when you took it, did you have some mental reservation, some Fifth or Sixth Amendment notion that you could measure what you would tell?

McCARTHY: I don't take the Fifth or Sixth Amendment.

"This is where Welch was beginning to get the spurs in deep," I said. "You can always tell when Joe is hurting. His eyes go glassy and he holds that upper lip so tight against his teeth and the pitch of his voice goes up and up and up."

"Interesting. Go on with it."

I continued to read:

WELCH: Have you some private reservation when you take the oath that you will tell the whole truth that lets you be the judge of what you will testify to?

McCARTHY: The answer is that there is no reservation about telling the whole truth.

"Welch is a master performer. He had the trap wide open now, and McCarthy stuck his head all the way in. There was no reservation about telling the whole truth. Then it goes like this":

WELCH: Thank you, sir. Then tell us who delivered the document to you.

McCARTHY: The answer is no. You will not get the information.

188

WELCH: You wish then to put your own interpretation on your oath and tell us less than the whole truth?

McCARTHY: You can go right ahead and try until doomsday. You will not get the names of any informants who rely upon me to protect them.

WELSH: Will you tell us where you were when you got it?

McCARTHY: No.

WELCH: Were you in Washington?

McCARTHY: The answer was I would not tell you.

"That was just about the end of it," I said, "and I can't reconstruct it the way it happened. But twenty million Americans saw it happen, and they saw a performance that never could have been explained to them."

"Even a solemn oath means nothing to him, even his own oath," Eisenhower said. "I think you may be right, Charlie. What decent American would not be repelled by this?"

"It will cost him every person who has any respect for decency and reason," I answered, "but he'll still keep his fanatics. They live on emotions, they want nothing to do with facts. They are the ones who say that maybe he's a little rough at times but, after all, he is driving out the Communists. I noticed that even Ray Jenkins, the Committee counsel, leans over backward to help Joe. After Joe refused to reveal who stole the Hoover letter, Jenkins ruled that Joe had a right to protect his source of information because he was a law-enforcing officer ferreting out crime, an absolutely incredible ruling.

"Then today, Joe continued to bite himself. He said that Bob Stevens was trying to block his investigations of Communism by prolonging this hearing. If there is one thing Bob Stevens does not want, it is more of what he has been going through the last few days. Then Joe said that General Zwicker had lied under oath.

"Today we received a letter from Attorney General Brownell

189

which said that Joe's use of the faked FBI letter was unauthorized, that it was classified as confidential. Joe went into a rage
over this. He said that no Truman directive or any other directive could prevent him from publishing secrets. There was no
connection between any Truman directive and Brownell's letter, but the way he says 'Truman directive' makes it sound like
an obscenity.

"All this was into the microphones and the television sets.
He was ordering his troops into open rebellion. And he said he
wanted to determine once and for all whether or not we are the
lackeys to obey a decision made by someone in the executive
department."

"By someone, he meant Brownell?" the President asked.
"Brownell is the highest legal officer in the country. So he defies
the law of the land."

"That wasn't all of it this morning. He accused Brownell of
releasing files about spies who were dead while he himself was
busy exposing live ones who are poised with a razor over the
jugular vein of this nation. He likes that phrase, he's used it
several times. He said that his committee's activities may determine whether this nation will live or die. It was one of his
semihysterical episodes, and he was using that strange, high-
pitched, whining voice."

"Charlie, didn't someone once say that patriotism is the last
refuge of a scoundrel?"

"Someone said it," I answered, "but it doesn't apply here.
Joe McCarthy isn't that kind of a scoundrel because he isn't a
patriot. Too bad he didn't live in Washington's time. That's
when we needed revolutionaries, and he might have been one
of the founding fathers."

"God forbid," the President said.

CHAPTER **23**

Dennis the Menace

I THINK I was the first one to know that
Ralph Flanders was considering a censure resolution against
Joe McCarthy. I found a message from him at my office when
I returned from one of the endless days of hearings late in May.
I called him and he said, "Charlie, if you can spare the time, I'd
like to come over and see you."

I knew something serious was on his mind. We had been no
more than cordial acquaintances. We had never served on the
same committees. But it was no secret to me, nor to anyone else,
that Flanders, to put it mildly, disapproved of Joe McCarthy.
Flanders was a man who had made little noise in the Senate
through all the years he served his people in Vermont. In the
few times we had talked together before this, I had found that
he had a snapping wit and a dry sense of humor.

He came over to my office, bringing a rough copy of a speech.

"Charlie, I want to talk to you about Dennis the Menace."

"What do you have in mind, Ralph?" I asked. I didn't have
to ask him who Dennis was.

"Charlie, have you ever considered that if he were in the pay
of the Communists, an agent right out of Moscow, he could not
possibly have done a better job for them?"

"He hasn't blown up the Pentagon or looted Fort Knox, Ralph," I said.

"Not quite. But he has done his best to smash the morale of the Army, and I would guess that he has just about succeeded. And when you talk about looting, have you read the report of the Gillette Committee?"

"I'm a television personality now. I don't have time to read much of anything. No, I have not read the Gillette report."

"I've been watching you, Charlie. I think you are one of the few we have left who is not afraid of him. You and Margaret Smith and one or two more. I watch the rest of them cringing and slobbering when he turns on them and it makes me sick."

"Some of the others have gone down, Ralph," I said.

"Let me read you this, Charlie," he said, flicking through the pages he had in his hand. " 'An America which has lost faith in the integrity of the government, the Army, the schools, the churches, the labor unions, and most of all, an America whose citizens have lost faith in each other—such an America would not need to bother about being anti-Communist; it would have nothing to lose. Such an America would have nothing to recommend it to freedom-loving men—nothing at all, not even the shining image of its victorious junior Senator from Wisconsin.' I didn't say that, Charlie, but I think every word of it is true. I lifted it from a speech made by Bishop Bernard Sheil of Chicago, and I think it sums up the situation as of right now. Charlie, would you mind glancing through this speech? Someone has got to stand up to the hatemongers and seditionists who support this man and it might as well be me."

"Have you got an asbestos mailbox, Ralph? An unlisted telephone?"

"I know what you mean. You may remember I gave a little talk about him before. Who are these people who write the letters? You never know because they never sign their names. Illiterate, ignorant, terrified by facts, full of venom, hating everything and everybody. And always gathered around some prominent rabble-rouser. It could happen here, Charlie. When fifty percent of the people approve the actions of a man who throws filth on his own President, his own church, his team- mates on his own political party and everyone else in sight, then the public is well along the road to accepting the whole pro- gram of Fascism or Communism or Nazism or McCarthyism, by whatever name you want to call it. I noticed that a recent Gallup poll indicated that fifty percent approved of Joe, about thirty did not, and the rest didn't know. Didn't know. My God!"

He tossed the speech over to me, leaned back in the deep leather chair and closed his eyes. I began to read it.

"Mr. President, I propose for a few minutes to address this body on the subject of the colossal innocence of the junior Sena- tor from Wisconsin, Mr. McCarthy. I am not using the word innocence in the meaning of freedom from guilt, for no ques- tion of guilt is involved. Rather the meaning is that of the blithe heedlessness of the young, who blunder innocently into the most appalling situations, as they ramble through the world of adults. Perhaps the best illustration of this kind of innocence is to be found in a popular cartoon series published daily under the title *Dennis the Menace*."

So he sees it too, I thought, the over-age delinquent who en- joys smashing windows, stealing hubcaps, writing obscene words on the sides of buildings. I continued to read.

". . . He spreads division and confusion wherever he goes. Note, for instance, the foreboding he inspires in our fellow citizens of Jewish blood and faith. Among them this is well nigh universal. . . . I have been led to remember the part the Sena- tor played in the investigation of the Malmédy massacres, and the strange tenderness he displayed for the Nazi ruffians in- volved.

"Perhaps this would not have been enough to perpetuate foreboding, but his anti-Communism so completely parallels that of Adolf Hitler as to strike fear into the heart of any defenseless minority. . . . It was not the Jews alone who had reason to be troubled. The former Chief of Staff of the Senator's committee, without a word of rebuke from his superior, charged the Protestant ministry with being, in effect, the center of Communist influence in this country. Here the attack was on a vigorous, indignant majority, and the Chief of Staff had to go."

(This, of course, referred to the episode of J. B. Matthews.)

"Clearer and clearer evidence came to light of the danger of setting church against church," the next paragraph said, "Catholic against Protestant. At a recent communion breakfast of the New York police force, the Senator made a characteristic speech, blaming the Pentagon for not compelling the release of the remaining prisoners of the Chinese Communists. He did not say how this could be done short of renewing the war. Then he referred to his own proudest achievement—the detection of the Pink dentist. Loud cheers from most of the audience—others silent. . . . Then Monsignor McCaffrey went into a eulogistic oration on the public service of our Senator. More cheers and silences. . . .

"Cardinal Spellman entered during the Monsignor's introduction and shook hands with our Senator. He arrived late and left early, but he did shake hands. Did this mean that the imprimatur of *nihil obstat* had been set by the Church on these debonair campaigns to divide Americans from each other on religious lines? . . . But soon, thank God, from Chicago another voice was heard. It was that of a high and respected member of the Catholic Church, Bishop Sheil. He said that our Senator was doing more harm than good, and was dividing the United States instead of uniting it. . . . Thus, it became evident that Dennis the Menace had driven his blundering axe deep into the heart of his own church."

I read on through a few more paragraphs and glanced across the table at Ralph Flanders. His eyes were still closed, he had not moved. You are seventy-four years old, I thought, exactly twice my age, but there is the heart of a lion in that old body.

I went back to the speech.

"Meanwhile, the investigation goes on and on. There are new synthetic and irrelevant mysteries served up each day, like the baker's breakfast buns, delivered to the door hot out of the oven. But the committee has not yet dug into the real heart of the mystery. That mystery concerns the personal relationships of the Army private, the staff assistant, and the Senator. . . . This hubbub centers on the Army private. What is it really all about? His usefulness as an investigator is continually asserted, but never documented. Let him also be investigated. When he is released for committee work, what does he do hour by hour? Whom does he see? What material does he analyze? What does he report? These questions are important and un-answered. . . . Then, there is the relationship of the staff assistant to the Army private. It is natural that he should wish to return the services of an able collaborator, but he seems to have an almost passionate anxiety to retain him. Why? . . . And then, there is the Senator himself. At times he seems anxious to rid himself of the whole mess, and then again, at least in the presence of his assistant, he strongly supports the latter's efforts to keep the Army private's services available. Does the assistant have some hold on the Senator? Can it be that our Dennis, so effective in making trouble for his elders, has at last got into trouble himself? Does the committee plan to investi-gate the real issues at stake?"

This was strong stuff. I looked at Ralph Flanders again, and my mind flicked over other Senators who had cringed and run from Joe McCarthy. Here was a man who could give us all lessons in courage. There was only one more page to go.

"Let us now leave these interesting domestic details and look at the worldwide strategy of Communism," the last page read. "Let us begin by remembering that a while ago the Sena-tor from Maine, Mrs. Smith, was denounced by the Moscow press as an enemy of the people—that is, of Communism. I

have myself been honored by the same accolade. If the junior
Senator from Wisconsin has ever been attacked by Pravda, it
has not come to my attention. . . . In every country in which
Communism has taken over, the beginning has been a successful campaign of division and confusion. Race is set against race,
party against party, religion against religion, neighbor against
neighbor, and child against parent. Until lately, we have been
free of that. We are so no longer. . . . The preliminary campaign is successfully under way. One of the characteristic elements of Communist and Fascist tyranny is at hand, as citizens
are set to spy upon each other. Established and responsible government is besmirched. Religion is set against religion, race
against race. Churches and parties are split asunder. All is division and confusion.

"Were the junior Senator from Wisconsin in the pay of the
Communists, he could not have done a better job for them. This
is colossal innocence, indeed."

"What do you think of it, Charlie?"

"It's a brilliant piece of writing, Ralph. No staff man wrote
this one. It needs to be said every hour of every day, but the
jackal pack won't listen. Those who know you are right already
know it but they keep silent too. You see it happen in any
gathering. If you're not one hundred percent for him, you're
a Commie lover. And I'm afraid there's a streak of brainless
idiocy in anyone who supports him."

"Idiocy and fear. Always the fear."

"Of course you have to say it, Ralph. Men like you, the
veterans here, have an important voice. I am a rookie, a gun-
bearer. I am a squeak while you are a roar. And yet, when
I squeak, they come piling into me. I've got a copy of a column
here that was printed in the Detroit *Times* a few weeks ago,
written by David Sentner. It's banging me on the head because
I criticized Joe for his treatment of General Zwicker. It says
I'm a naughty boy because Joe helped me to get elected in
1952, and because the Veterans organization supported me and

because I was against Communists when I was on the House committee. But now I've switched, it says here. And the reason I switched, it says, is that I'm being coddled by the anti-McCarthy Washington correspondents and because I'm a headline hunter."

"I get the same thing, Charlie," he said, "and I get more than you. I'm senile, they tell me."

"The American press is a strange animal. It's full of self-righteousness and yet here is a powerful chain of newspapers slandering every other paper which doesn't agree with it. It says in this column that the pro-Communist press makes much of the fact that I am a double amputee every time I issue a critical statement regarding the—what they call—Communist-hunting McCarthy.

"I particularly like this paragraph that says my pious attitude toward the tough attitude of McCarthy toward Red witnesses also fails to hold water after my recent headline-hunting project—whacking the Chinese Reds for atrocities against American prisoners of war. That was that hearing I had a few months ago."

"Typical," he said. "The writer sees no difference between torturing war prisoners and a Senator attempting to destroy a general of his own Army. How loony can you get?"

"I'd like to go over that Gillette report with you, Ralph," I said. "Why don't we go someplace for dinner?"

"Great idea, Charlie. I know a little steak house out in the northeast jungles near here. Nothing fancy but real good eating. Give me fifteen minutes to shut up shop and I'll bring my car around to the steps, the big steps going up to the rotunda."

CHAPTER 24

These Communists Are Real

MY headline-hunting project—as the newspaper writer called it—had been a three-day investigation by a special subcommittee on Korean war atrocities with myself as chairman. It had provided testimony by American soldiers, some of them former prisoners of the Koreans, on the barbaric acts committed against our troops during the three years of the Korean war. We called twenty-nine witnesses. Six of them were former Army field commanders in Korea and officials of the War Crimes Division. The other twenty-three were survivors, and all of them carried wounds inflicted during the atrocities. Several of them had been "murdered" along with other prisoners but had feigned death and survived. One had been shot, buried alive, and somehow managed to crawl away after the sun went down.

The first reports of war crimes committed by the North Korean armies in Korea against captured United Nations military personnel began to filter into General Headquarters early in July 1950, only a few days after the military action started. General Douglas MacArthur, Commander of UN forces, immediately set up legal machinery for the investigation of war crimes committed by the Communist aggressors. This, he hoped, would avoid the difficulties experienced after World War II when little effort was made to investigate war crimes until some time after the war ended.

During that delay, witnesses vanished, evidence became blurred. This time, an organized program was started. And, in order to define and clarify the limits of the investigations in Korea, war crimes were defined as those acts committed by enemy nations, or those persons acting for them, which constitute violations of the laws and customs of war, as well as outrageous acts against persons or property committed in connection with military operations. The War Crimes Division made on-the-spot investigations. Thousands of enemy prisoners of war were interviewed, and every effort was made to discover corroborating evidence to establish the facts surrounding the reported war crimes. Investigators collected evidence consisting of affidavits, photographs, statements of participants and perpetrators. They located bodies of victims, effecting their identification whenever possible.

When the documented case was completed and analyzed, it was then referred to the Command Staff Judge Advocate of the Armed Forces in the Far East, for possible prosecution.

War is not a game to be played on a manicured lawn on a Sunday afternoon, and no nation's record has ever been completely clear of brutalities and sadistic cruelties. However, massacres and the wholesale extermination of their victims is a calculated part of Communist psychological warfare. The atrocities in Korea against United Nations troops by Chinese and North Korean Communists were not unique in Communist history, nor could they be explained away on the grounds that inhumanity is often associated with so-called civilized warfare.

A previous House committee had conducted an investigation of the evidence in the notorious Katyn Forest massacre of World War II in which thousands of Poles were exterminated by Russian troops. There was a striking similarity between the Katyn episode and the tactics used in Korea. The Communists in Korea violated every provision of the Geneva Convention of 1929, as well as Article Six of the Charter of the International Military Tribunal at Nuremberg, Germany, of 1946. It was this Article which listed crimes against peace, war crimes, and crimes against humanity.

I sat in my office, giving Ralph Flanders time to clean up his affairs before we went to dinner, and looked through a stack of papers on my desk. There were several letters which said nice things about my activities; there were several more that, for one reason or another, labeled me a Red-lover, a Commie-coddler, a traitor, and a few other choice descriptions. I picked up a copy of the little twenty-eight-page report which I had submitted after hearing twenty-three soldiers tell us their experiences with the Communists in Korea. Included in the sick-making pictures which we submitted for evidence was one of Private Roy Paul Manrin, Jr., of New Albany, Indiana, sitting on a stretcher, wrapped in bandages, somewhere in Korea, and pointing to two North Korean soldiers whom he identified as members of an execution squad.

I remembered Roy Manrin in the witness chair during our hearings. He was a tousle-headed youngster, wearing glasses, limping from his permanent wounds and looking like a boy who should be concerned mostly with a high school basketball game.

I riffled through the report and found his testimony:

"They just kept us in a ravine in the daytime. Then at night they'd move us across country. On August 17, about the middle of the afternoon, they motioned for us to get up again, that they were going to move us out again. That's when it happened. That's when I started hearing shots. I looked around and I saw my buddies was falling, getting murdered with their hands tied behind their back."

"Did they hit you?" I had asked him.

"Yes. The first time they hit me I got hit in the leg and the upper part of the arm. What caused me to fall was a fellow in front of me. When he fell, then I fell and as he fell, the wire that they had tied us together with broke loose and left me by myself. My hands were still tied behind my back."

"Did they think that you were dead?" I said.

"Yes. I guess they thought we was dead. As they left, a couple of minutes later, I heard a sound like somebody was coming back, so I managed to wiggle my body underneath the fellow that was next to me—was dead—and they come by and they started kicking and you could hear the fellows hollering, grunting, groaning, and praying, and when they kicked me they kicked my leg and I made a grunting sound, and that's when I caught it in the gut, got shot in the gut at the time."

Then there was Private John E. Martin of Ferndale, Michigan, one of my constituents. In October 1950, at Pyongyang, when the fall of that city appeared imminent, the Communists loaded approximately 180 war prisoners into open railroad cars for transport northward.

These men were survivors of the Seoul-Pyongyang death march and were weak from lack of food, water, and medical care. They rode unprotected in the raw climate for four or five days, arriving at the Sunchon Tunnel on the railroad on October 30, 1950. Late in the afternoon, the prisoners were taken from the railroad cars in alternate groups of approximately forty to nearby ravines, ostensibly to receive their first food in several days. There they were ruthlessly shot by North Korean soldiers, using Russian burp guns. One hundred and thirty-eight American soldiers lost their lives in this atrocity: sixty-eight were murdered at the tunnel, seven died of malnutrition while in the tunnel, and the remainder died of pneumonia, dysentery, and malnutrition on the horror trip from Pyongyang. Private Martin told us about it:

"They had us all get off the train. We were all in the tunnel there. The highest-ranking officer, two sergeants, and another corporal had already left earlier. There was some money collected up by the prisoners, supposedly to buy food. They hadn't come back yet. They told us we were going to a small house to eat, and the reason we were going in groups was because it was so small."

"How many in a group?" I asked him.

"I would say on the average of forty men to a group. The first group went out and the guards were gone about twenty minutes to a half hour. When they left we heard a lot of small arms fire, but I never thought anything about it and I don't think too many other people did either.

"They came back for my group and we started out. We went down the track about 400 yards and I had fallen back to the rear. My feet were pretty bad and I had to keep falling back. I couldn't keep up with them. We went around the corner into this ditch. They said get down, the planes, get down, the planes. So when we all ducked down some more of them came up on us over a little rice paddy and they just opened up."

"They fired on you? Were you hit?"

"No, sir. I was the last man to come around the corner. As I came around I just sat down when they started to fire and I fell forward on the embankment. I was right just about at one of their feet and I suppose he thought I was hit and was firing over my head at other people. Then another fellow fell just about across me, more or less on my back, and when they did come down in the ditch and check, they were in a hurry. They didn't get all the way down to me before they went back up."

"What do you mean by check?" I asked.

"They went down and kicked somebody, and if they groaned, they shot them again or bayoneted."

Later, Major General Frank A. Allen, Jr., Assistant Division Commander of the First Cavalry Division, led a command of troops that discovered the bodies and survivers at Sunchon Tunnel. He testified for us:

"Our first visit to the tunnel brought out these seven cadaverous corpses. They apparently had starved to death. There wasn't a speck of flesh on their carcasses. They were in the tunnel. Then I heard a cry from another source of an American so we came down the hill, and there we came across the most gruesome sight I have ever witnessed. That was in sort of a sunken road, a pile of American dead. I should estimate that in that pile there were sixty men. In the pile were men who were not dead, who were wounded. We, incidentally, found a very shallow grave that must have contained at least sixty bodies, the other side of the road, down maybe fifty yards from that place."

Sergeant Carey H. Weinel of Hickman Mills, Missouri, was the sole survivor of an episode at the Taejon prison camp in North Korea.

"Toward the last, they was in a hurry to leave Taejon," he told us. "So they took approximately the last three groups pretty close together. I witnessed the group right in front of me shot. After they was shot, we was taken to the ditch and sat down in the ditch and shot."

I asked what happened to him when he was shot.

"I leaned over against the next man, pretending I was done for. In firing, they hit my hand. They was aiming at my head. I have a scar on my neck, another on my collarbone and another on my hand. They hit me three times. . . . After they thought everybody was dead, they started burying us. I came close to getting panicky about that time, but somehow or other I figured as long as I had some breath there was hope."

"How long were you buried alive?"

"That is hard to say, sir. As I say, I was shot around five o'clock in the morning and I stayed in the ditch until that evening, until what time it was dark. I would say approximately eight hours, eight or seven hours."

It wasn't only the soldiers. A group of North Koreans came upon Captain Linton J. Buttrey, a regimental surgeon, who was wearing a Red Cross armband and trying to help twenty seriously wounded American soldiers. There was a chaplain with them. I asked if he was marked as a chaplain with a white cross.

"Yes, sir, he was," Captain Buttrey replied.

"What happened to him?" I said.

"He got killed, sir."

"What was he doing at the time he was killed?"

"He was administering last rites, extreme unction, to the patients," Buttrey said.

"And how did they kill him?" I asked.

"He was shot in the back, sir."

And on it went, the nightmarish memories, the eyes looking up at me that could never again smile without pain.

Sergeant Barry F. Rhoden of MacClenny, Florida: "First, they took our boots, our fatigue jackets, or mine, and all of our identifications, our dog tags. The officer who was in charge of the group, sir—I guess he was making a collection of dog tags as he had a nice row of them, with chains, sir. He gave me a small piece of paper and on it was mimeographed the words 'you are about to die the most horrible kind of death.'

"He motioned for me to go back to where my buddies were, they were standing a short distance away, sir, approximately the distance from me to you, and as I turned around, sir, I was shot in the back. The bullet knocked me down, and I lay there pretending I was dead and praying while they shot the other fellows. After they shot the other fellows, they stepped over me, bayoneted the other fellows a couple of times, and after awhile they left."

Corporal Charles E. Kinard of Quincy, Florida: "First, they put rocks in my shoes and they would chase me around until I would fall. I had lost quite a lot of blood and when I would come to, they would be giving me the cigarettes to my feet and legs and various places. They had taken the C-ration can opener which was on a dog tag hanging around my neck. They inserted that into the wound in my left shoulder and gave it a half twist. I took it out. He slapped me and hit me on my shoulder, on the wound, with the butt of his rifle and put it back in. Well, I decided it would be best if I left it in there."

Lt. Col. Robert Abbot, a prisoner of war for thirty-three

months: "In this hospital, men were dying again daily. Men were sleeping on the floor, and they were covered with maggots, they were suffering from dysentery, pellagra, and in this hospital the Chinese had introduced an operation that they claimed was a cure-all for all diseases.

"They made an incision underneath the arm and injected into this incision a chicken liver. It was then resewed and allowed to heal. Under these conditions, any cut does not heal readily. They fester and become infected, and the majority of the men that underwent those operations had some pretty nasty-looking cuts under their arms. They seemed to feel that it was something new. They said that this was something that Russian medical science had just developed."

All this evidence clearly determined that the general Communist policy, governing the treatment of American prisoners of war, emanated from a command level. In virtually every instance uncovered by the various investigations, the killing of American prisoners was either ordered or performed by a North Korean or Chinese Communist officer. The confiscation of clothing and footwear, forcing the men to walk in bare feet through the subzero cold, the inadequate medical attention, the lack of food and water, the beatings and torture, were constant during all forced marches and in all prisoner of war camps. This deliberate Communist policy to weaken prisoners was closely connected with their program of incessant political probing and forced Communist indoctrination.

General Matthew B. Ridgway, a former commander of the United Nations forces in Korea and later Chief of Staff of the U. S. Army, told our hearing that the Communist brutalities in Korea were a studied and calculated course of criminal misconduct, carried out with such callous disregard of human life and suffering as to indicate a design on the part of the Communist leadership to exterminate prisoners of war in one way or another.

Lt. Col. Jack Todd, head of the War Crimes Division, described the Communist policy as one of deliberate destruction of the human will, of human dignity and worth. In short, the animalizing of helpless humanity through starvation, torture and neglect is one of the most scathing indictments of Communist-inspired brutality.

The testimony revealed that more than 1,800 cases involving many thousands of victims of Communist war atrocities had been opened by the War Crimes Division in Korea. At that time the most accurate estimate of American troops who died as a result of war crimes was 5,639. This figure would go much higher and would reach more than 20,000 when all United Nations forces were included. The final roundup would prove endless cases of murder, various acts of torture such as perforating the flesh of prisoners with heated bamboo spears, starvation, bayoneting, and several ugly experimental medical operations.

This was Communist policy. It was known in every command post of the Army. Its record was offered to the American public through the hearings I held in early December 1953.

The pattern was no different from that of the Nazis of Hitler and the Fascists of Mussolini, nor of the Mau Mau in Kenya in later years. It was the barbarian on the loose. It was the Communist that I was now being accused of coddling.

And with this record only a few months behind us, the entire United States had been bamboozled into a nationwide uproar over the welfare of one Army private and the future of one "Fifth Amendment dentist." And the super patriotic followers of Dennis the Menace were doing their bit against Communism by throwing rocks through the windows of the dentist's home in Brooklyn.

I headed for the elevator to meet Ralph Flanders.

CHAPTER 25

It's Time to Go to War

RALPH Flanders drove slowly up North Capitol Street and out New York Avenue to the market and produce section. It was a sleazy and sloppy area piled high each night with the refuse of the thousands of tons of meats and vegetables that come into Washington. But tucked in behind the piles of splintered crates and paper cartons was the Hendrix Steak House. There was nothing fancy about that either, but with its small bar and some twenty booths it was just about the best eating place in town. We sat in a booth and Flanders pulled out another sheaf of papers.

"I'm a great one for making notes on things, Charlie," he said. "I have one of the girls in the office clip them out and paste them up and sometimes type them up when I think it's something I may use someday. I'm a New Englander and most of us are pack rats. We save everything. Our attics are full of old bedsprings and empty cartons and clothes that went out of style fifty years ago and trunks full of papers. I've got file cabinets that would fill a freight car and they're all full of little collections like these. Every once in a while it's worth it if I can find what I'm looking for.

"Charlie, the Senate is a fabulous organization," he said. "It is the highest level that a man can reach anywhere in the world in the legislative area; it is also the perfect sanctuary for a rascal. Where else could a man throw filth on everything decent in his own country and still be known as The Honorable Senator Zilch? Where else could a man conduct a piratical looting operation without penalty?"

He shook the sheaf of papers at me.

"We're still talking about Dennis?"

"About Dennis and soy beans and about hundreds of thousands of dollars donated by frightened little people and about dozens of United States Senators with the courage of so many mice and about shakedowns and stock market gambling and an open defiance of the rules of honesty. Dennis has been a busy boy, Charlie. He has made me curious."

"I remember the Lustron affair," I said. "I was still in the House then and all I ever knew about it was the newspaper stories plus the rumors. As I remember it, he demanded and got a $10,000 fee from the Lustron people before they went bankrupt."

"Yes, he was on the Banking and Currency Committee then and that had jurisdiction over the RFC and Housing Agencies, and Joe was a far-out Liberal on housing in those days. In fact, he has been in favor of almost everything on the Liberal program although most of his admirers like to see him as the great Conservative.

"Anyway, one way or another, and with Joe twisting as many arms as he could, the Lustron people sandbagged thirty-seven million dollars, and when they went busted it cost the taxpayers more than thirty million. The details are all in the report of the Gillette Committee which investigated Joe through 1951 and 1952."

"He never did appear before the committee," I said. "It was Communist persecution, it was a smear."

"That's right," Flanders said, "but, if he had gone in and testified and they could have forced the truth out of him, he

Chairman Karl Mundt (*left*) tries to listen to two expert talkers at once: McCarthy and Special Counsel Ray Jenkins.

Special Army Counsel Joseph Welch exchanges pleasantries with Senator McCarthy.

Special Army Counsel Joseph Welch and Senator McCarthy talk to each other at the start of another session of the hearings.

Pvt. Schine, McCarthy, and Cohn huddle as a monitored Schine-Stevens phone call was read into the record.

Chief Counsel Ray Jenkins talks heatedly to McCarthy and Cohn during morning session of June 8.

Army Counsel Joseph Welch utters the awaited words "I rest" concluding his cross-examination of McCarthy, final witness in the hearings on McCarthy's dispute with the Army. Then, after some closing utterances, the proceedings begun on April 22 came to an end.

Sign-carrying McCarthy supporters gather at Pennsylvania Station in New York before leaving by train for Washington to protest the censure move against the Wisconsin Senator.

McCarthy covers a yawn during one of the duller moments of the May 4 session.

Gib Crockett's version of the mountain of testimony as it appeared in the Washington *Star*.

Wide World

Cy Hungerford's concept of Senator Potter's final statement at the Hearings in the Pittsburgh *Post-Gazette*.

might be sitting in a federal prison today. It's a strange thing, Charlie, but do you know that copies of the report of this investigation are harder to get hold of than some of the top secret security files? The committee did a marvelous job. They have an accountant who put together page after page after page of photostated exhibits. There are a couple of dozen samples of McCarthy's insulting letters to Guy Gillette, another stack of demands from the Appleton State Bank of Wisconsin which are most revealing, copies of bank deposits, suspicious telephone calls, election financial statements, bank deposits in several different accounts including that of his administrative assistant Ray Kiermas and the deposits of the thousands of little old ladies who sent him three dollars to fight Communism.

"It's an amazing display of money juggling, and I don't see how he ever had time to do anything else.

"This Gillette report goes into the Lustron case pretty thoroughly. In the summing up, it asks whether, under the circumstances, it was proper for Senator McCarthy to receive $10,000 from the Lustron Corp. Joe was the medicine man for prefabricated metal houses in those days. He romped all over the country making speeches that this would solve the housing problem. He got to be friendly with Lustron's executives, particularly Carl Strandlund, the president. Joe was acting chairman of the Joint Housing Committee when some charges were offered against Lustron, and he was able to push those into the wastebasket for the time being. But the full Senate Investigating Committee got interested, and, although Joe was a member of that too, the investigation started with Bill Rogers acting as chief counsel.

"So Lustron needed some muscle here, and—guess what— the vice-president of Lustron decided that was a good time to give Joe McCarthy $10,000 for a pamphlet on housing. It was called 'A Dollar's Worth of Housing for Every Dollar Spent.' It bore Joe's byline, and some eager researcher figured out that he got $1.43 a word for it, which was a new literary high. Then, of course—sometimes this man truly amazes me—he called a press conference to announce his literary adventure. He tried to create the impression that he had actually written the pamphlet but those incorrigible enemies of his, the Communist smearing brigade, dug into it a little further.

"It turned out that Miss Jean Kerr, the present Mrs. Mc-Carthy, had done most of the work with the help of several people from the Federal Housing Agency," Flanders added. "Then a professional writer in New York was hired to help some more, and finally a revised manuscript was the one that got published. Then someone asked Joe, What about the fee? He said that it was embarrassingly small! How many good writers ever make $10,000 out of one opus, even if they write it themselves? He said he had to split it with ten people who helped him. Then the Gillette group found that he listed the entire $10,000 as income for 1948. Also there was testimony about Strandlund cashing checks for Joe at the racetracks and tearing them up, and another episode about a crap game in Columbus and Joe welshing on a gambling debt he collected there. That was a little confused and you could believe it either way.

"But what about the $10,000 from Lustron?" Flanders continued. "Just before he got it, his bank in Appleton had notified him that he either must get a part of the $72,000 bank debt outstanding or his collateral would be liquidated. So now Joe had $10,000. Did he send it on to the bank? No sir, he bought more stock in the Seaboard Airlines Railroad, which had been in receivership since 1930 and was in debt to the RFC in excess of 15 million, and strong-armed the bank into accepting that as additional collateral. He had good information from somewhere because when RFC disposed of its Seaboard holdings, Joe came out with a profit of $35,000 plus.

"Joe had his answer. He said it was being stirred up, his part of it anyway, by the elements of the press which have been rather vigorously opposed to his fight against Communism. I suppose if he had been accused of statutory rape, he would have used the same defense."

"It seems to be a good defense," I said. "If John Dillinger or Al Capone had been able to set themselves up as great Communist fighters, they might never have had any trouble with the law. I know he collected thousands and thousands of dollars to fight Communism. Fulton Lewis, Jr., was panhandling for him by radio— send all you can to help McCarthy in his fight for Americanism—and I know something about the donations of a friend of mine, Michigan's Congressman Alvin Bentley and his wife. I believe the testimony was that Bentley sent in $3,000 and his wife sent $7,000 more."

"The Gillette Committee tried to trace all the listed contributions, and I would guess their accountant almost lost his mind," Flanders said. "The $10,000 from the Bentleys and $5,000 in cash went into a savings account in Joe's name. Three weeks later, he withdrew $10,000, bought a bank draft payable to an old-time friend who endorsed it, sent it to a Chicago stockbroker and bought, on margin, 30,000 bushels of soy beans. It was a good buy. Within five or six weeks, there was $17,500 profit. Joe increased the margin and back came a check for $10,000 through the same friend to be deposited in Joe's account at a different bank.

"The committee questioned the friend, and he claimed it was his own money. Then, when they informed him it was nothing of the kind, he claimed he considered borrowed money to be his own and would not give any further information.

Flanders continued: "The committee report asked some questions, such as: If Senator McCarthy obtained $10,000 for his anti-Communistic fight, was not this money, in a sense, a trust fund? And why would Senator McCarthy speculate with funds advanced to him for his anti-Communistic drive, or loan such funds to a friend for speculative purposes, particularly when the friend's only experience in the commodity market was

211

limited and unsuccessful? And also, did Senator McCarthy have confidential information with respect to the trend of the soy bean future market? And finally, why was the $10,000, supposedly donated to fight Communism, brought back to McCarthy's general account? Joe's answer to all this was, as usual, that it was a Communist smear."

Our steaks arrived with the delicious baked potatoes and the salad that I could have eaten by the bushel. We talked about baseball for awhile and about New England lobsters and about President Eisenhower. When we got to the coffee and pipes, Flanders flipped through his papers again.

"I'm going to let you take the committee report when we leave," he said. "The Bentley fund was peanuts. Or should I say soy beans? The money was rolling in, and Joe's gambling account with his bank in Wisconsin was about as active as such an account can get. At one time he owed them close to $200,000, almost $70,000 in excess of the bank's loan limitation. The bank helped him out that time by transferring $69,000 to a loan ledger sheet in the name of one of Joe's brothers.

"In fact, Joe used his brothers, his father, his brother-in-law and his administrative assistant to account for all kinds of fancy financial monkey business. They were poor people, they still are poor people, hardworking north country farmers. But all of a sudden one of the brothers, a truck driver in Chicago, opens an account with a brokerage firm by depositing $10,000. Checks flew back and forth and around and around. There was a $20,000 note, used for collateral and endorsed by the public relations man for the Pepsi Cola Company. During a four-year stretch, McCarthy's administrative assistant deposited nearly $100,000 in his own account. All through it, the president of the bank in Wisconsin is pleading for more security, threatening to liquidate, then going along with Joe. I don't know how any of these people had any time to do anything else."

"You're right, Ralph," I said. "The Senate is a sanctuary. I know the report was turned over to the Justice Department and that, apparently, was the end of it."

"Right you are. Tom Hennings and Carl Hayden submitted the report for action to the Attorney General and the Commissioner of Internal Revenue. The last I ever heard of it, Coleman Andrews, the Internal Revenue boss, said it would receive most careful consideration in connection with the determination of the tax liability of the taxpayer involved. The statute of limitations has run out on most of it by now, and Dennis the Menace doesn't even have to worry about it anymore."

"Are you planning some action on it?"

"I am indeed. In about ten days, I'm going to bring up a motion in the Senate that McCarthy be separated from the chairmanship of the Committee on Government Operations and be prohibited from being chairman or vice-chairman of any committee whatsoever. It's time to go to war, Charlie. I've spent 74 years in this country and enjoyed every one of them. But this man has fouled up the neighborhood. Am I going to have your support?"

"You have it."

CHAPTER **26**

An Oscar for Cohn

WE went rattling into the twenty-fourth day of the Army-McCarthy hearings on June 1, and it was quite a day. While most of the United States still beamed its eyes and ears into the Senate Caucus Room, the editorial page of the *Post* had the usual startling Herblock cartoon. This one showed the open entrance to a sewer with a sign standing beside it, SPECIAL OPENINGS IN SECRET ILLEGAL WORK. JOIN THE McCARTHY UNDERGROUND. In Knoxville, Virginia, lightning struck the house of Ray Jenkins, counsel for the committee during our hearings. And thunder struck the hearing rooms from the Senate floor where Ralph Flanders turned loose his Dennis the Menace speech.

McCarthy seemed far out of touch with reality all through that day. He was playing his part, always the ham actor, but it had slipped down the scale and his monologues had dropped to the level of the lesser television dramas. He seemed particularly stung by Flander's suggestion that if he were in the pay of the Communists he could not have done a better job for them. And so he demanded and got time on nationwide television from the Caucus Room to say that he thought he had been very patient with Flanders and that he wondered if the speech resulted from senility or viciousness. He said that Flanders had done more than any man to inflame racial and religious bigotry. He asked that the committee itself call Flanders to testify under oath as to what he knows about Dennis the Menace by which "he refers to me." This might have been a diverting interlude, with Dennis the Menace under trial as a Fifth Amendment Communist.

We were now listening to McCarthy's side of the case and a new pattern was developing. Ray Jenkins, the special counsel to the committee, seemed to be acting as straight man for Roy Cohn and McCarthy. During the mauling of Stevens and John Adams, he had attacked them like a prosecuting attorney, hellbent on conviction. Now, particularly with Cohn, there was no browbeating, no insistence on a direct answer, there were no leading questions. This was a friendly duet, and I remember sitting and watching Roy Cohn's performance with amazement. Whatever honors Cohn had won before or since—and there may be many on the final record of this unusual man—none would ever be so deserved as some sort of super-Oscar as a professional actor.

Here suddenly, sitting in the witness chair, was the Boy Crusader—modest, respectful, gentle, kind, a candidate for every Boy Scout merit badge. Here also was the most slippery witness I have ever seen.

Although it seemed that we had long since forgotten why we were holding these hearings, the basic charge was that Roy Cohn and Senator McCarthy, but mostly Roy Cohn, had tried to strong-arm the Army into special consideration for David Schine. Also, when the Army had not given Schine all the privileges Roy Cohn thought he should have, that Cohn had threatened to wreck the Army, to have Secretary Bob Stevens fired.

A long parade of witnesses had testified that these things were true, and I never had any reason to believe they were not true.

And, on the record, neither did Roy Cohn say they weren't true. He had a series of stock answers:

"I don't recall the exact words I used."

"I am pretty close to denying it."

"I don't recall those words, sir."

"I haven't the remotest idea of everything I said."

"I don't remember using those words."

"The best I can give you, if you press me, would be a guess."

"I can't give you a categorical yes or no."

"I have no recollection."

"I don't remember saying that."

The other Roy Cohn, so well known for his arrogance and brutal treatment of people without defenses, was sitting there too. He talked of Fifth Amendment spies, indicating that citation of the constitutional privileges of every American could be evidence of treason. He was firm in his belief that he and McCarthy were above the law, repeating McCarthy's determination to disregard the law when he disagreed with it, and broadcasting the word to all their fellow seditionists that they, too, could ignore the framework of our society. He talked of Fifth Amendment Communists, reducing the Bill of Rights to a dirty word, and, before it was over, under the stabbing attack of Joe Welch, even Cohn's bland denials failed to hide the source of all Joe McCarthy's troubles with the Army—Roy Cohn's unearthly devotion to David Schine.

Cohn had his worst moments when, after all strategic delays had been exhausted, he was forced to submit copies of David Schine's plan to fight Communism. This was to be the evidential proof that Schine should not have been asked to serve the Army as a soldier but to devote his talents to defending the heartland of America from internal aggression. It was also, apparently, the only visible proof of any work David had done in the past year.

Along with the others behind the Senate table, I read

through the Schine plan outline and I was very happy we still had the FBI and counterintelligence agents working for us.

In the opening statement, it said:

> This is a plan of long-range strategy for immediate execution. It is designed to operate in a sector the democracies have left unguarded and in which the enemy has established a salient of terrifying scope. The program outlined here is designed to complement, not supplant, existing measures of military defense, mutual aid, and economic cooperation. The broad battlefield is the globe, and the contest is for men's souls. We can fill their bellies, as we must, but man does not live by bread alone. We require of the free peoples of the world, their hearts, their consciences, their voices, and their votes. How to do this?

We were all skipping through the document. I glanced over at Senator Henry Jackson and noticed the beginning of a smile, and I felt sure that the next scene would bring some long-needed comic relief.

Under *Strategy,* Schine suggested:

> Fight fire with fire, that has inspired native leaders elsewhere to express democracy in every field of social action and to develop democratic groups and parties. The grass roots approach is basic. We must create a "Deminform" or association of democratic parties on the basis of mutual cooperation, free of the charge of American imperialism—democracy must be sold globally.

Then Jackson started his questioning:

JACKSON: Isn't that word "Deminform" pretty close to "Cominform"? Aren't some of the people going to get mixed up?

MCCARTHY: Your question is what?

JACKSON: I just asked the question, isn't "Deminform" pretty close to "Cominform"?

McCARTHY: This description that he gives certainly has nothing to do even remotely approaching Communism. Let's read the whole thing. Let's be fair, Mr. Jackson.

(I smiled to myself. The needle had gotten to Joe already.)

JACKSON: I just asked the question, Senator.

McCARTHY: Let's read the entire—let's not take it out of context.

JACKSON: I am not taking it out of context.

McCARTHY: He says under "Strategy"—you picked out part of it and I have no objection to what you picked out except he says: Fight fire with fire, that is, inspire native leaders everywhere to express democracy in every field of social action and to develop democratic groups and parties. I assume he is not referring to the Democratic party in this country?

JACKSON: I was going to ask you that. Right at that point you remember when we had the *Voice* hearings, to refresh your recollection now, Mr. Schine said—and the point was made, I think, by a number—that the Communists used the word democracy freely and some of the people in the *Voice* program were condemned for using the word democracy.

McCARTHY: You don't think anyone was condemned for using the word democracy?

JACKSON: No, but isn't it true that the Communists have used the word democracy to exploit it for their own use?

McCARTHY: My God, man, you run for office under that label.

JACKSON: Senator, you remember very well in the hearings in connection with the activities of the Latin-American desk quite a point was made of the use of the words democratic and democracy by the Communists. Isn't that true? The records will bear that out.

McCARTHY: I don't know what you are talking about.

JACKSON: All right. Let's go on through. Down under "Tactic" he has: Use all instruments and concepts that enlighten and form the spirit of men. He has a list of various items. He has religious groups (all faiths). He then has (b) Higher clergy, pastoral letters. Is he going to infiltrate the clergy?

McCARTHY: What do you mean, infiltrate?

JACKSON: I don't know. This is a document—

McCARTHY: Senator Jackson, you know that he is talking here about fighting Communism. He says to use all religious groups to fight Communism. I think you and I could agree that the religious groups are the strongest in fighting Communism.

JACKSON: There is no dispute about that. Look at (d) Separation of church and state. Is he for it or is he against it? What does that mean? This is a document that is all ready to put this plan into action. In Europe, one Protestant church, the Lutheran Church, believes in church and state. So does the Catholic Church in Europe. Is he for it or is he going in there and upset it? I don't know.

McCARTHY: Is that a question?

JACKSON: Yes. This is a document that is all set to go. This is the plan. I am trying to figure it out.

McCARTHY: Mr. Jackson, this is the first time I have seen this. This would indicate that he is for complete separation of church and state.

(It occurred to me right then that it was a little strange that McCarthy was admitting he had never seen Schine's plan for psychological warfare before, and that he really had little knowledge of what went on in the lower ranks of his committee. I also noted that the angelic expression was gone from Roy Cohn's face. His dark, brooding eyes were locked on Jackson. The audience was beginning to giggle and there was more of it to come.)

JACKSON: Wouldn't that be bad in those countries of the world where they believe—for instance in some areas in democratic countries, both Protestants and Catholics don't believe in separation of church and state.

McCARTHY: Mr. Jackson, that has nothing to do with the issues here and I would not get into an argument with you as to whether you should separate church and state in certain countries. In this country, we have complete separation of church and state.

JACKSON: All right, now let's look under "Trade Associations."

McCARTHY: All right.

JACKSON: He has "free entry to a free market." What does that mean?

McCARTHY: You can see it the same as I do. I haven't discussed this with him.

JACKSON: What does it mean? This is a document all ready to go. I don't understand it. I am just asking you. You handed it to me. It is not my document.

McCARTHY: You asked for it. I told you he had handled one document having some suggestions on psychological warfare to the State Department. You will have to discuss it with him. He has some pretty good ideas in here, I think.

JACKSON: Senator, let me ask a question. Let me ask, look under Item 9, under "Armed Forces." He has members of the Democratic party in key positions. Aren't you leaving out the Republicans? Let's take Item 10.

McCARTHY: Do you want me to answer your question?

JACKSON: This is the plan that has been handed to me. I am trying to figure it out.

McCARTHY: Mr. Jackson, one thing that you can say about Schine, he is not dumb. Dave makes the mistake I never make, of referring to the non-Communist Republican type of government as a Democratic forum. I wish he wouldn't make that mistake.

JACKSON: This is in the international field. Look under "Communist Leaders." He said—"Special appeal to leaders of community thought." This is all around the world—"Heads of fraternal and veterans' organizations and so forth, Elks—"

McCARTHY: What number?

JACKSON: That is on Ten A. He has the Elks and the Knights

of Columbus. I don't know whether they have an Elks lodge
in Pakistan. I belong to the Elks.

(The audience was laughing loudly now, and McCarthy was
burning.)

McCARTHY: Mr. Jackson, you apparently think this is humorous. Let's see what he says here. He suggests that in the information program you have—he is setting forth what he thinks
should be done. You will find that he lists one of the things to
make special appeals to the leaders of the community thought.
He says through fraternal and veterans' organizations. He gives
an example of two—Elks, Knights of Columbus. What is wrong
with that? Isn't that a good idea?

JACKSON: I understand, but he is talking about the native
areas of the world. Is there an Elks lodge in Africa, in Pakistan,
and so on? Under "Universal Appeal," he has pictures, cartoons,
humor, pinups. What kind of a program is he going to carry
out with the use of pinups?

(Everybody in the room guffawed at that one. Everybody except Joe McCarthy and Roy Cohn.)

McCARTHY: As to pinup, I don't know what he is referring
to as a pinup.

JACKSON: Just this last question. You also notice under "Advertising Media" he has billboards and car signs. Really, Senator, when you look at this document, in all seriousness, do you
think that this qualified a man to investigate a multimillion-
dollar information agency? In all seriousness, Senator?

It was my turn to question next, and I asked McCarthy about
the famous automobile ride from the courthouse in New York
when McCarthy, Cohn, Carr and John Adams had gotten into
a brawl over David Schine. I recalled that Adams had testified
that Cohn had ejected him from the car in the middle of the
street and he had had to catch a cab to get to the Pennsylvania
Station. And that Mr. Carr had later said, "If Adams was
treated badly, you should have seen what happened to Senator

McCarthy." I said that my curiosity had gotten the best of me, and I would like to know what happened to Senator McCarthy. Joe denied that there had been any difficulty between him and Cohn, and although this was of no great importance, it spot-lighted one more item of inconsistency. Then, as that afternoon session was about to end, Karl Mundt tried to put Schine's document in a better light.

MUNDT: May the Chair say this much, and I am sure the press will deal with it fairly, that the document prepared by Mr. Schine has now been released in its entirety. Let me say that it is not indeed a ludicrous piece of work. I read it over. It has some very worthwhile suggestions, Mr. Cohn, I agree to that.

This did not pacify Roy Cohn. As the crowd started out of the Caucus Room, I was watching him. He had sent a staff man out a few minutes before and now the man came back with a file marked *Jackson's record*. I watched Cohn approach Bobby Kennedy, the counsel for the minority Democrats, and there was a heated conversation between them.

Later, Kennedy told newsmen that Cohn had said, "You'd better tell Jackson we're going to get him on Monday. We're going to bring out stuff on his being favorably inclined to Communism." Later, Cohn denied that he had made the threat, and Henry Jackson said that this was not the first one aimed at him during the hearings.

It was unfortunate that this exchange between Roy Cohn and the future Attorney General was not beamed out to the television audience. It might have erased the completely false performance of Roy Cohn, boy investigator.

CHAPTER 27

Why Struve Hensel?

STRUVE Hensel should have been no more involved in the Army-McCarthy hearings than Shirley Temple. It is beyond my understanding why McCarthy hauled off and threw a pail of garbage at him, knowing, as he later admitted, that he had nothing whatsoever on which to base his slanderous charges.

Soon after the Army report on Roy Cohn's activities was printed, McCarthy filed his official answer in a letter to Karl Mundt. It was in this document that he made his counter-charges, that the Army was using Schine as a hostage, and repeated his previous statement that "Pentagon politicians" were responsible. This, at some times, was his description of Bob Stevens and John Adams, although at other times it became rather vague as to just whom he did mean. Before the hearing was over, he had switched the blame to the Democratic party, particularly Stuart Symington, and always the culprits were those mythical souls who were trying to protect Communists in the Army.

But suddenly Hensel was in the line of fire. He, McCarthy said, supervised the attempt to discredit the subcommittee because he was under investigation by the subcommittee for misconduct and possible law violation. There was never any logical explanation of why Hensel, any more than anyone else, should be the target for this instant investigation.

He had been named Assistant Secretary of Defense and General Counsel of the Department of Defense by President Eisenhower, and he had been Assistant Secretary of the Navy under both Presidents Roosevelt and Truman.

The charges with which McCarthy hoped to bomb Hensel involved a firm which supplied hash to the Navy from 1943 to 1945, nine years before McCarthy decided to use the hash for ammunition.

The fact that Hensel was only one of many dozens of people who had been hit by McCarthy's mudslinging does not excuse the delay that occurred before we forced McCarthy to admit that he had committed a foul in this episode. After we got into the hearings, all the members of the cast were too busy and too weary to make much sense about anything. And so it was not until an executive session of the subcommittee which we held on May 17 that I decided it was time to do something about Hensel.

The only reason he was brought into the line of fire was that he had signed the letter of transmittal which delivered the Army report to me. And so, in his answer, McCarthy nominated Hensel as the instigator of the report and added, in an almost automatic reflex action, that therefore Hensel had given greater aid and comfort to Communists than any other single obstacle ever designed.

He claimed that his subcommittee had examined and confirmed the allegation that Hensel, while he occupied a top procurement post with the Department of Navy, had helped to organize a ships' supply firm for the purpose of selling priority goods to the Navy. And, although this was absurd enough, McCarthy now charged that the entire Army complaint against himself, Cohn, and Schine was started by Hensel to discredit the committee and thereby block further investigation of his selling hash to the Navy nine years before.

All this, naturally, should have been filed under "how silly can you get?" but once again the newspapers sniffed the big, irresponsible headline and Hensel suddenly had troubles. It need hardly be mentioned that until he read it in the papers, he was not aware he was being investigated and could hardly have devised this complicated counterattack.

And so he waited for his chance, during the hearings, to sweep up the mess. But as the weeks dragged by, we were all eager to end it as quickly as possible and it would have been most unfair to Hensel to have ended it without giving him the chance to refute McCarthy's attack. At the executive session on May 17, I asked McCarthy if he thought he could present any case against Struve Hensel. He said it would be impossible. He said that when the Army report was published he saw Hensel's name and that he had been investigating Hensel in a "minor" fashion since the previous December. He said he put two and two together and assumed that was the motive. He was probably referring to his smear file which he seemed to have prepared against almost everybody.

I questioned him quite thoroughly and, without going into detail, he finally admitted that he had been guessing, and I was shocked at his candid admission of this reckless disregard of truth, fairness, and common decency.

A few days after that meeting I was the last one to leave the Caucus Room. The audience and the spectators and everyone else had gone before I finished making some notes and gathered my papers together. As I headed for the door, Struve Hensel stopped me. He questioned me about the executive meeting.

"I am drawing up an affidavit, Charlie," he said. "I have waited patiently for the committee to issue a statement but naturally McCarthy is blocking it. So I will file the affidavit and issue my own statement if they haven't got the courage to admit publicly that the charges against me were one more on the pile of vicious, malicious attacks that he believes he has the right to make."

"You're right, Struve," I said. "He has nothing whatsoever on which to make a case."

"He is an amazing man," Hensel commented. "When he builds a structure, the foundation is a lie. He uses lies for his bricks and viciousness for his mortar. I have met some strange specimens in my time but here, I think, is the 100 percent amoral man, and he has surrounded himself with henchmen, storm troopers, with the same lack of decency. Do you know, by the way, of the cute little maneuver that one of his men used when they started this alleged investigation of me?"

I shook my head.

"Incidentally, this great investigation started in late March, not in December," Hensel continued, "and I guess it was the work of the former FBI agent on McCarthy's staff, the one who was fired by Hoover for cause, the one who set up that slanderous attack on Anna Rosenberg. Anyway, they wanted to find the address of a man whose firm had sold the canned meat nine years ago. As you know, it was my connection with this man that they were trying to distort into something evil. And so this agent approached this man's aged mother-in-law—a woman in her high seventies—and told her that her daughter had been involved in a hit-and-run accident and that they must have her home address. This is the kind of tactic they used, straight out of Hitler's handbook.

"I met McCarthy the other day, after your executive hearing when he admitted he had nothing on me, and I asked him if he intended to withdraw the charge publicly. He said he was willing to if he could do it without appearing to be a damned fool. I told him I was not willing to accept a withdrawal without a confession of error. He refused to make that confession. I asked him why he ever made the charge against me when he knew he had no evidence.

226

"He was a bit talkative and his breath reeked of liquor, and he gave me that hideous giggle and explained that he had learned the trick from an Indian friend of his whose name, incidentally, was Charlie. He said Charlie had taught him that when anyone approached him in a not completely friendly fashion, he should start kicking that person in the balls and continue to kick until there was nothing but air where the balls used to be. He's a crude bastard."

I said, "He's drinking a lot more these days, under pressure, and I think he knows that he is destroying himself. He must go through some terrible moments when he's alone and faces his tremendous psychopathic need to be the center of attraction, to be something important. The monkey on his back is not his fault but he uses all the wrong methods to try to kill it."

"The monkey on his back and the problem boys in his office," Hensel continued. "The recent antics of Cohn and Schine, their monkey business that is involved in this hearing, is just minor stuff. Do you know anything about their past performance charts with the Army?"

"No, I don't. I have wondered why Roy Cohn never pulled any military service, and it seemed strange to me that Schine's first call-up by the draft board could have been when he was in his mid-twenties. He must have been of age during World War II."

"He was. We have looked into it pretty thoroughly. We don't intend to use the information during this hearing unless it becomes absolutely necessary. It would be too much like using McCarthy's own way of doing things. It is not actually pertinent to the present case but it is interesting, very interesting."

Previously, I had learned from Department of Defense documents that Schine had become eighteen in September 1945 and registered with his draft board in Gloversville, New York. He was in his second term at Harvard then and stated that he hoped to finish college before being drafted. The war with Japan was over by then, about a month over, and the Army needed a lot of replacements to relieve the men who had actually been out fighting. So Schine was classified 1-A in September and was ordered to report for his physical in October. Then he started his delaying tactics. He asked for a last-minute transfer of his examination to the draft board in Cambridge, Massachusetts, and then led them to believe that a physical was no longer required. He had a letter from the War Shipping Administration saying that he would be appointed as a cadet in the Merchant Marine in the spring of '46.

Back at Gloversville they discovered that he had not yet been examined and insisted that Cambridge proceed with the physical. So Schine took it and passed it in December, and Gloversville again reclassified him as 1-A but, at his request, postponed his induction until the end of the college term in January of '46. They ordered him to report on February 6th of 1946, but he managed to delay this by a last-minute request that he be inducted in Cambridge, which meant that the orders from Gloversville were revoked and new orders issued for him to report in Cambridge in March. The day before that date, Schine asked for and got a sixty-day postponement through the Naval Officer Procurement Office in Boston, pending the processing of his application for appointment in the Merchant Marine.

He then, according to my information, got an appointment as a midshipman in the Merchant Marine Cadet Corps in May and was again deferred by the Gloversville draft board pending his entry on active duty. He was supposed to report for training at San Mateo, California, in July, but he ducked out of that. In the meantime, eighteen- and nineteen-year-old boys were exempted from induction, but in July of that year, the President issued an order making nineteen-year-olds liable for induction and Schine was about to become nineteen.

He wrangled a temporary appointment as a junior ship's transportation clerk, the same thing as an assistant purser, on an Army Transportation Service ship in July. But he fooled them again, he resigned three days later. This information drifted

back to Gloversville where the draft board reclassified Schine as
1-A in September. He had outscuffled them for a year now and
once again they told him to report for a pre-induction physical
immediately after his nineteenth birthday. So he got himself
signed on to the Army Transportation Service as a purser and
off he sailed, bound for Yokohama, Japan. He served on that
ship and on another for about five months as a civilian, and it
was from this record that Roy Cohn tried to claim that Schine
had been commissioned and was therefore eligible for a new
commission when all this fuss started last year.

"Struve, have you ever been able to figure out why Roy
Cohn permitted himself to become so obsessed over Schine's
doings with the Army?" I asked. "I can understand any man
trying to help a friend, even if their mutual goal is as con-
temptible as this episode—trying to avoid military service with
a stack of lies and phony contentions. But, beyond that, Cohn
seems to have become unbalanced over this. He is not stupid.
In fact, he is about as shrewd as a young man can get. He is
politically ambitious—he is aiming at becoming Mayor of New
York, I heard him say one time. And he was serious.

"He made his play for Schine long ago and he got turned
down in all directions. And he knew Schine was completely
unqualified for a commission, and he also knew that Schine was
not doing anything important for the subcommittee. Still, by his
constant heckling of the Army, and his threats, he openly and
brazenly put himself in an untenable position. This is not
shrewd. It is about as stupid as one could get, a political blunder
that will, no doubt, cost him his political dream. I keep asking
myself why?"

"Beats me," Hensel said.

We walked out to the elevator together, went down to the
main floor and Hensel left me there where the long, black
Army limousine was waiting for him. I knew now that Hensel
would never get the opportunity to take the stand and tell his
story at the hearings. McCarthy knew that if he did it would be

another disaster for McCarthy. My own feelings were that Hensel was a top-quality man with all the courage he needed.

The subway to the Capitol was practically deserted this time and I rode alone in the rickety car on the way to my office. I thought to myself how glad I was not to be saddled with the war records of our two young committee staff members.

CHAPTER **28**

Nobody Believed It

THAT first day of June was the decisive day, so far as I was concerned, about what the verdict must be in this hearing. It was the day of testimony on the eleven memoranda which were supposed to support McCarthy's claim that Stevens and Adams had used blackmail and bribery in an attempt to block the subcommittee from what Joe liked to call "driving the Communists out of government."

Of all the documents presented, these were the most mysterious, the most important, the most unbelievable. At the time, ten weeks before, when the Army had first filed its charges against McCarthy and Cohn, and when I had gone to talk to him that morning about the charges, he had never mentioned anything about the memoranda. He had agreed to meet with Mundt, Dirksen and myself the next morning to discuss the thing further. As was history now, he had ducked out of that meeting, held his press conference in which he denied the charges, charged the Army with blackmail, and suddenly came up with the eleven memoranda.

I have always believed in the past-performance charts, whether you are considering horse racing or people, and I had been im-

pressed with Joe's use of faked photographs and phony documents. And so I must admit that I never believed in these
memoranda in the first place, and when the testimony of Joe's
secretary was ended that day, I believed in them even less.

She was called to the stand suddenly that afternoon by Ray
Jenkins. McCarthy, in obvious panic, demanded thirty minutes'
delay. It was granted and he rushed out of the Caucus Room.

Mary Brinkley Driscoll, the sister of David Brinkley, the famous news commentator, had been running Joe's office for six
years. She was a competent, thoroughly professional congressional secretary of the highest level, capable of handling a staff
of fifteen to twenty.

As she trembled her way into the witness chair that day,
I thought I could understand the problems she carried with
her. By a strange trick of timing and whim in the mind of Ray
Jenkins, she now faced the job of supporting the unsupportable
—to make the country believe that the implements of Joe's defense were real. It was obvious from the first moment they were
introduced that Joe Welch, the Army counsel, did not think
so. And I think it might have been difficult to find anybody
who did believe in them, then or any other time.

Jenkins must have known he had blundered as soon as Mary
Driscoll took the stand. His probing was gentle, careful. But
even his questions were too much for her. She could not recall
the dictation of the memos. She had not kept her shorthand
notebooks. She did not know when she had made these copies.
Was it after the Army release? She didn't think so. She could
not tell how she knew where to look for them.

Roy Cohn sat close to her, whispering advice. McCarthy
scribbled notes and pushed them over to her. Joe Welch
watched, intent now, and when it was his turn to question, she
was in complete terror.

The memoranda had been thoroughly examined by the Army
side. They were admitted to be copies of "previous" memoranda

and they had been typed on three different machines. Welch asked her on what typewriter the first memorandum was typed.

MRS. DRISCOLL: I couldn't tell you. I don't know.

WELCH: You don't know?

MRS. DRISCOLL: I don't recognize the typing.

WELCH: The one on your desk is an IBM. Is that right?

MRS. DRISCOLL: There is an IBM on my desk now.

WELCH: Was it there then?

MRS. DRISCOLL: I don't recall. I don't know.

WELCH: Don't you know when you got it?

MRS. DRISCOLL: No.

WELCH: You can't tell us whether you've had it a month or two or longer?

MRS. DRISCOLL: No, Mr. Welch, I can't.

WELCH: You have no memory at all?

MRS. DRISCOLL: No. A typewriter is a typewriter and I don't pay any attention to the type of typewriter.

Welch couldn't believe it. "You are a paragon of virtue," he said. "My secretaries are always kicking about them and wanting a new one. You don't pay any attention to them?"

Mary Driscoll was beaten at that moment and Joe McCarthy came galloping to her rescue. He said he couldn't imagine what Welch was interested in, in this irrelevant and absurd questioning.

Welch told him, "I am interested to know whether these memoranda are the real McCoy or not. You know that much, don't you?"

At that point, one of McCarthy's staff brought in some wire service reports, a copy of the Dennis the Menace speech. McCarthy immediately forgot the anguish of Mary Driscoll. Welch led her to testify that she had originally placed all the memoranda in a file that no one else could find, and then he read to her the last memorandum, written on March 10, the day that McCarthy learned of the Army report on Schine. It said that its writer, Frank Carr, was searching the files for memoranda dictated concerning Schine.

Now we were at the key to the whole case. Why would Carr have to "search the files"? Why would he not say—Mary, give me that file on the Schine affairs? The answer seemed obvious, and Joe Welch closed in on his witness.

WELCH: Were you startled when Carr dictated that to you?
MRS. DRISCOLL: No.
WELCH: Did you say to him, "Mr. Carr, look no further, I've got them all here in the slickest little package you ever saw"?
MRS. DRISCOLL: Absolutely not.
WELCH: Did you tell him his search was silly?
MRS. DRISCOLL: Of course I didn't.
WELCH: Well, you had them all together, didn't you?

She had to answer. There was nothing for Roy Cohn to tell her and Joe McCarthy sat sullen beside her, apparently growling inside about Dennis the Menace.

Finally she said, "Maybe I overlooked one."

Then, at last, McCarthy roused himself and his anger against Ralph Flanders turned now toward Joe Welch. His upper lip locked against his teeth and his voice started spiraling up like a siren on an ambulance. He now wanted Welch put under oath—Joe liked to make a big thing about being under oath although it had seemed to have little effect on the testimony up till now. He claimed that Welch had made the statement "or given the indication that you have some evidence to indicate that there is something wrong about these documents." He said that if Welch had one iota of evidence he should be willing to give that under oath. This was the old counterattack routine, based on nothing but noise.

After squabbling back and forth for a few minutes, Joe demanded lie detector tests for everybody concerned. Somehow now he wanted Secretary Bob Stevens to take a lie detector test although Stevens' days in the witness chair were far behind us. His voice was climbing higher and higher into hysteria, and it was the perfect time for the second act curtain. And Karl Mundt recessed the hearings until the next morning.

CHAPTER **29**

Squelch by Welch

IT was late on the thirtieth day of the Army-McCarthy hearings when Joe McCarthy first sat in the witness chair. We were now down to what the hearings were all about. We were now going to show the world that the only enemy Joe McCarthy had was the one within himself. He had already demonstrated this several times in a minor way during the hearings and in one appalling scene with Joe Welch just before he officially took the witness chair.

Attorney Joseph Welch was a man of fairness, compassion, reason, and wit. And it was his ability to pierce the clouds of nonsense with a gentle, explosive question which brought appreciative laughter from the audience that brought on his most serious clash with McCarthy. Neither McCarthy nor Roy Cohn could tolerate laughter, nor humor—if they were the target. Here was the total weapon which exploded the preposterousness of their charges, the absurdity of their claim that they alone were saving the country from internal disaster.

It was obvious that Joe Welch believed by now that the contribution of McCarthy and Cohn to the fight against Communism amounted to a big, fat zero. He had made a shambles

236

of Cohn's claim that David Schine had contributed an enormous amount of vital work, and now he turned to a new attack.

WELCH: I want to come back, Mr. Cohn, to the item we were talking about this morning. I gathered, to sum it up a little, that as early as this spring, which must mean March or April, you knew about the situation of possible subversives and security risks, and even spies at Fort Monmouth, is that right?

COHN: Yes, sir.

WELCH: And I think you have used the word "disturbing," that you found it a disturbing situation?

COHN: Yes, sir.

WELCH: And you had, so to speak, only a sort of glimpse in it, you couldn't tell how big it was or how little it was, could you?

COHN: Not at the beginning, sir.

WELCH: And you probably knew enough about Fort Monmouth or found out quickly enough about Fort Monmouth, to know that it was a sensitive place, didn't you?

COHN: Yes, sir.

WELCH: And I am sure the knowledge that you had was a source, Mr. Cohn, to one in your position, of some anxiety for the nation's safety, wasn't it?

COHN: It was one situation among a number of serious situations, yes, sir.

WELCH: Well, I don't know how many worries you have, but I am sure that was, to you, a disturbing and alarming situation.

COHN: Well, sir, it was certainly serious enough for me to want to check into it and see how many facts we could check out and—

WELCH: And stop it as soon as possible?

COHN: Well, it was a question of developing the—

WELCH: But the thing that we have to do is stop it, isn't it?

237

COHN: Stop what, sir?

WELCH: Stop the risk.

COHN: Stop the risk, sir?

WELCH: Yes.

COHN: Yes, what we had to do was stop the risk and—

WELCH: That is right, get the people suspended or get them on trial or fire them or do something. This is right, isn't it?

COHN: Partly, sir.

WELCH: Sir?

COHN: Partly, sir.

WELCH: But it is primarily the thing, isn't it?

COHN: Well, the thing came up—

WELCH: Mr. Cohn, if I told you now that we had a bad situation at Monmouth, you would want to cure it by sundown, if you could, wouldn't you?

COHN: I am sure I couldn't, sir.

WELCH: But you would like to, if you could?

COHN: No, what I want—

WELCH: Answer me. That must be right. It has to be right.

COHN: What I would like to do and what can be done are two different things.

WELCH: Well, if you could be God and do anything you wish, you would cure it by sundown, wouldn't you?

COHN: Yes, sir.

WELCH: And you were that alarmed about Monmouth?

COHN: It doesn't go that way.

WELCH: I am just asking how it does go. When you find there are Communists and possible spies in a place like Monmouth, you must be alarmed, aren't you?

COHN: Now you have asked me how it goes, and I'm going to tell you.

WELCH: No, I didn't ask you how it goes. I said aren't you alarmed when you find it is there?

(I was watching the audience and I could see smiles developing. There were some chuckles. Cohn looked puzzled and wary, and McCarthy was watching closely. Their danger sign was laughter.)

COHN: Whenever I hear that people have been failing to act on FBI information about Communists, I do think it is alarming. I would like the Communists out, and I would like to be able to advise this committee of why people who have the responsibility for getting them out haven't carried out their responsibility.

WELCH: Yes, but what you want first of all, Mr. Cohn, and let's be fair with each other, what you want first of all, if it is within your power, is to get them out, isn't it?

COHN: I don't know if I'd draw a distinction as to what ought to come first, Mr. Welch.

WELCH: It certainly ranks terrifically high, doesn't it?

COHN: It was a situation that I thought should be developed and we did develop it.

WELCH: When did you first meet Secretary Stevens?

COHN: I first met Secretary Stevens September 7th, I believe it was.

WELCH: And you knew that he was the new Secretary of the Army?

COHN: Yes, I did know he was the Secretary of the Army.

WELCH: And you must have had high hopes about him, didn't you?

COHN: I don't think I gave it too much thought, sir.

WELCH: Anybody wants the Secretary of the Army to do well, no matter what party he is from, do we not?

COHN: Surely, sir.

WELCH: And on September 7th, when you met him, you had in your bosom this alarming situation about Monmouth, is that right?

COHN: Yes, I knew about Monmouth then. Yes, sir.

WELCH: And you didn't tug at his lapel and say, Mr. Secretary, I know something about Monmouth that won't let me sleep nights? You didn't do it, did you?

COHN: I don't—as I testified, Mr. Welch—I don't know whether I talked to Mr. Stevens about it then or not. I know that on the 16th I did. Whether I talked to him on the 7th or not, is something I don't know.

WELCH: Don't you know that if you had really told him what your fears were, and substantiated them to any extent, he could have jumped in the next day with suspensions?

COHN: No, sir.

WELCH: Did you then have any reason to doubt his fidelity?

COHN: No, sir.

WELCH: Or his honor?

COHN: No.

WELCH: Or his patriotism?

COHN: No.

WELCH: And yet, Mr. Cohn, you didn't tell him what you knew?

COHN: I don't know whether I did or not. I told him some of the things I knew, sir. I don't think I told him everything I knew on the first occasion. After the first two or three sessions, I think he had a pretty good idea of what we were working on.

WELCH: Mr. Cohn, tell me once more: every time you learn of a Communist, of a spy anywhere, is it your policy to get them out as fast as possible?

COHN: Surely, we want them out as fast as possible, sir.

WELCH: And whenever you learn of one from now on, Mr. Cohn, I beg of you, will you tell somebody about them quick?

COHN: Mr. Welch, with great respect, I work for the committee here. They know how we go about handling situations of Communist infiltration and failure to act on FBI information about Communist infiltration. If they are displeased with the speed with which I and the group of men who work with me proceed, if they are displeased with the order in which we move, I am sure they will give me appropriate instructions along those lines, and I will follow any which they give me.

WELCH: May I add my small voice, sir, and say whenever

you know about a subversive or a Communist or a spy, please hurry. Will you remember those words?

Welch was a master at this type of needling. The live audience in the Caucus Room was laughing at Cohn now, and McCarthy must have been aware that at the other end of the television tubes, many millions of Americans were enjoying Cohn's unhappiness. It had been a bad day all around for Joe, and he was about to make it worse. The enemy within, within himself, took charge and now the whole world was going to see—not read about but see—what McCarthyism really was.

As Cohn made a pompous little speech in an answer to Welch, McCarthy started to interrupt. Mundt asked him if he had a point of order. He said no, but Mundt could not stop him. It was a shocking thing, so needless and so brutal that there was not another sound in the Caucus Room but the climbing whine of McCarthy's hysteria:

"Not exactly, Mr. Chairman, but in view of Mr. Welch's request that the information be given once we know of anyone who might be performing any work for the Communist party, I think we should tell him that he has in his law firm a young man, whom he recommended incidentally, to do work on this committee, who has been for a number of years a member of an organization which was named, oh, years and years ago, as the legal bulwark of the Communist party, an organization which always swings to the defense of anyone who dares to espouse Communists. I certainly assume that Mr. Welch did not know of this young man at the time he recommended him as the assistant counsel for this committee, but he has such terror and such a great desire to know where anyone is located who may be serving the Communist cause, Mr. Welch, that I thought we should just call to your attention the fact that your Mr. Fisher, who is still in your law firm today, whom you asked to have down here looking over the secret and classified material, is a member of an organization, not named by me but named by various committees, named by the Attorney General, as I recall, and I think I quote this verbatim, as the legal bulwark of the Communist party. He belonged to that for a sizable number of years, according to his own admission, and he belonged to it long after it had been exposed as the legal arm of the Communist party.

"Knowing that, Mr. Welch, I just felt that I had a duty to respond to your urgent request that before sundown, when we know of anyone serving the Communist cause, we let the agency know. We are now letting you know that your man did belong to this organization for either three or four years, belonged to it long after he was out of law school.

"I don't think you can find any place, anywhere, an organization which has done more to defend Communists—I am again quoting the report—to defend Communists, to defend espionage agents, and to aid the Communist cause, than the man whom you originally wanted down here at your right hand instead of Mr. St. Claire.

"I have hesitated bringing that up, but I have been rather bored with your phony request to Mr. Cohn here that he personally get every Communist out of government before sundown. Therefore, we will give you information about the young man in your own organization.

"I am not asking you at this time to explain why you tried to foist him on this committee. Whether you knew he was a member of that Communist organization or not, I don't know. I assume you did not, Mr. Welch, because I get the impression that, while you're quite an actor, you play for a laugh, I don't think you have any conception of the danger of the Communist party. I don't think you yourself would ever knowingly aid the Communist cause. I think you are unknowingly aiding it when you try to burlesque this hearing in which we are attempting to bring out the facts, however."

We watched this in horror and disbelief as McCarthy's pure hatred of Welch poured out. Welch, with his deft gift for ironic comedy, had made a boorish clown out of McCarthy and a fumbling adolescent out of Cohn. Perhaps the most horrifying part of the whole affair was that McCarthy had been grinning through the whole sarcastic attack and had punctuated it with his weird giggles. I remember being grateful at the moment that Joe Welch was a gentleman and a gentle man. I wondered how many others in the room would not have attacked McCarthy physically. But Welch was magnificent. He turned to Mundt, who was white-faced and shaken, who said, "Mr. Welch, the Chair should say he has no recognition or no memory of Mr. Welch's recommending either Mr. Fisher or anybody else as counsel for this committee. I will recognize Mr. Welch."

But McCarthy wasn't through yet. He interrupted to snarl that he would give the news story on that. Then he turned his back on Welch and, in a loud voice, told his assistant, Jim Juliana, to get the news story on Fisher and the citations showing the connection to the Communist party and the length of time he belonged and the fact that he was recommended by Mr. Welch.

Once again, McCarthy was lying as he had time and again through the hearings. Welch had never recommended Fisher to assist him. And, in his tense but dignified answer to McCarthy, he told us about it.

"You won't need anything in the record when I have finished telling you this," he said. "Until this moment, Senator, I think I never really gauged your cruelty or your recklessness. Fred Fisher is a young man who went to the Harvard Law School and came into my firm and is starting what looks to be a brilliant career with me.

"When I decided to work for this committee I asked Jim St. Claire, who sits on my right, to be my first assistant. I said to Jim, 'Pick somebody in the firm who works under you that you would like.' He chose Fred Fisher and they came down on an afternoon plane. That night, when we had taken a little stab at trying to see what the case was about, Fred Fisher and

243

Jim St. Claire and I went to dinner together. I then said to these two young men, 'Boys, I don't know anything about you except I have always liked you, but if there is anything funny in the life of either one of you that would hurt anybody in this case, you speak up quick.'

"Fred Fisher said, 'Mr. Welch, when I was in law school and for a period of months after, I belonged to the Lawyers' Guild,' as you have suggested, Senator. He went on to say, 'I am secretary of the Young Republican's League in Newton with the son of the Massachusetts governor, and I have the respect and admiration of my community, and I am sure I have the respect and admiration of the twenty-five lawyers or so in Hale and Dorr.'

"I said, 'Fred, I just don't think I am going to ask you to work on the case. If I do, one of these days that will come out and go over national television, and it will just hurt like the dickens.'

"So, Senator, I asked him to go back to Boston. Little did I dream you could be so reckless and so cruel as to do an injury to that lad. It is true that he is still with Hale and Dorr. It is true that he will continue to be with Hale and Dorr. It is, I regret to say, equally true that I fear he shall always bear a scar needlessly inflicted by you. If it were in my power to forgive you for your reckless cruelty, I would do so. I'd like to think I am a gentleman, but your forgiveness will have to come from someone other than me."

I watched Joe McCarthy while Welch was talking. His head was down and he was glaring up at Welch with pure venom. Roy Cohn was trying to get his attention and he knew it, but the enemy within himself was in complete charge now. It was a moment when he might have won the whole ball game with a quiet, sincere apology to Welch and Fred Fisher, but that would have been completely out of character and beyond his understanding. He had never apologized to anyone in his life and now he did the worst thing possible—he continued the attack.

His voice was climbing to that high-pitched whine that he always used under stress as he said, "May I say that Mr. Welch talks about this being cruel and reckless. He was just baiting; he had been baiting Mr. Cohn here for hours, requesting that Mr. Cohn, before sundown, get out of any department of government anyone who is serving the Communist cause. I just gave this man's record, and I want to say, Mr. Welch, that it has been labeled long before he became a member, as early as 1944—"

Welch interrupted. "Senator, may we not drop this? We know he belonged to the Lawyers' Guild, and Mr. Cohn nods his head at me. I did you, I think, no personal injury, Mr. Cohn."

Cohn said that he had not.

"I meant to do you no personal injury," Welch said, "and if I did, I beg your pardon. Let us not assassinate this lad further, Senator. You have done enough. Have you no sense of decency, sir, at long last? Have you left no sense of decency?"

McCarthy answered that quickly—he had, indeed, no sense of decency. Although Roy Cohn was shaking his head at McCarthy, his dark eyes imploring Joe to stop, and although Karl Mundt was trying to put an end to it, McCarthy plunged on. The key word was, of course, "decency." Welch knew instinctively where decency stopped and indecency began, where prosecution became assassination. Prosecution by due process of law is part of civilized government; assassination belongs in the mud of savagery.

"I would like to finish this," McCarthy said, and I wondered if he realized that what he was finishing was Joseph Raymond McCarthy. "Mr. Welch has been filibustering this hearing, he has been talking day after day about how he wants to get anyone tainted with Communism out before sundown. I know Mr.

Cohn would rather not have me go into this. I intend to, however. Mr. Welch talks about any sense of decency. If I say anything which is not the truth, then I would like to know about it." He then read from a piece of paper, one of his ever ready documents, some description of the Lawyers' Guild and then went on to repeat the lie, already denied by Mundt, that Welch had recommended Fisher to work with the committee.

"It seems that Mr. Welch is pained so deeply he thinks it is improper for me to give the record, the Communist front record, of the man whom he wanted to foist on this committee. But it doesn't pain him at all—there is no pain in his chest about the unfounded charges against Mr. Frank Carr; there is no pain there about the attempt to destroy the reputations and take the jobs away from the young men who were working on my committee.

"And, Mr. Welch, if I have said anything here which is untrue, then tell me. I have heard you and everyone else talk so much about laying the truth upon the table that when I hear— and it is completely phony, Mr. Welch, I have listened to you for a long time—when you say now, before sundown, you must get these people out of government, I want to have it very clear, very clear that you were not so serious about that when you tried to recommend this man for this committee.

"And may I say, Mr. Welch, in fairness to you, I have reason to believe that you did not know about his Communist front record at the time you recommended him. I don't think you would have recommended him to the committee if you knew that. I think it is entirely possible you learned that after you recommended him."

Here, of course, was the multiple lie at work, magnified in all its appalling extremes by the loud whine of McCarthy's voice.

Mundt again reminded McCarthy: "The Chair would like to say again that he does not believe that Mr. Welch recommended Mr. Fisher as counsel for this committee, because he has, through his office, all the recommendations that were made.

He does not recall any that came from Mr. Welch and that would include Mr. Fisher."

Still Joe blundered on. "Let me ask Mr. Welch," he said. "You brought him down, did you not, to act as your assistant?"

But Welch had had enough.

"Mr. McCarthy, I will not discuss this with you further. You have sat within six feet of me and could have asked me about Fred Fisher. You have brought it out. If there is a God in Heaven, it will do neither you nor your cause any good. I will not discuss it further. I will not ask Mr. Cohn any more questions. You, Mr. Chairman, may, if you will, call the next witness."

The audience, as if it were watching a high moment in a theater, broke into loud applause. Several policemen who had been assigned to the Caucus Room to prevent any demonstrations stood silent and motionless. The bounce was gone out of Roy Cohn as he rose and left the witness chair, moving like a tired old man. McCarthy, his face frozen, sat staring down at the table. He must have known now that he had wounded himself seriously, and I am sure that that was his only regret.

Mundt called a recess of five minutes and Joe Welch, his head bowed, walked out of the room. Several of the audience blocked him at the door to shake his hand.

McCarthy was completely alone now. He had isolated himself even from those who had blindly supported him. Finally he caught the eye of a newspaper reporter standing nearby and spread his hands, palms upward, asking, "What did I do?"

His tragedy was that he would never know the answer to that question.

CHAPTER **30**

Joe Faces the Jury

FINALLY, after twenty-nine days of pre-
liminaries, it was time for the main bout, and Joe McCarthy
took the witness chair. It was only a few minutes in camera
time after his disastrous clash with Joe Welch and after the
degrading testimony and maneuvers over the now-famous eleven
memoranda.

We had now reached the heart of the whole affair—Mc-
Carthyism. Although the hearings had supposedly been set up
to investigate the Army career of Pvt. David Schine, that had
not been the subject at all nor had the performance been "hearings" although certain investigative procedures had been followed. Schine had never been called as a witness to the charges
against McCarthy and Cohn.

McCarthy had dominated the circus for twenty-nine days.
Had he performed under reasonable control like any other member of the cast, we would have reached this point in less than
a week and we might have entered this phase of the showdown
capable of presenting a clear-cut case to the jury—the many
millions at the other end of our television cameras. But that
never could have occurred in any pageant which included
Joseph Raymond McCarthy.

"Looking at you, Senator McCarthy," Joseph Welch once said, "you have, I think, something of a genius for creating confusion, creating a turmoil in the hearts and minds of this country."

In this final skirmish it would be Joe McCarthy alone against the pack. Each member of the committee would be judged in his own solo confrontation and each would be restricted or made stronger by his own political belief, sense of decency and courage. And each, of course, knew he must enter the arena with caution because McCarthy played by his own rules and recognized no authority whatsoever. The element of political partisanship was, on the surface, involved. The three Democrats, Jackson, McClellan and Symington, understood, in basic cynicism, that this mass exposure of McCarthy was wrecking his image and bruising the Republican party.

However, in the intense emotional atmosphere, I think each of us put that factor aside. I do not believe one word would have been changed if McCarthy had been a Democrat with Dirksen, Dworshak, Mundt and myself as the delegation of the opposition.

McCarthy, because of the turmoil that raged within him, had a phenomenal ability to stir men deeply. Because he ignored the manners and niceties of human relations, it was difficult for even the most serene of men to deal with him without passion. This was the part he played within the Senate, the bad guy of the wrestling show. It bore no resemblance to the clumsy but friendly puppy that he was outside.

Karl Mundt, the son of a South Dakota hardware merchant, described himself as a middle-of-the-road Republican. He was a gentle, jovial man who had been a schoolteacher, a farmer, a writer on outdoor life. He was friendly and gregarious and proud of his conservative posture.

He had been the joint sponsor of the Smith-Mundt Act which provided a program of international exchange of scholars, a piece of legislation which McCarthy might well have attacked as a supplement to the Communist cause. Mundt had also sponsored legislation authorizing the United States to participate in the United Nations Educational, Scientific and Cultural Organization (UNESCO). When he served in the House, he volunteered for the Un-American Activities Committee. There, with the help of Dick Nixon, he gathered evidence to convict Alger Hiss.

As soon as he reached the Senate, Mundt volunteered to serve on the McCarthy subcommittee. He was now a true veteran Communist hunter, proud of the fact that he was one of the founders of the *Voice of America* and Overseas Information Service, and it must have been with much misgiving that he watched Roy Cohn and David Schine tear through these agencies like twin tornadoes, leaving shattered morale and destroyed reputations behind them.

When plans were being made for the Army-McCarthy hearings, Mundt argued that the controversy should be handled by a group other than ours. I agreed with him but we lost that debate. He also protested against serving as chairman, saying that he was not the right man for the job. Mundt knew that any effort to control McCarthy would be hopeless.

He was proven correct in this belief within the first minute of the hearings. When, on that opening day, McCarthy had reached far out of bounds to attack Samuel Reber the time had come to use whatever measures were necessary to stop this oratorical vandalism once and for all. It could not be stopped short of gagging McCarthy by force. Mundt tried when McCarthy asked General Reber, "Are you aware of the fact that your brother was allowed to resign when charges that he was a bad security risk were made against him as a result of the investigation of this committee?" This question was based on a triple-headed lie. Samuel Reber had resigned because he wanted to, no charges had been made against him, nor was there any such investigation.

When John McClellan objected that the question was incompetent, Ray Jenkins ruled that McCarthy's inquiry was perfectly legitimate. That made the farce complete. Joe Welch then asked General Reber if he knew why his brother had retired. McCarthy protested that it was a "completely unfair question" although his own insulting smear of Samuel Reber was, he said, "of the utmost importance."

When we first set up the hearings, it was necessary to find an outside attorney to represent the committee, actually to substitute for Roy Cohn while Karl Mundt replaced McCarthy as chairman. The first candidate was an attorney from Boston. We tentatively accepted him for the job, but it was not long before it became evident that he was a violently pro-McCarthy man and that his claims to impartiality were not quite believable.

Finally, at the suggestion of Everett Dirksen, we picked Ray Jenkins of Knoxville, Tennessee, politically a Taft Republican but with no recorded history of being biased one way or another about McCarthy. And so he came to Washington, bringing with him, it soon developed, the firm conviction that McCarthy was a great American engaged in the patriotic work of flushing Communists out of government. And even though Joe McCarthy occasionally gave him the Indian Charlie treatment, Ray Jenkins went back to Knoxville with his faith unshaken.

Jenkins arrived in Washington ten days before the hearings started and spent half of that time in the Pentagon reviewing the Army charges. From there, he brought two questions to Capitol Hill—how many of Private Schine's privileges had been volunteered by the Army, and why did the Army grant so much? Roy Cohn was happy to give him a cram course on the answers.

Cohn and McCarthy in their countercharge had summed it up this way: "The pattern followed by Secretary Stevens and Mr. Adams is clear. As long as only individual Communists were the object of the subcommittee's investigation, they made continual offers of cooperation with the investigation. But as soon as the probe turned to the infinitely more important question of who was responsible for protecting Communist infiltration and protecting Communists who had infiltrated, every conceivable obstacle was placed in the path of the subcommittee's search for the truth."

David Schine, they assured Jenkins, was a "prime mover in the successful exposure of Communists' infiltration." His knowledge was important to the security of the Nation, therefore, all his special privileges were proper.

On another page of the McCarthy document, Jenkins read these words: "Five days after the Secretary claimed that attempts were made to induce and persuade him by improper means to give preferential treatment to Private Schine, Mr. Stevens posed for smiling photographs with Private Schine at Fort Dix."

Jenkins never suspected while he was being briefed by Cohn that this paragraph contained a time bomb, that he would read it again, shaken with anger, when he learned a little more about this photograph. In fact, Roy Cohn gave the photograph to Jenkins and let Jenkins himself play the fool.

He introduced it while Bob Stevens was still in the witness chair, and the dramatic sincerity of Jenkins' performance, temporarily, was an impressive point in favor of McCarthy and Cohn and against Bob Stevens.

JENKINS: Mr. Stevens, did you ever have a photograph taken with G. David Schine?

STEVENS: Well, there were a lot of photographers down there at the hearing and it could be.

JENKINS: Did you ever at your suggestion at a meeting anywhere, any time, say that "I want my picture taken with David" and have it done?

STEVENS: I am sure I never made a statement just like you make it there.

(Jenkins thought he had Stevens trapped now. From under the pile of papers on the table before him, he pulled a blown-up photograph of Bob Stevens and David Schine in uniform, facing each other and smiling. It was a dramatic moment, and the audience all over the country had to believe that Stevens had been caught in a lie.)

JENKINS: Let me show you a picture, Mr. Stevens, for the purpose of refreshing your recollection. I ask you whether or not that is a photograph of you, the Secretary of the Army, and David Schine, a private in the Army?

(It rocked Bob Stevens. He could not deny that the picture was indeed himself and David Schine, but I could guess that he could not remember when and where it had been taken. Jenkins bore in on Stevens.)

JENKINS: Mr. Stevens, isn't it a fact that you were being especially nice and considerate and tender of this boy Schine . . . in order to dissuade the Senator from continuing his investigation of one of your departments?

Then, for the first time, Stevens exploded in anger. "Positively and completely not."

The timing was perfect. It was late afternoon. All through the evening the news commentators from coast to coast would be flooding the air with this devastating "evidence" against Bob Stevens. It was a typical McCarthy maneuver, grabbing the headlines for the counterattack. The morning papers would carry it too, and millions of Americans would be convinced.

However, sometime during that night, Ray Jenkins learned a little more about that photograph and so did Joe Welch. And the hearings the next morning were to open with thunder and lightning.

Welch wasted no time. He was beginning to understand McCarthy and the tactics he might expect. As soon as we reconvened the next morning, Welch said: "Mr. Chairman, Mr.

Jenkins yesterday was imposed upon and so was the Secretary of the Army by having a doctored or altered photograph produced in this courtroom as if it were honest."

He whipped out a large reproduction of a photograph which showed Bob Stevens, David Schine, Frank Carr and an Army officer who was identified as Col. Jack Bradley. It was evident that, by cropping out the others, one would have the picture of Schine and Stevens all alone together.

"I show you now a photograph," Welch said, "in respect of which I charge that what was offered in evidence yesterday was an altered, shamefully cut down picture so that somebody could say to Stevens, 'Were you not photographed alone with David Schine?' when the truth is he was photographed along with David Schine in a group."

I could see that Welch was incensed by this clumsy fraud and that Ray Jenkins was barely able to wait his turn. McCarthy and Cohn were whispering urgently together, and I thought it might be entirely possible that McCarthy and Cohn, until now, had never known that this photo was a fake although they had mentioned it as a strong bit of evidence.

Welch turned now to Jenkins and told him that he knew Jenkins would never participate in a trick like this and that he had been imposed upon. Jenkins quickly made his position clear. He said that the picture had been furnished to him by one of the people in the case, whom he identified as one of the adversaries of Stevens, and that it had been presented as a genuine, authentic photograph, that there had been no intimation or insinuation that it had been cut down or that any other person had been taken out of it. He said he had presented it in good faith.

The picture, the new picture, the real picture, was accepted as evidence, and Welch told us that the official photographer of the Air Force base had been summoned to testify. But an ugly rage was rising again inside Joe McCarthy. I could see the symptoms—the lowered puffy eyelids, the upper lip tightening against his teeth, the glancing around to be sure he knew where the television cameras were located. He interrupted, demanding a point of order, and already the nasal tone of his voice was rising toward hysteria. "I think, Mr. Chairman, when the counsel for Mr. Adams and Mr. Stevens and Mr. Hensel—"

The photographers were jumping up and clustering around. They knew when a big moment was about to take place. Mundt asked the photographers to please comply with the rules and now McCarthy turned on him.

"Couldn't we have an understanding here that when I start to make a point of order that I may finish without interruption?" he demanded, forgetting that he had already established a new world's record for interrupting other people. "The point of order is this: that Mr. Welch, under the guise of making a point of order, has testified that a picture was doctored. I say this: yesterday was the first time I saw either of these pictures, the picture that was introduced yesterday and the one Mr. Welch put in today, and he makes the completely false statement that this is a group picture, and it is not."

This, I suppose, brought up a fine point of terminology. How many people do you need to have a group? Is four enough? But that did not seem to be Joe's point— rather, by denouncing the picture he hoped to eliminate it. Mundt tried to stop McCarthy, who was obviously intent on making a speech. "The Chair is advised," he said, "that the Senator is engaging in a statement or cross-examination rather than a point of order."

But McCarthy was in high gear now and the siren was wailing. "I am getting rather sick of being interrupted in the middle of a sentence." Stuart Symington was incensed by now, as were all of us. Bad manners are unpleasant at any time and perhaps even more so early in the morning.

SYMINGTON: I would like to say that if this is not a point of order, it is out of order. The counsel says it is not a point of

255

order and it is not a point of order if the counsel says it is not a point of order.

MCCARTHY: Oh, be quiet!

SYMINGTON: I haven't the slightest intention of being quiet. Counsel is running this committee and you are not running it.

(And I wished at that moment that Symington had been right. McCarthy demanded the floor and got it. McCarthy had lost all control by now and was becoming incoherent. He said he could see no doctoring of the picture and he wanted the record clear that Joe Welch was not speaking the truth although before us was the photographic evidence that he was speaking the truth. Mundt made an effort to regain control, became involved in a word-scuffle with McCarthy and lost the battle.)

MUNDT: Do you have a point of order?

MCCARTHY: Call it a point of order or call it what you may, when counsel for Mr. Stevens and Mr. Hensel and Mr. Adams makes a statement and he is allowed to do it without interruption, and if that statement is false, do I have a right to correct it, or do we find halfway through my statement that Mr. Welch should not have made his statement and therefore, I cannot point out that he was lying? I think that is an important question.

(Finally it simmered down, and Henry Jackson took up the questioning of Bob Stevens.)

Five days later, when Roy Cohn was on the witness stand, the photograph was haunting Jenkins. He was well aware that Cohn had used him and led him into asking extravagant questions based on his belief that the photograph was what it purported to be. However, Cohn stuck to his statement that Stevens had requested the picture, and, since it was one of the few times that Cohn's memory did not fail him, I believed him.

Jenkins, however, won his merit badge for loyalty to McCarthy although he supposedly wore the uniform of impartiality at the hearings. He gulped down the insults of McCarthy, who at one time said of him, "This is the most improper exhibition I have ever seen. You have a lawyer here [Jenkins] who brags about being one of the greatest criminal lawyers in the country badgering this private [Schine]. I think it is indecent and I think that the Chair should condemn it."

However, Jenkins remained loyal. When it came time for McCarthy to take the witness chair, Jenkins led him into his questions with a fawning adulation. McCarthy had prepared a map of the United States for his opening lecture. The map was brightly colored, and the names and addresses of Communist leaders were listed for every state except Texas—we were asked to believe that there were no Communists in Texas, nothing but oil millionaires who supported Joe McCarthy.

The map had been prepared in the usual sloppy method used by Joe's staff. It listed dead Communists and wrong addresses. And I thought at the time that this was the story of Joe's life—careless staff work, unchecked rumors, inadequate research, a manic scramble for headlines and to hell with the facts.

We listened to, or tried to stay awake through, a long explanation of Communism by Joe McCarthy. His argument seemed to be that by chasing the Communists out of Washington and our Army—and the implication was that only he and his staff were capable of doing it, although we were still waiting for him to produce his first Communist that wasn't already known to the FBI—the United States would somehow erase the breeding grounds of Communism all over the world. His conclusion was that we were in a war which could not end except by victory or by death for this civilization, and only he could protect us.

When Jenkins prodded him to tell what each individual American could do to liquidate the Communist party, Joe said that they must depend upon those of us whom they send down here to "man the watchtowers of the Nation." He meant, of course, himself. He warned about subversive teachers in schools, and he called upon the voters to defeat all candidates for election who felt that we should help our Allies if they traded with

257

China. He did not mention that President Eisenhower happened to feel that we should continue to trade with them.

With Jenkins strumming the background music, McCarthy sang a song of admiration for himself, praising an America of the future where all the citizens would be able to pass a loyalty test devised by Senator McCarthy and, I am sure, Roy Cohn and David Schine.

There were always political overtones in the Army-McCarthy hearings. It was a political arena and the cast of characters, excepting the lawyers and their staffs and the men in uniform, were all politicians or appointed by politicians. The three Democrats on the subcommittee—Symington, McClellan, and Jackson—were a minority. In some ways they had most to gain by this public brawl.

In 1954, Stuart Symington of Missouri was the leading candidate for the Democratic nomination for President in 1956 although Adlai Stevenson, defeated by Dwight Eisenhower in 1952, was still, through courtesy, the top man on the Democratic list. This position he sacrificed, at least in part, when his moral outrage led him to oppose McCarthy to the limit of his ability during the hearings.

They clashed both on camera and off. During the episode of the faked photograph of Stevens and Schine, the name of Don Surine, a former FBI agent on McCarthy's staff, was brought into the testimony. Symington demanded that Surine be called to testify. Later, outside the Caucus Room, McCarthy stopped Symington and threatened an all-out smear attack on Symington if Surine were called. Symington laughed at him and walked away.

Symington had been Secretary of the Air Force from 1947 to 1950. During those years, he had become deeply concerned about morale in the Armed Services and it was this factor as much as anything else which led him to run for the Senate in 1952.

During that campaign, McCarthy had gone galloping into

Missouri to work for Symington's opponent, James Kem, and to spread his routine smears, attempting to link Symington to —what else?—Communism. He was a member of the Armed Services Committee when McCarthy and Cohn began bombarding the Pentagon, and he was incensed over McCarthy's attack on General Zwicker and its resulting demoralizing effect on all of the Army.

For these reasons, Symington, a Democrat, became a strong fighter for Stevens, a Republican, against another Republican, McCarthy.

Symington was often unsure of himself in a legal dispute, but his strength was his belief in the rule of reason. It was this factor that McCarthy despised and led him to one deplorable moment when he sneeringly referred to Symington as "sanctimonious Stu."

At one point, Symington told McCarthy, "I believe in America and you do not, and that is the great and fundamental difference between us."

There were few men in the Senate those days who were not afraid of Joe McCarthy, and Stuart Symington was one of them. Near the end of the hearings, he tore into Frank Carr about the security clearances of the subcommittee's staff and argued that the danger always existed that a poorly screened staff might stumble across government secrets and find therein the material for mischief.

McCarthy, who always seemed overprotective about his staff, which was supposed to be the staff of the whole committee but was always recruited by Roy Cohn and himself, interrupted and accused Symington of attempting to smear the staff. Symington had done nothing of the kind and continued to question Carr.

For some reason, McCarthy again exploded into one of his uncontrolled rages with his siren voice climbing up to an effeminate screech. He demanded that if Symington had any evidence, he should produce it. He was protecting his boys, protecting them from an imaginary danger. In the middle of his tirade, the buzzer sounded announcing a Senate roll call, and Mundt banged down the gavel to end the session. We all got up to hurry to the Senate floor, the audience began to move out and still McCarthy was ranting.

Symington stood watching him with a half smile and finally picked up a microphone so that he might be heard: "In all the years that I have been in government," he said, "based on the testimony given to this committee under oath, I think the files of what you call 'my staff, my director, my chief of staff' are the sloppiest and most dangerously handled files I have ever heard of." The audience applauded. McCarthy was strangling with rage and shouted at the official recorder to stay at his machine.

"He's running away," he screamed, "he's running away."

Symington moved through the crowd and we all followed him. As I passed behind McCarthy, he was still talking incoherently and finally I heard him say, "I guess I'd better go vote."

At another point in the hearings, when McCarthy had accused Symington of cowardice, the Missouri Senator had the answer ready: "You said something about being afraid. I want you to know from the bottom of my heart that I am not afraid of anything about you or anything you've got to say at any time, anyplace, anywhere."

Henry Jackson had a thorough understanding of law and proper Congressional procedures and a clear vision of what McCarthyism was all about. He also brought that deft sense of humor to bear when, on an otherwise gloomy day, he directed that good-natured barrage of questions at the David Schine plan to fight Communism. This episode proved more than anything else that the proper answer to Joe McCarthy and Roy Cohn was laughter.

All through the hearings Jackson was sane and judicious. He played his part, not for political glory but to try to get some facts, some sense, into the shambles that McCarthy was creating.

If anyone had kept score on personality clashes during the

hearings, I think it might have been recorded that the only people not insulted by Joe McCarthy were John McClellan and myself. I was never quite sure, although I had my own theory, why Joe McCarthy never attacked me personally although his mouthpieces in the newspaper and radio world had a lot of fun pounding on me. Our personal relationship outside the Senate Building was always cordial and friendly, the way Joe wanted it to be with everybody (the good guy-bad guy wrestler routine). I think McClellan escaped because he may have been one of the few men in the world of whom Joe McCarthy was just a little bit afraid, and for whom, although he would never have been able to admit it, he might have had considerable respect.

In a way, their backgrounds were similar. Both had come from painfully poor farming families, had worked at dreadful jobs for their education, their knowledge of law. McClellan had grown up in Arkansas, a state which ranked next to the bottom in money spent on each child's education. John McClellan worked harder than the mules on his father's farm when he was still a boy. His father had done the same, teaching school on the side and studying law. John McClellan followed the same trail, working the farm, reading and studying in his father's law office. At seventeen, he was approved by the Arkansas Legislature to practice law in the circuit courts. He had learned his lessons well. He served in the First World War and when he returned, he and his father took written law examinations together and were both admitted to practice before the State Supreme Court.

He was first elected to Congress in 1934 and became part of a standing committee of the Senate which developed into the Committee on Government Operations. In 1948, as its chairman, he appointed himself to the Subcommittee on Investigations. McCarthy replaced him as its chairman after the Republican victory of 1952 but would move out again in 1956 when the Democrats again gained control of Congress.

John McClellan believed in the Bill of Rights, and he refused to let it be abused. No one could be more harsh than he, but he worked within the structure of the rules and regulations. It was McClellan who led the Democrats off the committee nearly a year before, outraged when McCarthy insisted that the staff was his own personal instrument and that he, and he alone, would name its members. But McClellan was back now as the leader of the three Democrats, humorless, suspicious, and sardonic.

War and military service had hurt him deeply. One of his sons had landed with the first troops in North Africa in 1942, had suffered from exposure and died. On the day the first son was buried in Arlington Cemetery, the second son was killed in the crash of an Army plane. It was natural to assume that any attempts to gain preferential treatment in the Army were beneath McClellan's contempt.

He did much to save the Army-McCarthy hearings from complete disaster, and the essence of his principles were shown best, perhaps, in his way of handling McCarthy's charges against H. Struve Hensel.

In that particular episode, McClellan lost the debate—and so did the Bill of Rights.

And so it was finally ended, after thirty-six days of what John McClellan called one of the most disgraceful episodes in the history of our government. It was, as McClellan added, deplorable and unpardonable. There was no valid excuse or justification for this situation having occurred. We were all weary, long since ashamed of the whole affair.

I think Joe Welch, who faced the final curtain as the only one in the cast who need have no regrets, summed it up for all of us in his final, eloquent statement. "I alone, I alone came into this room from deep obscurity. I alone, will retire to obscurity. As it falls about me, softly as I hope it does quickly, the lady who listened and is called Judith Linden Welch will hear from me a long sigh of relief.

"I am sorry that this play had to take place in the fretful

lightning and the ominous roll of noises from Indochina and around the world. It saddens me to think that my life has been lived so largely either in wars or turmoil. I may say, as I have already indicated, that I could do with a little serenity. I allow myself to hope that soon there will come a day when there will, in this lovely land of ours, be more simple laughter."

Amen, Brother Welch, I said to myself. More simple laughter. Let all of us who took part in this ghastly farce be able to face ourselves in a mirror and rock the walls with belly-shaking laughter at ourselves, each only at himself. Here we were, the legislative leaders of our nation, chosen by our people with some wistful hope that we deserved that choice, and now veterans and collaborators in four years of idiotic absurdity.

I distributed a short statement on that final day. I thought it would be a healthy antidote to the let's-all-go-back-to-being-buddies-together oratory that I anticipated would dominate the final hour.

The statement said:

I am convinced that the principle accusation of each side in this controversy was borne out by the testimony. There is little doubt that the testimony on both sides was saturated with statements which were not truthful and which might constitute perjury in a legal sense. I believe there may have been suborna-tion of perjury.

As a result of the hearings, some people on both sides should be separated from the government service. I shall propose dis-missal of those employees who have played top roles on both sides. They have demonstrated a failure to understand the obli-gations that go with employment by the government.

On each side fundamentals were overlooked at the outset. Since the subcommittee staff was investigating a very serious condition which was alleged to have existed in the Army, there never should have been at any time any conversation about a commission or the military status of one of its members by any-one but the person concerned.

On the other hand, top executives of the Army should never have encouraged this sort of thing and should have put an end to the discussions for their own protection and in order to avoid what occurred later.

The staff of the subcommittee will have to be overhauled. It is also clear that the individual members of the subcommittee must devote more time and assume greater responsibility.

Since the Attorney General has been supplied with daily transcripts, I assume some current study has been made. I believe a criminal case against some of the principals might be developed if the case were taken to a grand jury room where the testimony would have to be repeated without others being present.

Joe Welch had been playing with McCarthy through part of the last day. He knew now that he had won his case and that he could depend on McCarthy to answer his humorous thrusts without grace but with a huffing-puffing display of indignation.

He was using the transcript, recorded in the Pentagon, of one of McCarthy's telephone calls to Bob Stevens about David Schine. In it, Joe had said, "For God's sake, don't put Dave in service and assign him back to my committee. . . . There is nothing the Left Wingers would like better. . . . There is nothing indispensable about him. . . . If he could get off weekends . . . It is one of the few things I have seen Roy completely unreasonable about. . . . He thinks Dave should be a general and work from the penthouse of the Waldorf." The audience was laughing, but there was no humor in McCarthy.

McCARTHY: That, Mr. Welch, is obviously a completely facetious remark.

WELCH: Do you think there should be a "ha-ha" after it? Is that right?

McCARTHY: Because neither Mr. Stevens nor Mr. Cohn nor I ever thought that you should have a general working from the penthouse at the Waldorf.

264

WELCH: Now let me go into your next sentence or next paragraph—Roy was next to quitting the committee—was that funny?

McCARTHY: You say was that funny?

WELCH: Yes. Were you trying to be facetious there?

McCARTHY: I don't think it would be funny if Roy would quit the committee.

And on it went. Welch was reestablishing his point that there was indeed nothing indispensable about David Schine, thus refuting the entire testimony of Roy Cohn.

Each member of the cast made his curtain speech. McCarthy, dominating the hearings to the end, showed that he had learned nothing, or perhaps something within him drove him to play his normal role to the end.

His difficulty, he said, had been with the "old Pentagon civilian politicians" who thought they should run the Army. Once again, he was apparently attacking Bob Stevens and John Adams. He claimed that members of the working press had been dishonestly distorting the news and deceiving the American people. He complained about the vast amount of time and expenditures spent on what he called fraudulent charges. He said that one of the very good things that had come out of the hearings had been the result of television. And yet, it was this massive exposure on television that was ending forever the threat of McCarthyism.

Fanatics of the Far Right would still follow him, deliberately blinding themselves to what they had seen. Ten years later he would be one of the patron saints of the John Birch Society. But hundreds of thousands of Americans who had thought that perhaps he was a healthy factor in American politics, knowing only what they had read in the newspapers, had now seen him perform and heard his hysterical tirades based on his distortion of truth.

Henry Dworshak, filling Joe McCarthy's chair only to bring

the committee up to its full count and hating every minute of it, had wasted no time during the hearings and had contributed little. He wasted no time at the end except to emphasize the disruption of the normal work of the Senate by pointing out that on that very afternoon a twenty-nine-billion-dollar defense appropriation bill was being discussed in the Senate while eight Senators played their parts in the Caucus Room.

Roy Cohn's contribution was a tribute to Joe McCarthy in the form of "evidence" that McCarthy was the No. 1 menace to the Communist movement.

Karl Mundt said he wanted to sit down quietly with the printed record, to search out certain statements and facts to be pieced together along certain chains of evidence. He admitted that there had been irrelevancies and diversions.

John McClellan was next. McClellan wasted no words: "I am compelled to say in conclusion, Mr. Chairman, that the series of events, actions, and conduct that precipitated the ugly but serious charges and countercharges that made these lengthy and unpleasant public hearings mandatory, I think will be recognized and long remembered as one of the most disgraceful episodes in the history of our government.

"Simply to say that this series of events is regrettable is a gross understatement. They are deplorable and unpardonable. There is no valid excuse or justification for this situation having occurred, and it will now become our solemn duty, the duty of this committee, to undertake to determine and fix the responsibility.

"It is easy to ask for cooperation, but the best way to get it is to reciprocate. I recall when I begged this committee not to take an action that would drive the Democrat members away from it. I begged you not to silence the voice of the Democratic members of this committee [he was talking now to Joe McCarthy]. Our voices were silenced and we left the committee. These things occurred during our absence. I would hate for the country to think, the people of the nation to think, that this

is a fair sample of the proceedings and the manner of con-
ducting proceedings in the highest law-making body in the
world."

Everett Dirksen followed. He said that Mundt had done a
magnificent job and that he wanted to bestow a salute to Ray
Jenkins for the constructive, objective, and great job he had
done. He said that the crusade against these sinister forces with
which we have been contending for a long time must go on
with renewed vigor in the interest of the perpetuity of a free
country.

When my own turn came, I kept my comment short. The
record shows that this is what I had to say: "Mr. Chairman, as
the curtain goes down on the final act of thirty-six days of hearings, I think there are two things that it would be well for the
American people to recognize. First, that this is not a typical
Congressional hearing. Even the structure and the format are
not typical. We have had outside attorneys brought in to act as
counsel for one of the principals and for the committee.

"The procedures, the rules, that we have adopted for this
particular hearing were unusual, and I doubt if they have ever
been used in any other type of Congressional hearing.

"I have been disturbed throughout the hearings to witness
the personality clashes. They reflect upon the dignity of the
Senate. I wish to assure the American people that are watching
that that is not normal. Because of certain testimony, some
people may believe that the government is overrun with disloyal
people. I feel sure that the administration downtown and the
committees of the Congress are all working with a singleness of
purpose to root out all persons that may be disloyal or security
risks.

"I feel that there is no one committee, that there is no one
individual, that carries this fight alone; that the President and
the members of the Executive Branch are equally concerned
about this problem.

"I sincerely hope, however, that as a result of these hearings there will be a greater degree of cooperation between the Executive Branch and the Legislative Branch of our government, in the work on this serious problem of endeavoring to ferret out Communists.

"When we get back to regular functions of our committees, I am sure we can work together and the personality difficulties that have developed in the course of these hearings will be removed."

Stuart Symington was next. He had clashed violently with McCarthy many times during the hearings, and in his brief comments he brought up again McCarthy's contention that it was perfectly all right for government employees to deliver confidential documents to him. This, Symington said, goes to the very heart of the fundamental theory of the separation of powers in the Government of the United States. Symington had no suggestion of what might be done to end this. It was already against the law, but McCarthy had said that he would respect no such law.

Ray Jenkins, counsel for the committee, was the anchor man. He sang a little hymn of praise to the seven Senators on the subcommittee, "Seven rocks of granite to whom the people in this country may anchor all of their hopes, their aspirations, their ambitions, their trust, and their faith."

By now the copies of my statement had been distributed to the committee and the press. I noticed that Joe McCarthy glanced at it casually, started to put it aside, then picked it up and read it. His face changed quickly to a mask of anger and, without looking at me, he passed it over to Everett Dirksen. Within a few seconds, Dirksen was whispering in my ear.

"Charlie, I think you should withdraw this statement." I shook my head.

"Charlie, this is a time for unity, for sweeping up the mess. I implore you to withdraw it."

"There was perjury by the basketful, and you know it,

Everett," I said quietly. "The evidence is in and now is the time to make my position known."

He stood there for a moment but must have sensed that I wasn't about to change my mind. This happened after Karl Mundt had officially ended the hearings and the audience was moving out. Newspapermen closed in on me as I tried to leave the hearing room but I told them I would not comment any further at that time. There had indeed been perjury in carload lots, and it was now up to the Attorney General, Herbert Brownell, Jr., and that day he had accused Joe McCarthy of setting himself above the law by openingly inciting government workers to violate federal secrecy laws.

CHAPTER **31**

Verdict

I BELIEVE that Joe McCarthy and Roy Cohn were guilty as charged, that they had brought improper pressures on the Army for the benefit of David Schine. On the other hand, although Bob Stevens' performance during that period had been degrading—his failure to put a stop to Cohn's antics—the countercharge that they had held Schine as a hostage and used him as an instrument of blackmail was beyond belief.

McCarthy's defense, if it could be called that, was a counterattack against Stevens and Adams and, almost as an afterthought, against H. Struve Hensel. The evidence for the defense was based on eleven memoranda which McCarthy, Cohn, Carr, and McCarthy's secretary claimed to have been written during the months-long negotiations about David Schine.

After the hearings were over, lawyer Joseph Welch and his staff prepared a brief. In it, Welch said flatly that the investigation of the circumstances under which these memoranda were alleged to have been written, and an analysis of the contents of the memoranda themselves, disclosed that they were not contemporaneously written, as they were purported to have been, and must instead have been manufactured at a later date. With the failure of this proffered documentary evidence, support for the countercharges collapsed, the brief said, and the invalidity of the countercharges themselves was laid here.

Thus, McCarthy's countercharges, which were no defense in the first place, were probably based on false evidence.

I was suspicious of the memoranda when I first heard about them. Joe McCarthy had not mentioned them when I confronted him with the Army charges and he promised to meet with me and the other Republicans the next morning. I knew that Cohn and Carr and the rest of the staff and secretaries worked late that night. Then, the next day, Joe had run out on his date with us, had held his news conference, and offered these memoranda as "proof" that the Army had offered to furnish to the committee dirt on the Navy and Air Force; that the Army was holding Schine as a hostage in an attempt to obtain concessions from the committee; that the Army was threatening reprisals against its own officers who had cooperated with the committee and was attempting to blackmail the committee by threatening to issue an embarrassing report on Cohn.

And suddenly, although they had never been mentioned before to my knowledge, here, Joe said, were the memoranda. I noted immediately the almost miraculous relevance to the charges and countercharges, and the seemingly impossible coincidence that these were the only memoranda pertaining to subcommittee relations with the Army which appeared to have been prepared by staff members or their chairman during a six-month period in which the committee held about fifty hearings on Army matters.

It seemed then, and it still seems now, that the eleven memoranda were a hurried and inept attempt to document a defense.

Neither Frank Carr nor Mary Driscoll won any medals for believability when they were on the witness stand, testifying about the memoranda. Much of Mrs. Driscoll's testimony was characterized by professed memory lapses and vague explanations of loose and improbable office procedures. She was attempting to testify that the original carbon copies of the memoranda had been reproduced into several copies for distribution when McCarthy and Cohn held their press conference. However, the "original originals" had conveniently become lost and thus could not be scientifically credited to any particular typewriter in the office.

There is no group of government workers in all the huge federal structure more efficient than secretaries to Senators, and I had always known that Mary Driscoll had, for six years, maintained order in McCarthy's office despite a sort of super-chaotic atmosphere there. But on the witness stand, she appeared to be able to remember nothing at all. She could not recall the name of a single one of her typists who had participated in the reproduction process, she was not even sure whether she herself had done any of it. She claimed she could not remember what typewriter she used—if she had done any—or what machine was on her desk or whether it was her present electric machine. Mrs. Driscoll also claimed that she had destroyed her original shorthand notebooks concerning the memoranda.

She did maintain that she had transcribed all eleven of the memoranda when they had first been dictated through the months. I could have accepted this if Joe McCarthy had been the author of all of them, but several of them were supposedly dictated by Roy Cohn and Francis Carr. A simple study of geography made this claim incredible. Mrs. Driscoll worked in McCarthy's office which was Room 428 on the fourth floor of the Senate Office Building. Cohn and Carr were in Room 101 on the first floor of the building.

Thus, a trip by Cohn or Carr from their office to dictate to Mrs. Driscoll required a walk down the entire Constitution Avenue side of the building and then two-thirds along the Delaware Avenue side, a distance of almost two city blocks, plus an elevator ride up three floors. In their own office, Cohn and Carr had seven or eight staff secretaries as well as their own secretaries, any one of whom could have, and did, take regular dictation from them both.

Equally incredible was Mrs. Driscoll's explanation of the ready accessibility of all the memoranda in a single package. She testified that starting with the October 2nd memorandum, she had placed them all in a single folder soon after they were transcribed. She undermined her own testimony by admitting she did not inform Carr of the existence of this folder at the time he was dictating to her the statement in his March 11th memorandum that "the writer was searching the files for memoranda dictated concerning Schine" and by saying that she did not know if all the memoranda were in one folder at that time.

Even more damaging was her inability to explain how, in the absence of any direction from her superiors, she managed to put these particular eleven memoranda in the same file. She did not and could not claim that the scant "Investigations Committee" label served as a guide. Instead, she said that she carried such filing information in her memory and filed each memoranda after studying "the text of the entire memorandum."

Such haphazard filing methods, if Mrs. Driscoll's testimony were to be believed, did little credit to the office of a United States Senator. Moreover, under interrogation, her definition of the subject matter shifted from "conversations with Mr. Stevens" to material which "had to do with Mr. Adams or Mr. Stevens or something pertaining to that." This did not explain the omission from the file of a letter Joe McCarthy sent to Bob Stevens on December 22, nor the inclusion of one of Carr's memoranda.

During her ordeal in the witness chair, McCarthy had interrupted Attorney Welch to say, "Anyone listening to your questions would assume that this did not have to do with the same subject matter. I wonder if you would make it clear that all the memoranda have to do with the attempted pressure to call off the investigation." For Mrs. Driscoll, without instructions from anyone, to have deduced from the wording at the time of the transcription that it concerned "attempted pressure" was a feat beyond all possible intuition.

In summing up Mrs. Driscoll's testimony, Welch said, "These considerations compel the conclusion that Mrs. Driscoll's amazing structure was built, not brick by brick, but all at once, when a shelter was badly needed."

Then too, some of the witnesses contradicted themselves and each other. One of the memoranda, dated November 17, was supposedly dictated by Roy Cohn. He testified that he dictated all four of his memoranda in Senator McCarthy's office. Mrs. Driscoll said that each was dictated on or before the date it bore. Other evidence showed that on November 17, Cohn was absent from Washington, apparently in New York City. He left Manhattan to go to Boston for hearings on November 18 and 19. Thus he could have dictated this memorandum only by telephoning it to Washington and even Mrs. Driscoll would not have testified to that.

Frank Carr stumbled over his own integrity on the memorandum of December 9, in which, he as the author said, "Again today John Adams came down here after the hearings." Carr acknowledged that "came down here" meant Room 101 on the first floor, a place where secretarial help was conveniently at hand. However, Carr also testified that he went all the way up to Senator McCarthy's office and dictated the memorandum to Mrs. Driscoll. This self-contradiction throws the authenticity of the document into grave doubt. This doubt is compounded when one compares the language of the document alleging unfair treatment of Schine with Carr's own testimony that, as of December 9, the Army had been fair to Schine and that he did not think the Army could hurt Schine.

One more example—a memorandum dated December 17, from Joe McCarthy to Cohn and Carr said: "In talking to John Adams today, I learned that General Lawton, who, as you recall, cooperated fully with the committee in exposure of subversives at Fort Monmouth, is about to be relieved of his command." The absurdity of McCarthy's dictating procedure—he claimed that he dictated this memorandum to Mary Driscoll by long-

distance telephone from New York—and the uselessness of telling Cohn and Carr, in a memorandum, something they had
known for three weeks and had discussed together at length, is
completely beyond belief.

I had made some notes on some of these items during the
testimony itself and one of them said, "Why would McCarthy
say, 'General Lawton, who, as you recall, cooperated fully with
the committee' unless the memorandum was intended for a
wider audience than Carr and Cohn?"

One other memorandum interested me. It was dated January
9, from Carr to Cohn. It said: "I called John Adams about the
question of the insert for the annual report *re* the change of the
Army security program. Also told him you had been trying to
reach him about Dave not being free Sunday to help with the
report. He was up in Amherst, Mass., and stated that he was
snowbound and that he couldn't do a thing about it from
Massachusetts. I am sure he doesn't want to do anything but I
told him you would call. I think he will duck you. It is obvious
that he doesn't want the part about Army laxity in the report,
so don't expect Dave to get off to help."

According to Frank Carr's own testimony, he had already
conveyed this information to Cohn by telephone, Cohn had
attempted to get Adams on the telephone at Amherst, and
Adams had hung up on him. Why then would Carr, sitting in
Washington, dictate a memorandum in which he used the
future tense, "I think he will duck you," when Adams had already ducked Cohn? Why would he say, "So don't expect Dave
to get off to help," when, in fact, Cohn had already found out
he could not expect Schine to get off? Carr's inability to present
a convincing explanation of the purpose served by such a document compelled me to believe that it was not written on January 9 but at a later date, when it was believed to be necessary
to document McCarthy's countercharges.

This analysis of the memoranda casts such a grave doubt on
the contemporaneity of the documents that I could not accept

them as a chronicle or record of events made at the time they occurred. If the memoranda were not written contemporaneously, their probative force was still further lessened by two considerations—first, if contrived at a later date, they must have been composed for a purpose, for a documenting of a defense. And secondly, those who testified that the documents were contemporaneous, and that meant McCarthy, Cohn, Carr and Mrs. Driscoll, were, in my opinion, casting doubt on their own credibility in all other matters to which they had testified.

With these things in mind, I had written my statement on perjury which I offered at the close of the hearings.

Perhaps it all boiled down to credibility. There had been so much testimony by the McCarthy side which was not easily believable that it was difficult to give his case the benefit of doubt at any point. On the other side, Bob Stevens testified to nothing that I could not believe. He had been foolish, indecisive, naïve, but there was no reason to think that he was not telling the truth. John Adams, who backed up Stevens' story and gave more of the details of the skirmishing with McCarthy and Cohn, was also a credible witness. On top of this, the basic absurdity of McCarthy's countercharges—that high Pentagon officials were reluctant to eliminate alleged Communists from the Armed Services and its civilian centers—was too bizarre to accept without overwhelming evidence that it was true. No such evidence was produced.

Had improper means been used in an attempt to obtain a direct commission for David Schine? It certainly had. When McCarthy and Cohn first inquired of the Army whether it would be possible to obtain a direct commission for Schine, there would have been nothing improper had this been a routine request for information about how a young man, about to be drafted, could serve in a commissioned, rather than in an enlisted, status.

What made it improper was that McCarthy and Cohn made their inquiry in their capacities as chairman and chief counsel of the Senate Permanent Investigating Subcommittee. Then, they exerted continuing pressure by following it up with a barrage of daily phone calls to the Pentagon at a time when their committee was engaged in an embarrassing investigation of the Army.

General Miles Reber had testified that never in his many years of handling similar cases had so much pressure been put upon him. I believed him. It was brought out at that time that Cohn had told Reber that Schine had had a year of service as an officer in the Army Transport Service, but Reber soon found out that Schine had had no previous military experience whatsoever and had no special training of any kind which qualified him for a commission. He had not been an officer in the Army Transport Service at all but had been employed as a civilian in a capacity similar to that of a purser.

Under Cohn's demands, Reber had exhausted all possibilities to get a commission for Schine in the Army, the Navy, and the Air Force. Cohn then showed his appreciation of this special treatment by going to Under Secretary of State General Walter Bedell Smith and telling him that the Army had not been cooperative and had not honored a "promise" to arrange a direct commission for Schine. I found amongst my notes that General Smith, when testifying, had discussed the possibility of Schine's being offered to the Central Intelligence Agency and that Cohn had expressed the view that it would be improper to ask favors from an agency that the committee was about to investigate.

But McCarthy and Cohn did not seem to be following this policy in connection with the Army. During that period, according to Reber's testimony, he had been bombarded with phone calls. Although both McCarthy and Cohn tried to minimize the calls, and McCarthy claimed that he couldn't remember any at all, records of the Telephone Company showed that McCarthy had made at least one long-distance call to Reber from Wisconsin, that Cohn had made at least five toll calls, and that Schine himself had instigated at least ten to General Reber from New York. On top of that, there were innumerable calls from Washington which are not recorded by the Telephone Company.

It seemed to me that the credible evidence established that McCarthy and Cohn had indeed used great pressure in an attempt to obtain a direct commission for David Schine.

The second Army charge was that improper use of the office of the Permanent Investigating Subcommittee had been made to obtain special consideration for Private Schine after he was inducted. Although Joe McCarthy was screaming—and making page one—that the Army charges had been proven fraudulent and were obviously a Communist smear, I felt quite strongly that he and Cohn were both guilty on this second complaint.

When it became evident that Schine would not get a commission and that his induction was certain, Cohn shifted his efforts and attempted to have Schine exempted from basic training and given a special, non-combat assignment.

By that time, a full-scale investigation of Fort Monmouth by the committee was in operation and this gave Cohn ready access to high Army officials. Even before Schine was inducted, Cohn suggested to Bob Stevens that Schine be assigned to New York without basic training. During his bobbing and weaving performance on the witness stand, Cohn did not agree that he made such a request, but he did concede that the Secretary specifically stated that Schine must take basic training along with his fellow soldiers—a remark which would have been superfluous on the Secretary's part had not Cohn asked for the exemption.

Later, during an automobile ride in New York City, Schine himself, not yet inducted, told Stevens that he thought it would be more logical for him (Schine) to become a special assistant to Bob Stevens, to assist in the Communist-hunting program rather than be inducted into the Army. It was during this conversation that Schine told Stevens he thought Stevens was doing a good job in ferreting out Communists—high praise indeed from this expert on the Red menace. However, Stevens did not give in on the demands that Schine avoid basic training, and Cohn now shifted his target to John Adams, making it clear that he hoped Schine would be assigned to New York immediately after he was drafted.

When this didn't work out, Cohn pressed for a direct assignment to the CIA for Schine. Up to this moment, neither McCarthy nor Cohn had made any pretense that it was necessary to have Schine available for committee work in the future. This pretense was put forward when it was apparent that all efforts to forestall Schine's induction had failed. This pattern seems to erase the validity of the claim that Schine was needed for committee business after his induction and upon the claims that he performed valuable services for the committee when he was supposed to be a trainee at Fort Dix.

Cohn was relentless. When Schine's induction date was set, he asked Bob Stevens to give Schine a two-week furlough immediately, and now, suddenly, Schine was needed to finish pending committee work. Again Stevens gave in and Schine was granted a fifteen-day furlough. This was cut to four days when McCarthy himself began to get leery of possible unfriendly publicity.

At this point, one might have expected McCarthy to order Roy Cohn to knock it off. A few moments of reflection should have made it obvious to Joe that Cohn's obsession over Schine was heading for trouble. However, Cohn continued to demand, and obtain, a series of passes for Schine. During the sixty-eight days Schine spent at Fort Dix, Schine was away from the post on all, or part, of thirty-four days. In contrast, the average Fort Dix trainee received three or four passes, did not receive passes on both the Christmas and New Year's holidays as Schine did, and would have received not a single pass during the first four weeks of basic training.

In one incident, when assigned for guard duty and KP during the New Year's holidays, Schine vanished from his company area. When his commanding officer sent a telegram to Schine to return at once, it was Cohn who answered. He telephoned Fort Dix and said that Schine was needed for committee business during the New Year's holidays. At the end of the sixty-eight days, this most unusual private obtained a two-week furlough. Perhaps he needed the rest after doing so much to "help the committee." Telephone Company records show that Schine placed 181 outgoing calls of his own to non-committee parties and that most of these calls to his own personal friends preceded his taking off with a special pass.

General Cornelius Ryan, commandant at Fort Dix during this unhappy period, testified that the unusual arrangement which Cohn and the staff had secured for Schine had its effect upon the other trainees and made Schine "a man set aside . . . a man apart." Schine himself was not averse to taking full advantage of his unique situation. According to the testimony of his company commander, Schine explained that his purpose was "to remake the American military establishment along modern lines." Evidence of this unique role, coupled with the unusual number of special passes and the phenomenal number of incoming and outgoing telephone calls, could point to only one conclusion—that Cohn's activities amounted to little short of a siege of Fort Dix in behalf of his very special friend.

There seemed to be no end to the harassment of Stevens, Adams, and other Army officials. There was one episode about which Francis Carr and Roy Cohn contradicted each other in their testimony. In early December, John Adams went to Sioux Falls, South Dakota, to visit his mother and sister for a few days. Before he left he told Carr that he would be grateful for four days undisturbed by calls concerning David Schine, but he did not go far enough. And so long as the taxpayers were picking up the telephone bill, the harassment continued.

Adams said that he received telephone calls from Carr on two different dates, both of which alluded to Schine and one of which had Schine as its principal purpose. Carr testified that although the telephone records indicated both calls, he could recollect only one, and he claimed this was to find out if any immediate action was going to be taken concerning General Lawton. He said that Cohn had asked him to find out from John Adams what and when any action on this removal of Lawton would take place.

Cohn contradicted this in his standard manner of testifying: "I have no recollection of ever suggesting to Mr. Carr that he call Mr. Adams in South Dakota." This striking discrepancy between the testimony of Cohn and Carr makes completely unacceptable the attempt to refute Adams' testimony that Carr called him in South Dakota about an assignment for David Schine.

I had made a note to myself that I thought it was important to consider that on each occasion where the conduct of the McCarthy side required explanation, they consistently substituted General Lawton as the subject matter of discussion when necessary to contradict Adams' testimony that the subject was Schine. The repeated resort to the Lawton thesis exposed its own falsity. Evidence indicated that actually the Lawton discussions took place long before.

As the skirmishing went into its sixth month and into the new year, Adams mentioned to Cohn that Private Schine might be sent overseas. According to Adams, Cohn became very upset and said, "Stevens is through as Secretary of the Army," and "We will wreck the Army." Cohn and Carr attempted to deny that Cohn made any specific threats against the Army or Stevens. Yet Cohn's testimony was vague. He said he had "no recollection of having said that" but he refused to make a flat denial. Carr admitted that there had been a heated discussion.

According to testimony David Schine reported to Camp Gordon in Georgia the first week in February, and already Cohn had started to butt in. He said that this was "much too far from New York and would not do." He demanded the name of the person who would serve as the contact at Camp Gordon to relieve Schine from duty for "committee business." He tried to cut short Schine's basic training at Camp Gordon and have him assigned to an advanced school before he was qualified to enter it.

Adams testified that these proposals were channeled to him through columnist George Sokolsky who, in return for favorable consideration, said he would undertake to "soften this pressure on the Army which is coming from Senator McCarthy and to move in and stop the investigation of the Army." When Adams told Sokolsky that Schine would have to complete his basic training as scheduled, Sokolsky said that the Army was just asking for a two-year fight. Sokolsky was not called as a witness at the hearing and it is too bad that he was not.

Cohn attempted to build up the proposition that the committee could not do without David Schine. However, way back in July, McCarthy and Cohn had been alerted that Schine's services must soon be lost. And Schine was available to the committee, full time, for four additional months, more than enough time to wind up any pending work he might have been doing. His inability to complete this work has never been satisfactorily explained although I might make a guess that no one can complete work that hasn't even been started. No evidence appears in the record which ever served to contradict McCarthy's own admission that Schine was "a good boy, but there is nothing indispensable about him."

While Cohn was demanding that Schine be absent from his basic training more than half of the time, I wondered if Schine was actually engaged on any committee business whatsoever while away from Fort Dix. The conditions under which he was alleged to have worked were so inefficient and bizarre that it was hardly credible that there was any serious intention for him to work at all.

First, and most important, it was not satisfactorily explained why Schine conducted his work in New York City and in Trenton, New Jersey, rather than at Fort Dix. A substantial portion of the total pass time had to be consumed on each occasion by the long automobile rides—four hours round trip in the case of New York and two hours on journeys to Trenton. General Ryan had set aside a special room at Fort Dix where Schine could have worked in private.

When Cohn was under fire to show evidence of the allegedly massive amount of work Schine had produced while in the Army, he claimed that Schine had submitted his efforts in longhand and that Cohn himself would then type it up on his typewriter. He was able to produce only two and a half pages of notes. Cohn was finally forced to admit under cross-examination that Schine did only a "very limited" amount of work during this period. Cohn's transparent evasiveness when requested to bring forward Schine's work highlights its remarkable scantiness.

When asked to produce only those files which contained memoranda by Schine, Cohn presented a large box full of committee papers and precipitated a long and time-wasting discussion about the right of the subcommittee to receive the material. These tactics became obvious when at last he admitted that the only documentary evidence of Schine's work was the two-and-a-half-page masterpiece.

CHAPTER **32**

The Censure

LYNDON B. Johnson expressed the feelings of most of us in the Senate as we neared the final vote on the inevitable censure motion against Joe McCarthy in December 1954. Joe's attack on the Watkin's committee, which had recommended the censure, Johnson said, "does not belong in the journal of the Senate but would be more fittingly inscribed on the walls of a men's room. If we sanction this abuse the Senate may as well close up shop."

As I had told President Eisenhower during one of our huddles at the White House, Joe McCarthy had committed political suicide as twenty million Americans watched the Army-McCarthy hearings. None but the most hate-loving, facts-hating fanatics could have failed to see, during the hearings, that Senator Joseph R. McCarthy had become a major liability to the cause of anti-Communism. He had played directly into the hands of the Communists and had made it tougher for the many others who were fighting to stop the spread of Communism at home and abroad long before he had dropped his own Communist support to become a self-elected savior of humanity.

He had distorted the picture of Communism in the United

States out of all semblance to reality. He had introduced a slam-bang, rabble-rousing, hit-and-run technique into a serious business which required exceptional professional skills.

As the hearings ended in June 1954, a new atmosphere spread through the Senate Building. Many Senators who had lived in complete terror of Joe McCarthy, who had been avoiding their responsibilities to save their political lives, were suddenly brave again. They talked openly now, instead of in whispers; they poured out the anger they had held back so long. They had seen him strike down Tydings of Maryland and Benton of Connecticut and had trembled when he invaded many states to wage a vicious campaign against them and had sent his hatchet men into others. They knew now that he was finished and they closed in for the kill.

But it was not the messy slaughter of a wounded leader that it might have been. The Senate, acting through the agency of the Watkins committee which had been chosen to study the censure charges, completed the unpleasant task with the courage, dignity and integrity that it had failed to use during the five years of McCarthy's rampages.

On July 30, Ralph Flanders had submitted Senate Resolution No. 301 to censure Joe McCarthy, and Senator Arthur V. Watkins of Utah was named chairman of the select committee. The other Senator members were Edwin C. Johnson of Colorado, John C. Stennis of Mississippi, Frank Carlson of Kansas, Francis Case of South Dakota, and Sam J. Ervin, Jr., of North Carolina. None of them, by any wild reach of imagination, could have been described as Left Wing, pro-Communist admirers. However, McCarthy saw fit to so describe them before the episode ended. It cost him an additional penalty in the final verdict.

Arthur Watkins was the perfect answer to McCarthyism. As his committee sifted the forty-six charges submitted against McCarthy, Watkins made it clear at the beginning that Joe's attempts to make a shambles of this adventure as he had during the Army hearings would not be tolerated. An additional restraint came from Joe's own lawyer, Edward Bennett Williams, the brilliant young Washington attorney who took the case only after Joe agreed that Williams would be in charge and that McCarthy would not go into any of his inflammatory outbursts during the hearings. Williams later said that he regretted not extending this agreement outside the hearing room. He might have known that Joe would bombard Watkins and the rest of the committee with mud and garbage gathered in the gutters he had known so long.

There were forty-six specific and well-documented charges for the Watkins committee to consider. And it was fortunate for Joe McCarthy that these charges were considered without passion but with a deep feeling of legality, justice and fair play that he could not have expected before any other group or in any other country. On all but two of the charges McCarthy was "acquitted"; too leniently, I thought, in many cases, particularly the one concerning General Ralph Zwicker.

Most of the charges were a replay of all the headlines Joe had promoted through his glory days: the long list of unwarranted attacks on the reputations of those who could not fight back through the barricade of Senatorial immunity; the baseless charges that resulted from poor staff work; and McCarthy's own inability to realize the dangers in accepting "information" from the grubby parade of fanatics who trailed him wherever he went.

All his regrettable episodes were dragged out into the open to be studied again—the $10,000 fee from the Lustron Corp.; his attack on Gen. George C. Marshall; his responsibility for the Cohn-Schine-Army abuse; his hiring of staff members with questionable backgrounds; his irresponsible threats to subpoena former President Truman and several newspaper reporters who had offended him; his endless attempts to intimidate the press with threats against its writers and letters to its advertisers urging them to withdraw their advertisements; his building of smear-file information against his fellow Senators; his distorted, innuendo attacks against a long list of prominent citizens; his public disclosure of restricted security information; his irresponsible hanging of the Communist label on individuals and newspapers which disagreed with him; his lying about his military record and false claims about wounds which he did not suffer; his rude and ruthless disregard of the rights of other Senators; his public threats to withdraw the second-class mailing privileges of newspapers which had offended him.

All these charges were eliminated by the Watkins committee for a variety of reasons. Some they decided were not censurable, others they called "too vague," some lacked proper documentation, a few, if upheld, would tend to place unwarranted limitations on freedom of speech.

McCarthy was indeed fortunate that he was being judged by a committee that seemed to lean over backward to be certain that the defendant's rights would be honored. I have wondered if he ever understood that this was the exact opposite, the total refutation, of his own performance.

There were some Senators who fought for McCarthy and against the censure down to the final vote. Everett Dirksen and Karl Mundt of our own committee, along with William Jenner and William Knowland, the GOP Senate majority leader, used every maneuver and strategy to either kill the resolution completely or to tone it down. Barry Goldwater worked diligently to arrange a compromise for Joe and was enraged when McCarthy refused to do anything that might have brought about a peaceful solution

I stayed out of it as much as I could until a defensive maneuver developed to eliminate the charge that McCarthy should be censured for his treatment of General Zwicker. This ill-mannered and groundless attack against one of our outstanding military heroes was just too much for me to swallow. Arthur Watkins yielded the Senate floor to me and this was part of what I had to say:

"As to the question relating to General Zwicker, no greater insult can be hurled at a military man or one more calculated to destroy his reputation than to say, whether he be a general or a private, that he is unfit to wear the uniform of his country. I am sure that if I had been in uniform and such a statement had been made to me, my reaction would have been much more violent than that of General Zwicker.

"We have heard a great deal said about the prestige, the honor, and the dignity of the Senate. When we, with the power of a subpoena, summon a citizen of this country to appear before a Congressional committee, that citizen, whether he be a private, or a general, or a civilian, has every right to expect courtesy and fair treatment from a dignified body.

"I hold no brief with the leadership of the Army in this instance. They have bungled, by being evasive, the entire question of General Zwicker and Major Peress. I would not be standing here today speaking as I am if the spleen of the junior Senator from Wisconsin had been directed to the responsible persons in the Army who prohibited General Zwicker from testifying. I hold no brief for their actions; but what was done was much like whipping a grandchild for the actions of his grandfather. It was a case where General Zwicker was under orders from his superiors in the Army not to testify on certain matters. If he had testified, he would have acted in violation of those orders. I am sure all Senators know the pattern of military service, and that a soldier does not violate orders of his superiors. If the spleen of the junior Senator from Wisconsin had been directed against Secretary Stevens or John Adams in this case, I would have no quarrel. But here was a man who, though acting under orders from his superiors, was humiliated by the statement that he was not fit to wear his uniform when, as a matter of fact, he was under orders not to testify.

"I would feel derelict in my duty if I let this opportunity pass without expressing my sentiments, because the people of the country would assume that the Senate of the United States condones and approves of a committee representing the Senate referring to an officer in uniform as unfit to wear that uniform, when he was carrying out the orders and directives of his superiors."

Senator Mike Monroney backed me strongly in this protest but we lost; the censure motion concerning McCarthy's treatment of General Zwicker was dropped. The Watkins committee was on record that McCarthy's conduct was inexcusable in his controversy with General Zwicker.

In the final decision, Joe McCarthy was condemned rather than censured on two charges. The first was for his performance against the Gillette Committee which had attempted to get his explanation of his strange financial dealings. McCarthy had consistently refused to appear and repeatedly abused and insulted the members of the committee by letters and public statements. They were, he had said, "completely dishonest" and "guilty of stealing just as clearly as though the members had engaged in picking the pockets of taxpayers and turning the loot over to the Democratic National Committee." It was the decision of the Watkins committee that "when the personal honor and official conduct of a Senator of the United States are in question before a duly constituted committee of the Senate, the Senator involved owes a duty to himself, his state and to the Senate to appear promptly and cooperate fully." The full Senate agreed.

If Joe had been able to overcome his compulsive reaching for headlines through extravagant statements, this would have been the only charge on which he was finally condemned. The Watkins committee completed its investigation of all forty-six charges by early autumn but final Senate consideration was delayed until after the elections in early November. This was done under the direction of Senate majority leader William

Knowland so that the campaign would not be overshadowed by the McCarthy dispute.

However, although candidates preferred to forget they had ever heard of McCarthy, another group was busy. It called itself Ten Million Americans Mobilizing for Justice and its goal was ten million signatures opposing the censure of McCarthy. Its lineup was sprinkled with prominent names, many of them former generals and admirals who, it seemed strange to me, could condone McCarthy's treatment of General Zwicker and General Marshall. A vote to censure McCarthy, it said, would establish a dangerous precedent that could only lead to the destruction of constitutional government. It pointed out that the Communists and their un-American cohorts, by vicious propaganda and through willing stooges and blind but innocent dupes, already had victimized certain members of the United States Senate. The censure movement, it alleged, was an all-out campaign of smear, slander, pressure, and political intimidation in a final attempt to destroy Joe McCarthy. Finally, an armored truck appeared outside the Senate Office Building and, with a flourishing of guns, the guards of the trucking company delivered what was purported to be ten million signatures of Americans who were opposed to censure.

Other strange groups appeared. From New York came a trainload of Joe's supporters headed by Rabbi Benjamin Schultz, director of the American Jewish League against Communism. Their slogan was: "Strike terror into the hearts of Flanders and Malenkov." They waved placards, made pests of themselves through the corridors of the Senate Building. There was a rally in Constitution Hall where many prominent Right Wingers adorned the stage, waiting until Joe and his wife made a "surprise" appearance. This support by the super-conservative groups in this country always amazed me. Joe's domestic voting record was always extremely liberal, much more so than my own.

In late November we finally got down to business, and once more McCarthy ran true to form. This time it was another speech, written by one of his favorite apologists, and released to the press before he delivered it in the Senate. It was the usual nonsense that anti-McCarthyism equaled pro-Communism, and part of it said, "I would have the American people recognize and contemplate in dread the fact that the Communist party, a relatively small group of deadly conspirators, has now extended its tentacles to the most respected of American bodies, the U. S. Senate. That it has made a committee of this Senate its unwitting handmaiden." As Joe had planned, this speech reaped a harvest of big headlines and also became a new censure charge and was approved.

Finally, in early December, it was ended. There had been a long series of ugly skirmishes on the Senate floor and a half-dozen amendments tossed in by the McCarthy troops. All of them were beaten down by a 3 to 1 margin. On no amendment was Joe able to count more than 24 of 96 possible votes.

And then, after weeks of silence, President Eisenhower spoke. Arthur Watkins, he said, had done "a very splendid job."

CHAPTER **33**

McCarthy Was Not Alone

THE purpose of a Congressional hearing is to provide factual information to aid the Congress in the proposal of any necessary legislation and to assist the Congress in appraising the execution by the administrative agencies of related laws.

Unfortunately, it has been used many times by irresponsible Senators and Congressmen in a selfish hunt for headlines or as a punitive device. The wise men who founded our government authorized the first investigating committee in 1792. The objective of that first hearing was to find out why General St. Clair and an expedition of American troops had been clobbered by a small group of Indians. This committee of Congressmen was given the right to subpoena witnesses; it conducted its affairs with dignity. There could have been no thought in the minds of our early leaders that these Congressional rights would be distorted and abused by a long list of committees of which Joe McCarthy's became the most regrettable only because it was the most widely publicized.

Alan Barth has written in his fine book, *Government by Investigation:*

292

Congress has authorized and conducted close to a thousand special investigations, more than half of them during the last quarter of the century. Some of these have been frivolous, and some have served only the interest of headline hunters. Some have undoubtedly produced real mischief. Some undertook legislative trials, disgracefully invading the domain of the judiciary. Some trespassed grievously on the rights of individuals.

But if Congressional use of the power to investigate produced occasional excesses, it also produced tremendous boons to the democratic process. Through it, Congress effected valuable reforms in American life and imposed a salutary check on the Executive Branch of the government. It would be as foolish to condemn the investigating power because it is now and then abused as to condemn the principle of freedom of the press because some newspapers sometimes behaved irresponsibly.

It is unfortunate that in human society bad news finds more general interest than good news. Many Congressional committees quietly perform the function to which they are assigned, conduct their hearings with dignity, and supplement existing laws so that American society will benefit in some way. These minor improvements, however, produce no big headlines. At the same time, the news media are delighted with the production of scandal. The Kefauver crime show, televised from coast to coast in the early 1950's, served no legislative purpose whatsoever and was a clear-cut invasion of the rights of many people. Although Frank Costello, Virginia Hill and the rest of Kefauver's cast provided interesting entertainment for the public, it was a regrettable misuse of Congressional power. Although many of these witnesses were listed among the "bad guys," they have, in this country, the same legal rights as the "good guys." And it is a fortunate thing for us all that they do.

In more recent years, we have seen the same abuses in television circuses built around Jimmy Hoffa and Bobby Baker.

The hearings involving Bobby Baker were particularly reprehensible. The Senate had no possible excuse for approving them

293

in the first place. If Baker had done anything illegal, which he may have, it should be decided in a court of law. And so, once again on television, we could watch a smear versus anti-smear brawl during which otherwise admirable Senators and committee members screamed "liar" at each other and generally disgraced themselves and their office.

Fortunately there has been a healthy change in the newspaper world since Joe McCarthy's glory days. Although there have been many outbreaks of McCarthyism in Congressional committee raids all over the country, they no longer get the big front-page headline except in the area involved.

There have been disgraceful abuses in Congressional committee actions of so little importance that they never make the newspapers at all. A friend of mine who appeared as a sympathetic witness before the Merchant Marine and Fisheries Committee was put through a verbal horsewhipping by a committee member who apparently had never learned the meaning of courtesy. In a reverse operation a few years ago, Joe Valachi, a small-time hoodlum, was given a welcome close to that usually saved for minor statesmen when he was summoned to appear before a Senate group. The advance publicity claimed that he was ready to testify to such startling information that his life was in danger. The buildup was tremendous but Valachi told nothing that was not already public information, and his testimony could have caused little concern in the higher levels of gangland society. As in the Kefauver crime hearings, the questioning was carefully steered away from any discussion of the interlocking of the underworld with politicians which, through all history, has been the strength of the lawless. The Valachi episode wasn't even an interesting show.

But there is no end to the grabbing for headlines. Time and again we see pictures of Jack Dempsey and Gene Tunney posing with committee chairmen; calling Casey Stengel to the witness stand always guarantees newspaper coverage which might otherwise be lacking; the appearance of actress Lucille Ball can inject a few delightful moments into an otherwise dull and dreary performance and, of course, bring the photographers.

However, the legislative hearing provides a privileged forum for vicious and vindictive abuses of private citizens. There are often no standards of judgment, no rules, no appeals, no boundaries of irrelevance. Any witness, to whom the committee or its chairman is unfriendly, has no protection but whatever minor restraint these men care to give.

There will always be irresponsible men who, when elected to a powerful government office, will become bemused with their new capacity for mischief. And, although there have been occasional halfhearted beginnings to create restrictive laws and regulations to control investigative committees, it is doubtful if they will ever be passed and more doubtful that they would ever be enforced. The rules and regulations of Congress as they now stand prohibit the type of abuses which have, in recent years, carried the label of McCarthyism. The abuses continue. It seems hardly necessary to add that there have been throughout history, laws against murder and theft but this has not stopped killing and stealing.

The defense against outrages aimed at a private citizen by a government agency is, of course, public opinion. The tyrannies of Joe McCarthy lost all their tremendous power to injure individuals when he demonstrated them through millions of television outlets across the nation in the Army-McCarthy hearings.

The public watched and the verdict of the overwhelming majority was clear—the freedom of any one individual depends on the freedom for all, the right of every man and woman to think and speak within their own conscience.

It was the end of a period of strange and hysterical nonsense, brought on by a haunted man who had an overpowering need to be the center of attraction but whose ambitions had no substance. In the less than thirty months still remaining of his life after the censure verdict, he still went through the motions, bombarding old and new targets, but no one was taking him seriously anymore.

I think he was the loneliest man I ever knew.

Index

INDEX

52; arrangement for staff appointments, 64; bank debt, 210, 212; baseless charges strategy, 226-227; Benton's resolution to impeach, 160-170; as brawler, 63; Brownell accused, 190; cancels meeting, goes to Wisconsin, 113-114; Carr's appointment date squabbled over, 151; censure, 284-291; after censure, 295-296; as clown, 184; and Cohn, 28-30 (*See also* Cohn, Roy); committee control of his excesses, 117; as Communist hero, 132; countercharges probably based on false evidence, 270-274; defends plan to fight Communism, 217-221; defies his party and friends, 108-111; as Dennis the Menace, 193; device to handle disagreement, 164; distorted questioning by, 92-96; Driscoll testimony, 234-235; and Eisenhower (*see* Eisenhower, Dwight D.); eleven memoranda on blackmailing by Army, 231-235; European reaction to, 134; fact-finding tactics, 226; family used for financial manipulation, 212; Fisher slandered, 241-247; Flanders considers censure, 191-197; Fort Monmouth "spy ring," 178-181; Hensel as target, 139-141, 223-230; and Hitler as anti-Communists, 193-194; Hoover document rewritten, 185; housing pamphlet, 209-210; impeachment resolution, 160-170; increased drinking, 227; Jenkins insulted, 257; Jones put up for Senator, 152-159; on Lewis' radio program, 108-109; as Liberal, 208; as lonely rebel, 186; Lustron affair, 208-213; lying strategy, 141; "McCarthy committee," 28; as Malmédy murderers' attorney, 130-132; Matthews fired, 117; and Moss, Annie Lee, 107-108; as one-man committee, 154; "Pentagon politicians," 140; Peress questioned, 82-84, 89-90; points of order, 140-141; Potter, relationship with,

261; Potter threatened, 24-25; press support (*see* Press support for McCarthy); protects his informants, 187-189; public support (*see* Public support for McCarthy); publications, 134; Reber, Sam, slandered, 149-151; record for unmasking Communists, 109; responsibility for not stopping him, 117-118; rise to power, 54-57; role-player, 25-26, 100; Rosenberg, Anna, falsely charged, 171-175; St. Claire attacked, 169-170; and Schine, 38, 43-44 (*See also* Schine, G. David); Smith, Margaret, challenges him, 167-169; Smith, Margaret, as foe, 152-159; speculates with donations, 211-212; Stevens call played back, 264-265; Stevens as victim, 180; Stevens-Schine photograph, 183, 255-256; Symington as foe, 258-260; Tyding's photograph faked, 161; under oath, 187-189; vindictiveness, 59-60; as vote-getter, 21; Welch outsmarts him, 184, 187-189, 241-247; Wheeling speech, 25-26, 57; Zwicker judged, 85-86; Zwicker questioned, 99-105

McCarthyism, the Fight for America, 134

McClellan, John, 14, 72; background, 261-262; final statement at hearings, 266-267; principles, 262; protests hearsay evidence, 108; protests questioning of Reber, 149-150, 250; speaks for minority Democrats, 139

McGranery, James, 35

McGraw, James, 173-174

McManus, Major John J., 89-90

Malmédy atrocities trial, 129-132; included in McCarthy impeachment resolution, 162; McCarthy's performance, 52

Manrin, Roy Paul, Jr., 200-201

Marquette University, 27

Marshall, George, book published by McCarthy on, 134; Eisenhower's support, 19-20;

301

INDEX

235; as gentleman, 176; monitored call from McCarthy, 264-265; opening statement, 17; as "Pentagon politician," 140; photograph faked with Schine, 183, 252-253; victim of McCarthy's mania, 180; reminded about his Peress promise, 134; Wilson's assessment of, 64

Stevenson, Adlai, 27; charges McCarthy with splitting party, 58, 108

Strandlund, Carl, 209-210

Sunchon Tunnel, 202-203

Surine, Don, 162, 258

Swift, Reverend Wesley, 172

Symington, Stuart,
believes Annie Lee Moss, 107; blamed by McCarthy, 223; on committee, 14; final statement at hearings, 268; hassles with McCarthy, 255-256; logic of, 150; opposing McCarthy affects career of, 258; questions Carr on security clearances, 259-260

Taejon prison camp, 203

Television's influence on McCarthy, 182, 189, 265

Ten Million Americans Mobilizing for Justice, 290

Todd, Lt. Col. Jack, 205-206

Truman, Harry, 171, 190, 224; loyalty order, 177

Tunney, Gene, 294

Tydings, Millard, 19, 161, 183

USA Confidential, 154

U. S. Information Agency, 21

Valachi, Joe, 294

Veterans of Foreign Wars, 22-23

Voice of America, 61, 250

Vote-getter, McCarthy as, 21

Washington *Evening Star*, 120-121

Washington *Post*, 27, 114-115, 214

Watkins, Arthur V., 285

Watkins committee, 284-291

Weinel, Sergeant Carey H., 203

Welch, Joseph,
brings out Cohn's devotion to Schine, 216; claims memoranda invalid, 270-271; discloses tampered photograph, 183, 254-255; final statement from, 262-263; plays telephone monitor of McCarthy, 264-265; protects Fred Fisher, 241-246; questions Cohn, 237-240; questions Mary Driscoll, 232-234; questions Reber, 145-146; traps McCarthy, 187-189; treats McCarthy as comic, 184

Welker, Herman, 165

Wheeling speech, McCarthy's, 25-26, 57

Williams, Edward Bennett, 286

Wilson, Charles, 17, 27; alerts Potter, 31; insists on firing Cohn, 30, 63-64

Winchell, Walter, 26, 35, 51, 154

Wisconsin's Communist Party, 26

Wright, Dr. Louis B., 115

Zwicker, General Ralph,
Anastos monitors conversation, 81-82; confidential file information, 97; discussed by Watkins committee, 286-289; Eisenhower's support, 20; first hears of Peress, 78-79; infuriating effect on McCarthy, 100; insulted by McCarthy, 86, 104; Potter protests treatment of, 287-289; refuses to criticize President, 105; as "sacred cow," 64-65; testifies before the committee, 99-105; war record, 66-69

304